HIGH COURT CASE SUMMARIES

EVIDENCE

Keyed to Fisher's Casebook on Evidence, 2nd Edition

Memory Graphics by Stu Rees (www.stus.com)

WEST®

A Thomson Reuters business

Mat #40870061

© West, a Thomson business, 2006
© 2009 Thomson Reuters
 610 Opperman Drive
 St. Paul, MN 55123
 1–800–313–9378
Printed in the United States of America

ISBN: 978–0–314–90532–1

Table of Contents

Page

INTRODUCTION **1**
Tanner v. United States 3

CHAPTER ONE.   General Principles of Relevance **5**
United States v. James 7
Cox v. State 9
State v. Bocharski 11
Commonwealth v. Serge 13
United States v. James 15
United States v. Myers 17
People v. Collins 19
United States v. Jackson 23
Old Chief v. United States 25

CHAPTER TWO.   The Specialized Relevance Rules **27**
Tuer v. McDonald 29
Bankcard America, Inc. v. Universal Bancard Systems, Inc. 31
Williams v. McCoy 33
United States v. Biaggi 35

CHAPTER THREE.   Character Evidence **37**
People v. Zackowitz 39
United States v. Trenkler 41
United States v. Stevens 45
United States v. DeGeorge 47
Huddleston v. United States 49
Lannan v. State 51
State v. Kirsch 53
United States v. Guardia 55
United States v. Mound 57
Michelson v. United States 59
Halloran v. Virginia Chemicals Inc. 61

CHAPTER FOUR.   Impeachment and Character for Truthfulness ... **63**
United States v. Whitmore 65
United States v. Brewer 67
Luce v. United States 69
Ohler v. United States 71

CHAPTER FIVE.   The Rape Shield Law **73**
People v. Abbot 75
State v. Sibley 77
State v. Smith 79
Olden v. Kentucky 81
Stephens v. Miller 83
United States v. Knox 85

CHAPTER SEVEN.   The Rule Against Hearsay **87**
Mahlandt v. Wild Canid Survival & Research Center, Inc. 91
Bourjaily v. United States 93
United States v. Barrett 95
United States v. Ince 97
Fletcher v. Weir 99
Tome v. United States 101
Commonwealth v. Weichell 103

Page

United States v. Owens 105
United States v. DiNapoli 107
Lloyd v. American Export Lines, Inc. 111
Williamson v. United States 113
Shepard v. United States 115
United States v. Gray 117
Mutual Life Insurance Co. v. Hillmon 119
Shepard v. United States 121
United States v. Iron Shell 123
Johnson v. State 125
Palmer v. Hoffman 127
United States v. Vigneau 129
Beech Aircraft Corp. v. Rainey 131
Dallas County v. Commercial Union Assurance Co. 133
United States v. Laster 135

CHAPTER EIGHT. Confrontation and Compulsory Process **137**
Mattox v. United States 139
Crawford v. Washington 141
Davis v. Washington Hammon v. Indiana 143
Bruton v. United States 147
Cruz v. New York 149
Gray v. Maryland 151
Chambers v. Mississippi 153

CHAPTER NINE. Lay Opinions and Expert Testimony **155**
United States v. Ganier 157
United States v. Johnson 159
Jinro America Inc. v. Secure Investments, Inc. 161
Hygh v. Jacobs 163
State v. Batangan 165
United States v. Hines 167
Frye v. United States 169
Daubert v. Merrell Dow Pharmaceuticals, Inc. 171
Daubert v. Merrell Dow Pharmaceuticals, Inc. 173
United States v. Crumby 175
Kumho Tire Company v. Carmichael 177
State v. Kinney 179

CHAPTER TEN. Authentication, Identification, and the "Best Evidence" Rule **181**
United States v. Stelmokas 183
State v. Small 185
Simms v. Dixon 187
Wagner v. State 189
Seiler v. Lucasfilm 191
United States v. Jackson 193

CHAPTER ELEVEN. Privileges: General Principles **195**
Jaffee v. Redmond 197
In Re: Grand Jury Subpoena, Judith Miller 199
Morales v. Portuondo 203

CHAPTER TWELVE. The Lawyer–Client Privilege and the Privilege Against Self–Incrimination **205**
People v. Gionis 207
Howell v. Joffe 211
Koch Foods of Alabama, LLC v. General Electric Capital Corp. 213
Swidler & Berlin v. United States 215
United States v. Zolin 217
In Re: Grand Jury Investigation [Rowland] 219
United States v. Hubbell 223

	Page
CHAPTER THIRTEEN. Familial Privileges	**227**
Tilton v. Beecher	229
Trammel v. United States	231
United States v. Rakes	233
In re Grand Jury Proceedings	235

*

Alphabetical Table of Cases

Abbot, People v., 19 Wend. 192 (N.Y.Sup.1838), 75

Bankcard America, Inc. v. Universal Bancard Systems, Inc., 203 F.3d 477 (7th Cir.2000), 31
Barrett, United States v., 539 F.2d 244 (1st Cir.1976), 95
Batangan, State v., 71 Haw. 552, 799 P.2d 48 (Hawai'i 1990), 165
Beech Aircraft Corp. v. Rainey, 488 U.S. 153, 109 S.Ct. 439, 102 L.Ed.2d 445 (1988), 131
Biaggi, United States v., 909 F.2d 662 (2nd Cir.1990), 35
Bocharski, State v., 200 Ariz. 50, 22 P.3d 43 (Ariz.2001), 11
Bourjaily v. United States, 483 U.S. 171, 107 S.Ct. 2775, 97 L.Ed.2d 144 (1987), 93
Branzburg v. Hayes, 408 U.S. 665, 92 S.Ct. 2646, 33 L.Ed.2d 626 (1972), 199
Brewer, United States v., 451 F.Supp. 50 (E.D.Tenn.1978), 67
Bruton v. United States, 391 U.S. 123, 88 S.Ct. 1620, 20 L.Ed.2d 476 (1968), 147

Chambers v. Mississippi, 410 U.S. 284, 93 S.Ct. 1038, 35 L.Ed.2d 297 (1973), 153
Cohen v. Jenkintown Cab Co., 238 Pa.Super. 456, 357 A.2d 689 (Pa.Super.1976), 215
Collins, People v., 68 Cal.2d 319, 66 Cal.Rptr. 497, 438 P.2d 33 (Cal.1968), 19
Commonwealth v. _____ (see opposing party)
Cox v. State, 696 N.E.2d 853 (Ind.1998), 9
Crawford v. Washington, 541 U.S. 36, 124 S.Ct. 1354, 158 L.Ed.2d 177 (2004), 141, 144
Crumby, United States v., 895 F.Supp. 1354 (D.Ariz.1995), 175
Cruz v. New York, 481 U.S. 186, 107 S.Ct. 1714, 95 L.Ed.2d 162 (1987), 149

Dallas County v. Commercial Union Assur. Co., 286 F.2d 388 (5th Cir.1961), 133
Daubert v. Merrell Dow Pharmaceuticals, Inc., 43 F.3d 1311 (9th Cir.1995), 173
Daubert v. Merrell Dow Pharmaceuticals, Inc., 509 U.S. 579, 113 S.Ct. 2786, 125 L.Ed.2d 469 (1993), 171
Davis v. Washington, 547 U.S. 813, 126 S.Ct. 2266, 165 L.Ed.2d 224 (2006), 143
DeGeorge, United States v., 380 F.3d 1203 (9th Cir.2004), 47
Delli Paoli v. United States, 352 U.S. 232, 77 S.Ct. 294, 1 L.Ed.2d 278 (1957), 147
DiNapoli, United States v., 8 F.3d 909 (2nd Cir.1993), 107
Doyle v. Ohio, 426 U.S. 610, 96 S.Ct. 2240, 49 L.Ed.2d 91 (1976), 99

Fletcher v. Weir, 455 U.S. 603, 102 S.Ct. 1309, 71 L.Ed.2d 490 (1982), 99
Frye v. United States, 293 F. 1013 (D.C.Cir.1923), 169

Ganier, United States v., 468 F.3d 920 (6th Cir.2006), 157
Gionis, People v., 40 Cal.Rptr.2d 456, 892 P.2d 1199 (Cal. 1995), 207
Glasser v. United States, 315 U.S. 60, 62 S.Ct. 457, 86 L.Ed. 680 (1942), 93
Grand Jury, In re, 103 F.3d 1140 (3rd Cir.1997), 235
Grand Jury Investigation, In re, 399 F.3d 527 (2nd Cir.2005), 219
Grand Jury Subpoena, Judith Miller, In re, 397 F.3d 964, 365 U.S.App.D.C. 13 (D.C.Cir.2005), 199
Gray v. Maryland, 523 U.S. 185, 118 S.Ct. 1151, 140 L.Ed.2d 294 (1998), 151
Gray, United States v., 405 F.3d 227 (4th Cir.2005), 117
Guardia, United States v., 135 F.3d 1326 (10th Cir.1998), 55

Halloran v. Virginia Chemicals Inc., 41 N.Y.2d 386, 393 N.Y.S.2d 341, 361 N.E.2d 991 (N.Y.1977), 61
Hines, United States v., 55 F.Supp.2d 62 (D.Mass.1999), 167
Howell v. Joffe, 483 F.Supp.2d 659 (N.D.Ill.2007), 211
Hubbell, United States v., 530 U.S. 27, 120 S.Ct. 2037, 147 L.Ed.2d 24 (2000), 223
Huddleston v. United States, 485 U.S. 681, 108 S.Ct. 1496, 99 L.Ed.2d 771 (1988), 49
Hygh v. Jacobs, 961 F.2d 359 (2nd Cir.1992), 163

Ince, United States v., 21 F.3d 576 (4th Cir.1994), 97
In re (see name of party)
Iron Shell, United States v., 633 F.2d 77 (8th Cir.1980), 123

Jackson, United States v., 405 F.Supp. 938 (E.D.N.Y.1975), 23
Jackson, United States v., 488 F.Supp.2d 866 (D.Neb.2007), 193
Jaffee v. Redmond, 518 U.S. 1, 116 S.Ct. 1923, 135 L.Ed.2d 337 (1996), 197
James, United States v., 169 F.3d 1210 (9th Cir.1999), 7, 15
Jinro America Inc. v. Secure Investments, Inc., 266 F.3d 993 (9th Cir.2001), 161
Johnson v. State, 967 S.W.2d 410 (Tex.Crim.App.1998), 125
Johnson, United States v., 575 F.2d 1347 (5th Cir.1978), 159

Kinney, State v., 171 Vt. 239, 762 A.2d 833 (Vt.2000), 179
Kirsch, State v., 139 N.H. 647, 662 A.2d 937 (N.H.1995), 53
Knox, United States v., 1992 WL 97157 (AFCMR 1992), 85
Koch Foods of AL LLC v. General Elec. Capital Corp., 531 F.Supp.2d 1318 (M.D.Ala.2008), 213
Kumho Tire Co., Ltd. v. Carmichael, 526 U.S. 137, 119 S.Ct. 1167, 143 L.Ed.2d 238 (1999), 177

Lannan v. State, 600 N.E.2d 1334 (Ind.1992), 51
Laster, United States v., 258 F.3d 525 (6th Cir.2001), 135
Lloyd v. American Export Lines, Inc., 580 F.2d 1179 (3rd Cir.1978), 111
Luce v. United States, 469 U.S. 38, 105 S.Ct. 460, 83 L.Ed.2d 443 (1984), 69

Mahlandt v. Wild Canid Survival & Research Center, Inc., 588 F.2d 626 (8th Cir.1978), 91
Mattox v. United States, 156 U.S. 237, 15 S.Ct. 337, 39 L.Ed. 409 (1895), 139
Michelson v. United States, 335 U.S. 469, 69 S.Ct. 213, 93 L.Ed. 168 (1948), 59
Morales v. Portuondo, 154 F.Supp.2d 706 (S.D.N.Y.2001), 203
Mound, United States v., 157 F.3d 1153 (8th Cir.1998), 57
Mutual Life Ins. Co. of New York v. Hillmon, 145 U.S. 285, 12 S.Ct. 909, 36 L.Ed. 706 (1892), 119
Myers, United States v., 550 F.2d 1036 (5th Cir.1977), 17

Ohler v. United States, 529 U.S. 753, 120 S.Ct. 1851, 146 L.Ed.2d 826 (2000), 71
Old Chief v. United States, 519 U.S. 172, 117 S.Ct. 644, 136 L.Ed.2d 574 (1997), 25
Olden v. Kentucky, 488 U.S. 227, 109 S.Ct. 480, 102 L.Ed.2d 513 (1988), 81
Owens, United States v., 484 U.S. 554, 108 S.Ct. 838, 98 L.Ed.2d 951 (1988), 105

Palmer v. Hoffman, 318 U.S. 109, 63 S.Ct. 477, 87 L.Ed. 645 (1943), 127
People v. _____ (see opposing party)

Rakes, United States v., 136 F.3d 1 (1st Cir.1998), 233

Seiler v. Lucasfilm, Ltd., 808 F.2d 1316 (9th Cir.1986), 191

Serge, Commonwealth v., 586 Pa. 671, 896 A.2d 1170 (Pa. 2006), 13

Shepard v. United States, 290 U.S. 96, 54 S.Ct. 22, 78 L.Ed. 196 (1933), 115, 121

Sibley, State v., 131 Mo. 519, 132 Mo. 102, 33 S.W. 167 (Mo.1895), 77

Simms v. Dixon, 291 A.2d 184 (D.C.1972), 187

Small, State v., 2007 WL 4395621 (Ohio App. 10 Dist.2007), 185

Smith, State v., 743 So.2d 199 (La.1999), 79

State v. _____ (see opposing party)

Stelmokas, United States v., 100 F.3d 302 (3rd Cir.1996), 183

Stephens v. Miller, 13 F.3d 998 (7th Cir.1994), 83

Stevens, United States v., 935 F.2d 1380 (3rd Cir.1991), 45

Swidler & Berlin v. United States, 524 U.S. 399, 118 S.Ct. 2081, 141 L.Ed.2d 379 (1998), 215

Tanner v. United States, 483 U.S. 107, 107 S.Ct. 2739, 97 L.Ed.2d 90 (1987), 3

Tome v. United States, 513 U.S. 150, 115 S.Ct. 696, 130 L.Ed.2d 574 (1995), 101

Trammel v. United States, 445 U.S. 40, 100 S.Ct. 906, 63 L.Ed.2d 186 (1980), 231

Trenkler, United States v., 61 F.3d 45 (1st Cir.1995), 41

Tuer v. McDonald, 347 Md. 507, 701 A.2d 1101 (Md.1997), 29

United States v. _____ (see opposing party)

Vigneau, United States v., 187 F.3d 70 (1st Cir.1999), 129

Wagner v. State, 707 So.2d 827 (Fla.App. 1 Dist.1998), 189

Weichell, Commonwealth v., 390 Mass. 62, 453 N.E.2d 1038 (Mass.1983), 103

Whitmore, United States v., 359 F.3d 609, 360 U.S.App.D.C. 257 (D.C.Cir.2004), 65

Williams v. McCoy, 145 N.C.App. 111, 550 S.E.2d 796 (N.C.App.2001), 33

Williamson v. United States, 512 U.S. 594, 114 S.Ct. 2431, 129 L.Ed.2d 476 (1994), 113

Zackowitz, People v., 254 N.Y. 192, 172 N.E. 466 (N.Y.1930), 39

Zolin, United States v., 491 U.S. 554, 109 S.Ct. 2619, 105 L.Ed.2d 469 (1989), 217

INTRODUCTION

Tanner v. United States

Instant Facts: Tanner (D) was convicted of fraud and attempted to challenge the guilty verdict by showing misconduct by individual jurors.

Black Letter Rule: Juror testimony may not be used to impeach a verdict unless the testimony relates to an outside influence that affected the jury.

Tanner v. United States

(Fraud Defendant) v. *(Prosecuting Authority)*

483 U.S. 107, 107 S.Ct. 2739 (1987)

JUROR TESTIMONY USUALLY CANNOT OVERTURN A VERDICT

Dude, you're drunk.

It makes jury duty bearable.

stus.com

■ **INSTANT FACTS** Tanner (D) was convicted of fraud and attempted to challenge the guilty verdict by showing misconduct by individual jurors.

■ **BLACK LETTER RULE** Juror testimony may not be used to impeach a verdict unless the testimony relates to an outside influence that affected the jury.

■ **PROCEDURAL BASIS**

Appeal from an order of the Eleventh Circuit denying motions for a new trial.

■ **FACTS**

Tanner (D) was convicted of mail fraud and conspiring to defraud the United States. Before he was to be sentenced, his attorney received an unsolicited telephone call from one of the jurors. The juror told him that several of the jurors had consumed alcohol during lunch breaks, which made them sleep through the afternoon sessions.

The court held a hearing on the jury misconduct issue to decide whether Tanner's (D) attorney should be allowed to interview the jurors. The court did not admit the whistle-blowing juror's testimony, but allowed Tanner (D) to present evidence from non-jurors. Tanner's (D) attorney testified that he thought that one of the jurors seemed to be in a "giggly" mood, but he did not bring it to anyone's attention. The judge made reference to an exchange with Tanner's (D) attorney early in the trial, in which the possibility that jurors were falling asleep was discussed. During that exchange, the judge directed counsel to notify him if jurors were falling asleep, but the matter was not brought up again.

The trial court denied the motion to interview the jurors. While the denial of the motion was on appeal, Tanner (D) filed a second motion for a new trial. The affidavit in support of that motion stated that a juror made an unsolicited visit to the home of Tanner's (D) attorney. That juror stated that seven of the jurors drank alcohol during the noon recess, and that he and other jurors smoked marijuana regularly during the trial. The juror also stated that he saw two other jurors use cocaine during the trial, and that one juror sold a quarter pound of marijuana to another during the trial. The second motion for a new trial was denied.

■ **ISSUE**

Could the testimony of the jurors relating to juror misconduct be used to impeach their verdict?

■ **DECISION AND RATIONALE**

(O'Connor, J.) No. Juror testimony may not be used to impeach a verdict unless the testimony relates to an outside influence that affected the jury. Questions of a juror's state of mind have long been held to be internal questions, not questions of outside influence. And substance abuse is not an outside influence on the jury. The legislative history of the Federal Rules of Evidence notes that intoxication of a juror was rejected as a reason for which a verdict might be attacked.

The policy against inquiring into jurors' mental states is a strong one. Jury deliberations are meant to be private, with the jurors free to have open and frank discussions of the evidence. Inquiry into juror misconduct would lead to the invalidation of some verdicts, but it would also seriously disrupt the finality of the process. The trust of the community in the decisions rendered by laypeople, as well as the willingness of jurors to render an unpopular verdict, would be undermined by public scrutiny of the process by which the verdict was rendered.

The right to an unimpaired jury is protected during the trial, first at *voir dire,* when the mental state of the potential juror may be evaluated, and throughout the trial, by observation by court personnel and other jurors. In addition, nonjuror testimony may be used to impeach a verdict due to juror misconduct. In this case, however, there was insufficient evidence to merit overturning the jury's verdict due to juror misconduct. Affirmed.

■ **CONCURRENCE AND DECISION**

(Marshall, J.) The policy requiring jury deliberations to be kept secret is an important one. In this case, however, the inquiry is not about the jury's deliberations themselves, or about the effect of anything on those deliberations. Even if the proposed evidence is considered to relate to the deliberations of the jury, evidence of juror intoxication should be admitted under the "outside influence" exception. Drugs and alcohol are outside influences, no less than a virus, poorly prepared food, or a lack of sleep.

Analysis:

Allegations of jury misconduct can take many forms. The allegation may be a claim that evidence was overlooked, or that a juror stubbornly, against all reason, refused to credit a witness's testimony. The allegation may likewise be of the type at issue here, where there is specific testimony regarding identifiable misbehavior. The first type of "misconduct" is inherent in the nature of the jury system, and such claims may fairly be dismissed as "sour grapes" from a losing party. The type of misconduct here, however, does not criticize the verdict, or how the verdict was reached, but goes to the integrity of the jury itself.

■ **CASE VOCABULARY**

IMPEACHMENT OF VERDICT: A party's attack on a verdict, alleging impropriety by a member of a jury.

VOIR DIRE: A preliminary examination of a prospective juror by a judge or lawyer to decide whether the prospect is qualified and suitable to serve on a jury. Loosely, the term refers to the jury-selection phase of a trial.

CHAPTER ONE

General Principles of Relevance

United States v. James

Instant Facts: James (D) claimed she acted in self-defense when she handed her daughter a gun that was used to kill Ogden, and she sought to introduce evidence of homicides and assaults committed by Ogden to corroborate her story.

Black Letter Rule: Evidence that directly corroborates a witness's credibility is admissible, even if the evidence relates to facts not known to the witness.

Cox v. State

Instant Facts: Cox (D) was convicted of murder, and the prosecutor introduced evidence that his motive was revenge for a friend whose bail was not reduced.

Black Letter Rule: Evidence that is relevant only if another fact is proven will be admitted if the court concludes that a reasonable jury could make the required finding of fact with the evidence before it.

State v. Bocharski

Instant Facts: At Bocharski's (D) trial for murder, photographs of the victim's body were introduced, and Bocharski (D) claimed that they should have been excluded as inflammatory.

Black Letter Rule: Relevant evidence should not be admitted if the only effect of the evidence would be to inflame the jury.

Commonwealth v. Serge

Instant Facts: The prosecution in a criminal case introduced a computer-generated animation of the crime scene that illustrated the forensic and physical evidence established by its experts' testimony.

Black Letter Rule: Computer-generated animation is admissible as demonstrative evidence if it is a fair and accurate representation of the evidence it purports to portray, it is relevant under the rules of evidence, and its probative value is not outweighed by the danger of unfair prejudice.

United States v. James

Instant Facts: James (D) claimed she acted in self-defense when she handed her daughter a gun that was used to kill Ogden, and she sought to introduce evidence of homicides and assaults committed by Ogden.

Black Letter Rule: Evidence that is unfairly prejudicial to either party should be excluded.

United States v. Myers

Instant Facts: Myers (D) was convicted of bank robbery after the judge instructed the jury that it could consider evidence of flight and could decide whether flight constituted evidence of a consciousness of guilt.

Black Letter Rule: Evidence of flight is admissible to show consciousness of guilt only if the evidence is sufficient to support inferences (1) from the defendant's behavior to the defendant's flight, (2) from flight to consciousness of guilt, (3) from consciousness of guilt to consciousness of guilt of the crime charged, and (4) from consciousness of guilt of the crime charged to actual guilt.

People v. Collins

Instant Facts: The prosecutor introduced mathematical evidence that purported to show the probability that a couple matching the description of Collins (D) and his wife committed a robbery.

Black Letter Rule: Statistical evidence will not be admitted unless it has a foundation in evidence and statistical theory, and it must not distract the jury from its duty to weigh the evidence on the issue of guilt.

United States v. Jackson

Instant Facts: Jackson (D) was accused of bank robbery and moved to exclude evidence that, shortly after the robbery, he was arrested in a different state while using a false name.

Black Letter Rule: Exclusion of evidence may be conditioned on a stipulation that acknowledges the truth of a part of the excluded evidence.

Old Chief v. United States

Instant Facts: Old Chief's (D) offer to stipulate to the fact of a prior felony conviction was refused.

Black Letter Rule: A court abuses its discretion if it rejects an offer to stipulate to a prior conviction when a prior conviction is an element of the offense charged.

United States v. James

(Prosecuting Authority) v. *(Mother of Shooter)*
69 F.3d 1210 (9th Cir. 1999)

EVIDENCE IS RELEVANT IF IT CORROBORATES A WITNESS'S TESTIMONY

Sorry, I couldn't keep your police record out of court. Your killers want to use it to make themselves look honest.

Here Lies
OGDEN
Totally Violent Jerk

stus.com

■ **INSTANT FACTS** James (D) claimed she acted in self-defense when she handed her daughter a gun that was used to kill Ogden, and she sought to introduce evidence of homicides and assaults committed by Ogden to corroborate her story.

■ **BLACK LETTER RULE** Evidence that directly corroborates a witness's credibility is admissible, even if the evidence relates to facts not known to the witness.

■ **PROCEDURAL BASIS**

Rehearing en banc of a decision affirming a conviction for aiding and abetting manslaughter.

■ **FACTS**

James (D) was convicted of aiding and abetting manslaughter after she handed her daughter a gun and the daughter used it to kill Ogden. James (D) testified that Ogden had boasted about killing a man and getting away with it, and that he claimed to have stabbed a man in the neck with a pen during a dispute about a watch. Ogden also claimed that he once tore a side mirror off a car and beat a man unconscious with it, and that he robbed an old man at knifepoint by holding him down and threatening to cut his eyes out. Ogden had also acted violently towards James (D), and on one occasion James's (D) daughter used a carving knife to keep Ogden away from James (D). Ogden seemed frightened of James's (D) daughter, who, although only fourteen, had beaten him three different times.

Before Ogden was killed, James (D), Ogden, James's (D) daughter, and the daughter's boyfriend were at a party. When they left the party, Ogden punched the boyfriend in the face, breaking his nose, and knocking him unconscious. The daughter chased Ogden and asked her mother for her gun. James (D) testified that she gave her daughter the gun to protect herself and other family members. She said she thought her daughter would use the gun just to scare Ogden away, and that she didn't want her to shoot him.

At trial, the judge allowed James (D) and her daughter to testify about Ogden's violent acts of which they had personal knowledge. The court did not allow the introduction of court records about other violent acts about which James (D) had no knowledge at the time of the killing. The jury asked for further information about those acts, wanting to know if there were police or court documents to prove what had taken place, or if it was just "bragging." The judge denied the request for additional information. The judge explained that, if court or police records had shown that the incidents Ogden bragged about had never taken place, he would have sustained a defense objection to the introduction of the records, because the outside record could not have affected James's (D) state of mind. James (D) was convicted, and the Ninth Circuit affirmed her conviction.

■ **ISSUE**

Should the outside evidence of victim's violent acts have been admitted to show that the defendant acted in self defense?

■ DECISION AND RATIONALE

(Noonan, J.) Yes. Evidence that directly corroborates a witness's credibility is admissible, even if the evidence relates to facts not known to the witness. It was necessary for James's (D) defense that the jury believe her, and that she was not merely making up stories. The records would have corroborated her testimony. Without the additional evidence, the jury might well believe that the testimony about such violent atrocities was fabricated. Exclusion of the additional evidence was prejudicial and more probably than not affected the verdict. Reversed.

Analysis:

The majority's holding rests on the logic that, if a person actually did something, a witness who testifies that the actor bragged about his conduct is more likely to be telling the truth. There may be some notion that if the boasting is about something illegal or immoral, a person would not lie in order to look bad. This reasoning overlooks the fact that, in many social circles, violent or criminal activity is a badge of honor. The jury here seemed to recognize that fact and asked if Ogden's violent past actually happened, or if it could have been just boasting.

■ CASE VOCABULARY

HARMLESS ERROR: An error that does not affect a party's substantive rights or the case's outcome.

INDIAN COUNTRY: The land within the borders of all Indian reservations, the land occupied by an Indian community (whether or not located within a recognized reservation), and any land held in trust by the United States but beneficially owned by an Indian or tribe; historically, any region (especially during the U.S. westward migration) where a person was likely to encounter Indians.

MATERIAL EVIDENCE: Evidence having some logical connection with the consequential facts or the issues.

RELEVANT EVIDENCE: Evidence tending to prove or disprove a matter in issue. Relevant evidence is both probative and material and is admissible unless excluded by a specific statute or rule.

Cox v. State

(Friend) v. *(Prosecuting Authority)*

696 N.E.2d 853 (Ind. 1998)

CONDITIONALLY RELEVANT EVIDENCE IS ADMISSIBLE

Don't be coy...
I heard the prosecution
said you killed for me.
Now we really are
best friends forever!

stus.com

■ **INSTANT FACTS** Cox (D) was convicted of murder, and the prosecutor introduced evidence that his motive was revenge for a friend whose bail was not reduced.

■ **BLACK LETTER RULE** Evidence that is relevant only if another fact is proven will be admitted if the court concludes that a reasonable jury could make the required finding of fact with the evidence before it.

■ **PROCEDURAL BASIS**

Direct appeal of a conviction for murder.

■ **FACTS**

Leonard was shot in the eye while asleep in his bedroom. He died three days later. Police questioned Cox (D) about the crime, but he denied involvement. Police later learned that Cox (D) told a friend that he looked in Leonard's window, fired a shot, and fled. The friend also said that Cox (D) told him that "Leonards [sic] probably ain't gonna have a dad after last night." Another friend also testified that she bought bullets for Cox (D) at his request, and that she and other friends were with Cox (D) at Helen Johnson's home until Cox (D) left, at the approximate time of the shooting.

Helen Johnson was the mother of Hammer, a close friend of Cox (D). Hammer was in prison pending trial on charges brought by Leonard that Hammer had molested Leonard's young daughter. The prosecution's theory was that Cox (D) killed Leonard in retaliation for the charges. Evidence was introduced that, a few days before the murder, a bond reduction hearing was held in Hammer's case. At that hearing, the court was informed that additional charges would be filed against Hammer. Hammer's mother testified at the hearing, and Hammer's bond was not reduced. Cox (D) objected to the admission of that evidence, stating that the evidence would be relevant to show his motive only if he knew what happened at the hearing. Cox (D) claimed that the prosecution was unable to prove conclusively that he had that knowledge. The trial court allowed the evidence to come in, reasoning that because Hammer's mother knew what happened, other members of Hammer's circle were reasonably likely to know about it.

■ **ISSUE**

Was evidence of an occurrence, which would substantiate the prosecution's theory of the defendant's motive, admissible even if there was no proof that the defendant had knowledge of the occurrence?

■ **DECISION AND RATIONALE**

(Boehm, J.) Yes. Evidence that is relevant only if another fact is proven will be admitted if the court concludes that a reasonable jury could make the required finding of fact with the evidence before it. The relevance of the evidence here depends upon a finding of an additional fact—that Cox (D) knew what happened at Hammer's bond reduction hearing. If he did know what happened, the evidence was probative of the State's (P) theory that Cox (D) killed Leonard because of Hammer's situation. If Cox (D) did not know about the hearing, the evidence would be inflammatory and highly prejudicial.

Conditionally relevant evidence, such as the testimony at issue here, will be admitted if the court makes a preliminary finding of fact that there is sufficient evidence to support a finding that the conditional fact exists. The court is not required to make formal findings, or to weigh the credibility of the evidence. In this case, the evidence showed that Cox (D) was a close friend of Hammer's, and that Cox (D) was at the house where Hammer's mother lived almost daily. The evidence is sufficient to support an inference that Cox knew what happened at the bond reduction hearing. Affirmed.

Analysis:

It is difficult to imagine an assertion of fact that does not depend on whether something else is proven or assumed. For example, in this case, even something as basic as the day on which Leonard was shot depends on someone knowing what day it was, which in turn depends on knowing the basis for that conclusion. The inquiry could be stretched out to an absurdity just by asking, "how do you know?" as a response to any affirmative statement. At a certain point, we have to assume that a basic fact is known, or accept that we have reason to believe it is known.

■ CASE VOCABULARY

BOND: A bond given to a court by a criminal defendant's surety to guarantee that the defendant will duly appear in court in the future and, if the defendant is jailed, to obtain the defendant's release from confinement. The effect of the release on bail bond is to transfer custody of the defendant from the officers of the law to the custody of the surety on the bail bond, whose undertaking is to redeliver the defendant to legal custody at the time and place appointed in the bond.

State v. Bocharski

(Prosecuting Authority) v. *(Accused Murderer)*

22 P.3d 43 (Ariz. 2001)

INFLAMMATORY EVIDENCE SHOULD NOT BE ADMITTED

$5 a day for nightmares for the rest of my life?!?

stus.com

■ **INSTANT FACTS** At Bocharski's (D) trial for murder, photographs of the victim's body were introduced, and Bocharski (D) claimed that they should have been excluded as inflammatory.

■ **BLACK LETTER RULE** Relevant evidence should not be admitted if the only effect of the evidence would be to inflame the jury.

■ **PROCEDURAL BASIS**

Direct appeal from a conviction for first-degree felony murder.

■ **FACTS**

Bocharski (D) lived on a campsite next to a woman named Brown, who was eighty-four years old. A friend of Bocharski (D), Sukis, testified that Bocharski (D) suggested killing Brown, supposedly to put her out of her misery from arthritis. A few days after that conversation, it was observed that Brown's dog appeared to be unattended and that Brown had not been seen lately. Sukis and another man went into Brown's trailer and found her dead. When police arrived, the initial conclusion was that she had died of natural causes. An autopsy showed, however, that she died from multiple stab wounds to her head. A search was made for the knife Bocharski (D) was known to have carried, but the knife was never found. Bocharski (D) was arrested and tried for Brown's murder.

At trial, six photographs of Brown's body were introduced and admitted into evidence. Two of the photographs showed the state of decomposition of Brown's body and the wounds to her face. Another photograph showed superficial head wounds, and one showed a cut on Brown's finger. Two other photographs showed Brown's skull, with the contents removed. Bocharski (D) conceded that the photographs were relevant, but he claimed that they were so gruesome as to be inflammatory. The fact of Brown's death, the extent of her injuries, and the manner in which she died were not contested by Bocharski (D). Bocharski (D) was convicted of burglary, for which he received a sentence of twenty-one years, and he was convicted of felony murder, for which he was sentenced to death.

■ **ISSUE**

Were the gruesome photographs of the murder victim admissible?

■ **DECISION AND RATIONALE**

(Zlaket, C.J.) Yes. Relevant evidence should not be admitted if the only effect of the evidence would be to inflame the jury, but there has been no showing here that the photographs had any particular adverse effect on the jury. The trial judge has broad discretion to determine what evidence should be admitted. Photographs of a homicide victim's body generally are admissible, because the fact and the cause of death are always relevant in a murder case. The photographs that showed the decomposition of Brown's body related to the question of how long she had been dead before she was found. The photographs that showed the head wounds and the cut on the finger were marginally relevant, at best.

The cut on the finger was not a defensive wound, and there were other diagrams that showed Brown's most serious injuries.

The photographs of Brown's skull present a closer issue. The State (P) claimed that those photographs were necessary to show the angles and depths of the wounds, and that information was important because a juror had asked the medical examiner about it. However, the manner of death was not in issue, and the State (P) did not introduce any testimony concerning the angles or their significance. The photographs met the bare minimum standard of relevance, but they had little tendency to establish a contested issue in the case. The only purpose for introducing the photographs was to inflame the jury. The court abused its discretion by admitting the photographs.

Nonetheless, there has been no showing that the photographs affected the jury's verdict. Jurors showed some distress at seeing the pictures of Brown's body, but the trial judge thought that they took them "in stride." The verdict showed careful deliberation and attention to detail. The verdict is affirmed, but the case is remanded for resentencing.

■ CONCURRENCE

(Martone, J.) The trial court did not err in introducing the photographs. Bocharski (D) conceded the relevance of the photographs. There was no appeal to emotion, sympathy, or horror. Jurors do not need to be protected from themselves.

Analysis:

In portions of the opinion not in the excerpt, the court noted that Bocharski (D) grew impatient with the pace of the investigation of mitigating factors in his case and waived the right to further mitigation. The Arizona Supreme Court found his waiver to be ineffective. The excerpt also does not say why Bocharski (D) was accused of the crime in the first place. In the omitted portions, the court noted that he told a friend that he had killed and robbed an old woman. Other friends saw him in possession of more money than they would have expected him to have, and they testified that he gave implausible explanations for having the money.

■ CASE VOCABULARY

FELONY MURDER: Murder that occurs during the commission of a dangerous felony (often limited to rape, kidnapping, robbery, burglary, and arson).

FELONY MURDER RULE: The doctrine holding that any death resulting from the commission or attempted commission of a felony is murder. Most states restrict this rule to inherently dangerous felonies such as rape, arson, robbery, and burglary.

Commonwealth v. Serge

(Prosecuting Authority) v. (Convicted Defendant)

586 Pa. 671, *cert denied*, 549 U.S. 920, 127 S.Ct. 275 (2006)

ANIMATION IS ADMISSIBLE EVIDENCE

Please admit me. I promise to be fair and accurate.

stus.com

■ **INSTANT FACTS** The prosecution in a criminal case introduced a computer-generated animation of the crime scene that illustrated the forensic and physical evidence established by its experts' testimony.

■ **BLACK LETTER RULE** Computer-generated animation is admissible as demonstrative evidence if it is a fair and accurate representation of the evidence it purports to portray, it is relevant under the rules of evidence, and its probative value is not outweighed by the danger of unfair prejudice.

■ **PROCEDURAL BASIS**

On appeal to review the defendant's conviction.

■ **FACTS**

In 2001, Serge (D) shot his wife three times in their home, killing her. Serge (D) was arrested and charged with first-degree murder. Before trial, the Commonwealth (P) filed a motion in limine seeking permission to use a computer-generated animation (CGA) of the crime scene. The court granted the motion, provided that the Commonwealth (P) first established that the animation was a fair and accurate depiction of its experts' reconstructive testimony, and that any inflammatory features that may cause unfair prejudice to Serge (D) were excluded. At trial, Serge (D) claimed that he acted in self-defense as his wife attacked him with a knife. The Commonwealth (P) responded that, as a former police detective, Serge (D) tampered with the crime scene to make it appear as self-defense. The Commonwealth (P) presented the CGA as demonstrative evidence to illustrate its experts' testimony that the forensic and physical evidence suggested that Serge's (D) wife had been shot in the lower back and then through the heart as she knelt on the floor. Serge (D) was convicted and sentenced to life in prison.

■ **ISSUE**

Was the court's admission of the CGA depicting the Commonwealth's (P) theory of the case proper?

■ **DECISION AND RATIONALE**

(Newman, J.) Yes. Computer-generated animation is admissible as demonstrative evidence if it is a fair and accurate representation of the evidence it purports to portray, it is relevant under the rules of evidence, and its probative value is not outweighed by the danger of unfair prejudice. Had the Commonwealth (P) chosen to illustrate its theory of the case through chalk diagrams or sketches, there would have been little doubt that the evidence would be admissible with proper authentication by the Commonwealth's (P) experts. The law does not prohibit the use to technological advances to illustrate what has always been admissible. Evidence is not inadmissible simply because it is more persuasive than other means of presenting the evidence. Here, the evidence established that the CGA was a strict depiction of the Commonwealth's (P) expert opinions. Although it contained images of the victim kneeling on the floor and engaging in a combat-style crouch, any prejudice caused by these images derives not from the CGA but from the act of murder itself. It contained no sounds, facial expressions, or life-like movements. In the end, the CGA depicted the trajectory of the bullets and conclusions from ballistics and blood splatter that the body had been moved after the murder. Moreover, although in some cases financial disparity between the parties can give rise to unfair prejudice, the court determined from the facts here that the cost of creating the CGA was not prejudicial, even though the defendant did not have the resources to create his own CGA. Finally, the court appropriately issued a limiting instruction to the jurors, instructing them that the CGA did not depict the events of the shooting, but merely the Commonwealth's (P) theory of the case. In all, the probative value of the CGA outweighed any prejudicial effect against the defendant. Affirmed.

■ CONCURRENCE

(Cappy, C.J.) Just as with all demonstrative evidence, the admissibility of CGAs is guided by the requirements of the rules of evidence, including relevance and authentication, and by weighing the probative value against the prejudicial effect. In weighing these considerations, the court must be mindful of the defendant's opportunity to mitigate the prejudicial impact of the Commonwealth's (P) evidence. The economic disparity between the parties is a relevant consideration in this balancing process.

■ CONCURRENCE

(Castille, J.) When both parties are well funded, the danger of unfair prejudice is minimized by the opportunity to prepare countervailing demonstrative evidence. When one party is indigent, however, the means to challenge the accuracy of the Commonwealth's (P) CGA are unavailable unless adequate funding is provided by the Commonwealth (P). If such funding is denied, the appointed defense counsel must educate himself sufficiently to attack the technological processes used to create the CGA. Trial courts may wisely exclude CGAs altogether in such circumstances to avoid prejudice.

■ CONCURRENCE

(Eakin, J.) The respective finances of the parties are irrelevant to the admissibility of evidence. A party should not be limited in its choice of demonstrative evidence, and therefore the proof of its theory of the case, by the financial resources available to its opponent. Relevance, not money, governs admissibility.

Analysis:

The admission of computer images at trial may present a substantial threat of unfair prejudice. Visual images can have a stronger and longer lasting impact on jurors than charts or even live testimony. Like video, computer animation gives the jury a visual depiction of the events of the case. Unlike video, however, computer animation does not capture the true events and cannot stand alone as evidence. It must be created and supported based on the testimony of other witnesses. While video can be definitive proof of its contents, computer animation cannot.

■ CASE VOCABULARY

DEMONSTRATIVE EVIDENCE: Physical evidence that one can see and inspect (such as a model or photograph) and that, while of probative value and usually offered to clarify testimony, does not play a direct part in the incident in question.

PROBATIVE: Tending to prove or disprove. Courts can exclude relevant evidence if its probative value is substantially outweighed by the danger of unfair prejudice.

RELEVANT EVIDENCE: Evidence tending to prove or disprove a matter in issue. Relevant evidence is both probative and material and is admissible unless excluded by a specific statute or rule.

UNDUE PREJUDICE: The harm resulting from a fact-trier's being exposed to evidence that is persuasive but inadmissible (such as evidence of prior criminal conduct) or that so arouses the emotions that calm and logical reasoning is abandoned.

United States v. James

(Prosecuting Authority) v. *(Mother of Shooter)*

169 F.3d 1210 (9th Cir. 1999)

UNFAIR PREJUDICE IS NOT LIMITED TO A DEFENDANT'S CLAIMS

When the jury sees the victim's record, it'll corroborate your testimony AND make him look like a total jerk.

stus.com

■ **INSTANT FACTS** James (D) claimed she acted in self-defense when she handed her daughter a gun that was used to kill Ogden, and she sought to introduce evidence of homicides and assaults committed by Ogden.

■ **BLACK LETTER RULE** Evidence that is unfairly prejudicial to either party should be excluded.

■ **PROCEDURAL BASIS**

Rehearing en banc of a decision affirming a conviction for aiding and abetting manslaughter.

■ **FACTS**

James (D) was convicted of aiding and abetting manslaughter after she handed her daughter a gun and the daughter used it to kill Ogden. James (D) testified that Ogden had boasted about killing a man and getting away with it, and that he claimed to have stabbed a man in the neck with a pen during a dispute about a watch. Ogden also claimed that he once tore a side mirror off a car and beat a man unconscious with it, and that he robbed an old man at knifepoint by holding him down and threatening to cut his eyes out. Ogden had also acted violently towards James (D), and on one occasion James's (D) daughter used a carving knife to keep Ogden away from James (D). Ogden seemed frightened of James's (D) daughter, who, although only fourteen, had beaten him three different times.

Before Ogden was killed, James (D), Ogden, James's (D) daughter, and the daughter's boyfriend were at a party. When they left the party, Ogden punched the boyfriend in the face, breaking his nose, and knocking him unconscious. The daughter chased Ogden and asked her mother for her gun. James (D) testified that she gave her daughter the gun to protect herself and other family members. She said she thought her daughter would use the gun just to scare Ogden away, and that she didn't want her to shoot him

At trial, the judge allowed James (D) and her daughter to testify about Ogden's violent acts of which they had personal knowledge. The court did not allow the introduction of court records about other violent acts about which James (D) had no knowledge at the time of the killing. The jury asked for further information about those acts, wanting to know if there were police or court documents to prove what had taken place, or if it was just "bragging." The judge denied the request for additional information. The judge explained that, if court or police records had shown that the incidents Ogden bragged about had never taken place, he would have sustained a defense objection to the introduction of the records, because the outside record could not have affected James's (D) state of mind. James (D) was convicted, and the Ninth Circuit affirmed her conviction.

After a rehearing en banc, the court of appeals reversed James's (D) conviction, holding that the court and police records of prior acts by Ogden corroborated James's (D) claims of what Ogden had told her.

■ **ISSUE**

Should outside evidence of a murder victim's earlier violent acts have been admitted when the defendant claimed self-defense?

■ DISSENT

(Kleinfeld, J.) No. Evidence that is unfairly prejudicial to either party should be excluded. The rules of evidence do not limit unfair prejudice to one side in a case. Unfair prejudice means a tendency to persuade a court or jury to make a decision on an improper basis. The records were relevant to corroborate James's (D) story of what Ogden told her, but admissibility alone does not mean that excluding the evidence was an abuse of discretion. The records were not direct evidence, but were only corroboration of James's (D) state of mind.

There was also considerable risk of unfair prejudice to the prosecution. The jury's question may have been a way of asking whether Ogden "deserved" to be shot. The majority says that the evidence went to James's (D) credibility, but the question suggests that the jury was wondering whether Ogden really did what he claimed to have done. James (D) was entitled to prove self-defense, but she was not entitled to claim that Ogden's death was justified because he was a bad person. It was up to the judge to determine whether the evidence was being introduced for a permissible or an impermissible purpose. Evidence that shows only that a victim was a bad person should not be admitted because of the likelihood of unfair prejudice. The judge's decision to exclude the records because James (D) did not know about them made sense and was not an abuse of discretion.

Analysis:

The possibility of prejudice by itself is not a sufficient reason to exclude otherwise relevant evidence. Arguably, the purpose of all evidence is to "prejudice" the finder of fact, so that a particular result is reached or not reached. The question is whether the evidence is "unfairly prejudicial." In a case in which a defendant makes a claim of self-defense based on the violent character of the victim, there is always the possibility that evidence of a victim's violent propensities will make the jury believe that the victim "had it coming."

■ CASE VOCABULARY

AIDING AND ABETTING: To assist or facilitate the commission of a crime, or to promote its accomplishment. Aiding and abetting is a crime in most jurisdictions.

MANSLAUGHTER: The unlawful killing of a human being without malice aforethought.

United States v. Myers

(Prosecuting Authority) v. *(Convicted Bank Robber)*

550 F.2d 1036 (5th Cir. 1977), *cert. denied*, 439 U.S. 847, 99 S.Ct. 147 (1978)

EVIDENCE OF FLIGHT MAY BE ADMISSIBLE TO SHOW GUILT

■ **INSTANT FACTS** Myers (D) was convicted of bank robbery after the judge instructed the jury that it could consider evidence of flight and could decide whether flight constituted evidence of a consciousness of guilt.

■ **BLACK LETTER RULE** Evidence of flight is admissible to show consciousness of guilt only if the evidence is sufficient to support inferences (1) from the defendant's behavior to the defendant's flight, (2) from flight to consciousness of guilt, (3) from consciousness of guilt to consciousness of guilt of the crime charged, and (4) from consciousness of guilt of the crime charged to actual guilt.

■ **PROCEDURAL BASIS**

Appeal from a conviction for bank robbery.

■ **FACTS**

Myers (D) was convicted of a bank robbery in Florida. The only question before the jury was whether Myers (D) was the lone gunman who committed the robbery. Coffie, a friend of Myers (D) who bore a close physical resemblance to Myers (D), pleaded guilty to committing that robbery. After the robbery, FBI agents tried to contact Myers (D) through Dunn, a woman with whom Myers (D) shared an apartment. The agents told her they were looking for Coffie. Myers (D) was not at home when the agents called, and he told Dunn that he did not want to speak with them. Approximately three weeks after the Florida robbery, Myers (D) called Dunn and asked her to bring some of his clothes to a shopping mall. The FBI agents were waiting nearby. One of the agents went towards Myers (D) without identifying himself, and Myers (D) fled. Sometime after that incident, Myers (D) left the state.

After the incident in the mall, Myers (D) and Coffie went to Pennsylvania, where they were involved in another bank robbery. After that robbery, Myers (D) and Coffie traveled to California. Approximately two months after the Florida robbery, FBI agents followed Myers (D) and Coffie while they were riding a motorcycle. One FBI agent, who was approaching from the opposite direction in an unmarked car, crossed over into their lane of travel and drove straight towards them. Coffie swerved, but collided slightly with the car. Another unmarked car with an FBI agent in plainclothes pulled up alongside the motorcycle. One agent testified that Coffie and Myers (D) each moved about three feet, in opposite directions. Another agent, Hanlon, testified that when he exited his car and identified himself as an FBI agent, Myers (D) and Coffie began to flee, each one moving in opposite directions, about fifty feet from the motorcycle. On cross-examination, Myers (D) introduced evidence from his trial in Pennsylvania, in which Hanlon said that neither Myers (D) nor Coffie was attempting to flee. Coffie testified that, when he swerved to avoid the oncoming car, he did not know that it contained police or federal agents.

The jury was instructed that it could consider evidence of flight in light of all the other evidence presented. The jury was instructed that flight alone was not sufficient to establish guilt, but that it could show consciousness of guilt. Myers (D) was found guilty.

■ ISSUE

Was the evidence of the defendant's flight admissible to show his consciousness of guilt?

■ DECISION AND RATIONALE

(Clark, J.) No. Evidence of flight is admissible to show consciousness of guilt only if the evidence is sufficient to support inferences from the defendant's behavior to flight, from flight to consciousness of guilt, from consciousness of guilt to consciousness of guilt of the crime charged, and from consciousness of guilt of the crime charged to actual guilt. Flight evidence has only marginal probative value as evidence of guilt or innocence, so all four inferences must be supported before it may be admitted.

In this case, the evidence regarding the incident in California does not show that Myers (D) or Coffie attempted to flee. The agents' testimony was inconsistent and contradicted Hanlon's prior testimony that he did not think anyone was attempting to flee. Furthermore, the evidence does not support an inference that Myers (D) fled out of consciousness of his guilt about the Florida robbery. Myers (D) had been involved in a robbery in Pennsylvania before the incident in California, and it is possible that he fled because of his consciousness of guilt for that robbery. It was error to instruct the jury that flight in California could be used as evidence of consciousness of guilt in Florida.

The Florida incident is also inadmissible. The evidence showed only that agents could not contact Myers (D) at his usual place of residence, that three weeks later he asked Dunn to bring his clothes to him at a mall, that he fled when an unidentified man came towards him, and that he left the state three to six weeks after the robbery. Flight evidence is relevant because it shows an instinctive or impulsive action that shows fear of apprehension. The more remote in time, the less likely it is that flight is due to consciousness of guilt of a particular offense, and the more likely it is that it is for some other reason. The jury should not have been instructed that it could infer consciousness of guilt from the Florida incident. The error was not harmless. The conviction is reversed.

Analysis:

The inference from consciousness of guilt to consciousness of guilt for a particular offense is one that is all too easy for a jury to make. Myers (D) might be able to offer an innocent explanation for his conduct at the mall in Florida that would not show consciousness of guilt for anything at all. On the other hand, assuming that what happened in California was flight, an innocent inference would be a harder to make. Imagine the reaction of a jury that was told Myers (D) was fleeing because he was conscious of his guilt in the Pennsylvania robbery, not the Florida one.

■ CASE VOCABULARY

CIRCUMSTANTIAL EVIDENCE: Evidence based on inference and not on personal knowledge or observation; all evidence that is not given by testimony.

People v. Collins

(Prosecuting Authority) v. *(Accused Robber)*
68 Cal.2d 319, 438 P.2d 33 (1968)

STATISTICAL EVIDENCE REQUIRES A STRONG FOUNDATION

The culprit had big eyes, big ears, and big teeth. Statistically, the chance of it being anyone other than the defendant is only one in 12 million.

stus.com

JURY

■ **INSTANT FACTS** The prosecutor introduced mathematical evidence that purported to show the probability that a couple matching the description of Collins (D) and his wife committed a robbery.

■ **BLACK LETTER RULE** Statistical evidence will not be admitted unless it has a foundation in evidence and statistical theory, and it must not distract the jury from its duty to weigh the evidence on the issue of guilt.

■ **PROCEDURAL BASIS**

Appeal from a conviction for robbery.

■ **FACTS**

Collins (D) and his wife were convicted of robbery. The victim said that she was walking in an alley and was pushed down. She saw a young woman running away. The woman was described as wearing dark clothes and having hair a little darker than Collins's (D) wife. Another witness saw a woman run out of the alley and get into a yellow automobile driven by an African–American man with a mustache and a beard. He described the woman as white, with a dark blonde ponytail, and wearing dark clothing. Her ponytail was described as being just like the one Collins's (D) wife wore in a police photograph taken a few days after the robbery. Collins (D) and his wife denied any involvement in the robbery and claimed they were visiting a friend when it happened.

At trial, the prosecutor (P) called as a witness a professor of mathematics to testify regarding the mathematical likelihood that Collins (D) and his wife committed the robbery. The prosecutor (P) presented the professor with a list of probabilities for the various characteristics allegedly shared by the guilty couple: the probability of someone driving a yellow car, of a man having a mustache, of a woman having a ponytail, of a woman having blonde hair, of an African American man having a beard, and of an interracial couple in a car. No evidence was introduced to show the basis for the probabilities assigned. The professor testified that the probability of the joint occurrence of a number of mutually independent events was equal to the product of the individual probability that each independent event will occur. Based on the figures given to him by the prosecutor (P), the professor concluded that there was only a one in twelve million chance that any couple would share all of the characteristics of Collins and his wife. The prosecutor (P) used the professor's testimony to argue that there was only a one in twelve million chance that Collins (D) and his wife were innocent and that another couple with the same characteristics committed the robbery. The prosecutor (P) also argued that the probabilities were conservative estimates, and that the actual likelihood that Collins (D) and his wife were innocent was closer to one in a billion.

The trial court denied the motion to strike, stating that the testimony had been received only for the purpose of illustrating the mathematical probabilities of certain matters. Collins (D) and his wife were convicted of robbery.

■ ISSUE

Was the professor's testimony on the statistical probability of the defendants' guilt admissible?

■ DECISION AND RATIONALE

(Sullivan, J.) No. Statistical evidence will not be admitted unless it has a foundation in evidence and statistical theory, and it must not distract the jury from its duty to weigh the evidence on the issue of guilt. The statistical evidence in this case failed both of these tests.

There was no foundation for the testimony. No evidence was introduced regarding the statistical probabilities of the six characteristics used by the prosecutor (P). For example, the professor was asked to assume that there was a one in ten probability of a yellow car, but no basis was given for making that assumption. In fact, the prosecutor (P) himself said that the figures were only conservative estimates, and he invited the jury to supply their own estimates. Likewise, there was no evidence that the six factors were mutually independent, and that there was no overlap among any of them. Some of the factors were certain to overlap—some African American men with beards also are men with mustaches, for example. Without an adequate evidentiary foundation, and without proof of statistical independence, the professor's testimony could lead only to wild conjecture, with no demonstrated relevance to the issues presented.

The best result that could come from the professor's testimony would be an estimate as to how infrequently bearded African Americans drive yellow cars while accompanied by blonde women with ponytails. It does not supply guidance on the issue of who was guilty of the robbery. The evidence relied on the assumption that a couple with the described characteristics committed the robbery. There was no way a mathematical formula could establish beyond a reasonable doubt that the witnesses were reliable, or that the people described by the witnesses were the same people.

Traditionally, it has been up to the jury to weigh the risks that testimony may be inaccurate. The likelihood of human error cannot be quantified, and no number can be assigned to the probability of guilt or innocence. Juries would be tempted to give disproportionate weight to such a figure. It is a rare juror or defense attorney who could keep in mind that the figure represents only the likelihood that a random couple would share the characteristics of Collins (D) and his wife, and not necessarily the characteristics of the couple that was in fact guilty.

Furthermore, the most a mathematical computation could show would be the probability of a random couple having the same characteristics. Even if the figure arrived at for this probability is accurate, it does not show that Collins (D) and his wife are the guilty couple. In the case at bar, if the prosecutor's (P) figures are accepted, there is actually a forty percent chance that there is at least one other couple that could have committed the robbery.

The prosecutor (P) urged the jury to disregard reasonable doubt because of the strength of the mathematical proof. The jurors were undoubtedly impressed by the mystique of the mathematical demonstration, but were ill equipped to assess its relevancy or value. The use of mathematical or statistical evidence must be evaluated in light of the substantial unfairness to defendants that may result from ill-conceived techniques beyond the abilities of the trier of fact. In this case, Collins (D) was so disadvantaged by the evidence that there was a miscarriage of justice. Reversed.

Analysis:

As the court points out, it is normally the function of the jury to assess the weight of evidence and to decide how flaws in reasoning affect the weight to be given to that evidence. The danger in this case is that the jury will be "blinded by science" and accept the mathematical proof uncritically. The court notes that many defense attorneys, as well as jurors, are unable to deal with mathematical evidence. It is possible that the court may not have excluded the evidence if defense counsel had been able to mount an effective challenge to the mathematical evidence and point out to the jury the manifold errors in the statistical testimony.

■ CASE VOCABULARY

FOUNDATIONAL EVIDENCE: Evidence that determines the admissibility of other evidence.

MATHEMATICAL EVIDENCE: Loosely, evidence that establishes its conclusions with absolute certainty.

United States v. Jackson

(Prosecuting Authority) v. *(Accused Bank Robber)*

405 F.Supp. 938 (E.D.N.Y. 1975)

STIPULATIONS MAY BE USED TO ALLOW ADMISSION OF A PART OF EVIDENCE

My client will admit he left the state and used a fake name.

Okay, then I won't mention his other arrest.

Whatever. I don't care about "total truth". I just want to get this trial over with.

stus.com

■ **INSTANT FACTS** Jackson (D) was accused of bank robbery and moved to exclude evidence that, shortly after the robbery, he was arrested in a different state while using a false name.

■ **BLACK LETTER RULE** Exclusion of evidence may be conditioned on a stipulation that acknowledges the truth of a part of the excluded evidence.

■ **PROCEDURAL BASIS**

Decision on a motion to exclude evidence.

■ **FACTS**

Jackson (D) was accused of robbing a bank in New York. At the time of the robbery, Jackson (D) was under indictment for assault, which ultimately led to a felony conviction. Approximately two months after the robbery, he was arrested in Georgia while using a false driver's license, and guns were found in his car. Jackson (D) later escaped from the Georgia jail. Before his trial for the bank robbery, Jackson (D) moved to exclude evidence that he used a false name when he was arrested in Georgia. Jackson (D) claimed that the probative value of that evidence was outweighed by the risk of unfair prejudice.

■ **ISSUE**

May potentially prejudicial evidence of guilt be excluded if the defendant acknowledges the truth of part of the excluded evidence?

■ **DECISION AND RATIONALE**

(Weinstein, J.) Yes. Exclusion of evidence may be conditioned on a stipulation that acknowledges the truth of a part of the excluded evidence. Such a stipulation may be used to balance the probative value of the evidence against the possibility of unfair prejudice. Jackson's (D) presence in Georgia is arguably proof of flight that stemmed from a consciousness of guilt. The use of a false name increases the probative force of this evidence. It is possible that Jackson (D) left New York to avoid trial for the assault, but that possibility is made less likely by the fact that he was in New York until shortly after the robbery. However, positive identification from the surveillance photographs and eyewitnesses is unlikely, so the probative value of the evidence is high. The probative value must be balanced against the potential for unfair prejudice to Jackson (D). There is a risk that evidence of the Georgia arrest will bring unrelated crimes to the attention of the jury, thus violating the protective policy of the rule excluding the use of evidence of other crimes to prove a propensity to criminal acts. The jury might infer that Jackson (D) was on a nationwide crime spree. The inferences of the evidence of flight may not be evaluated without revealing the assault indictment. There is also the possibility of delay in completing the trial that could result from calling the Georgia officer to testify, as well as issues relating to the possible illegality of the Georgia arrest.

In this case, evidence of Jackson's (D) Georgia arrest will be excluded if Jackson agrees to stipulate that he was in Georgia shortly after the robbery and that he used a false name while he was there. Eliminating reference to the arrest will protect Jackson (D) from the inference that he is a national crime figure, while giving the jury a basis for the inference that Jackson (D) left New York to avoid prosecution for the bank robbery. There is the possibility that jurors will use their imaginations to fill in perceived gaps in the evidence, but arriving at the "total truth" is not the goal of a trial. Motion granted, subject to agreement to the stipulation.

Analysis:

Evidence of other crimes is excluded because of the strong possibility of prejudice. If a defendant committed one crime, jurors may reason, he probably committed this crime, too. At the same time, the evidence may be necessary to help a prosecutor make a case. For example, in this case, jurors may have wondered why Jackson (D) was arrested at all, particularly since the identification evidence seems weak.

■ **CASE VOCABULARY**

PROBATIVE VALUE: Tending to prove or disprove. Courts can exclude relevant evidence if its probative value is substantially outweighed by the danger of unfair prejudice.

STIPULATION: A voluntary agreement between opposing parties concerning some relevant point; especially, an agreement relating to a proceeding, made by attorneys representing adverse parties to the proceeding.

Old Chief v. United States

(Accused Gun Possessor) v. *(Prosecuting Authority)*

519 U.S. 172, 117 S.Ct. 644 (1997)

COURTS MUST ACCEPT OFFERS TO STIPULATE TO PRIOR CONVICTIONS

■ **INSTANT FACTS** Old Chief's (D) offer to stipulate to the fact of a prior felony conviction was refused.

■ **BLACK LETTER RULE** A court abuses its discretion if it rejects an offer to stipulate to a prior conviction when a prior conviction is an element of the offense charged.

■ PROCEDURAL BASIS

Appeal from an order of the Ninth Circuit Court of Appeals affirming a conviction for possession of a firearm by a person convicted of a felony.

■ FACTS

Old Chief (D) was charged with assault with a dangerous weapon, using a firearm in relation to a crime of violence, and possession of a firearm by a person who has been convicted of a felony. The felony for which Old Chief (D) was convicted was assault causing serious bodily injury. He moved the court for an order barring introduction of any evidence relating to his prior conviction, except to state that he had been convicted of a felony. Old Chief (D) argued that revealing the name of his prior felony would unfairly tax the jury's ability to hold the prosecution (P) to its burden of proving the current offense beyond a reasonable doubt. He offered to stipulate to the fact of the conviction and proposed a jury instruction that instructed the jury that Old Chief (D) had been convicted of a crime punishable by imprisonment for more than one year. The prosecutor (P) refused to agree to the stipulation, and the court allowed introduction of the order of judgment and commitment for the prior conviction. Old Chief (D) was found guilty, and the Ninth Circuit affirmed his conviction.

■ ISSUE

Should the evidence of the prior conviction have been excluded?

■ DECISION AND RATIONALE

(Souter, J.) Yes. A court abuses its discretion if it rejects an offer to stipulate to a prior conviction when a prior conviction is an element of the offense charged. Introduction of the name and nature of a prior offense generally carries a risk of unfair prejudice to the defendant. The unfair prejudice is that the jury may generalize the earlier crime into bad character, taking that as raising the odds that a defendant committed the crime charged. The risk of such unfair prejudice is especially obvious when the prior offense was, as it is in this case, a firearm offense. Old Chief (D) was justifiably concerned that the prejudicial effect of the prior conviction would take on added weight from the related assault charge.

The prosecution (P) argued that a prosecutor is entitled to prove his or her case by the evidence he or she chooses. A defendant is not allowed to stipulate his or her way out of the full evidentiary force of the government's case. As a general rule, this argument is correct. Evidence has a value beyond a linear scheme of reasoning, and the persuasive power of particular facts is often essential to allow jurors to make a decision. Furthermore, there is a need for evidence that supports the juror's expectations of what is to be proven. Jurors who hear a story may be puzzled by the gaps and abstractions.

The recognition of a prosecutor's need to tell a story with continuity has no application when the point at issue is a defendant's legal status. That legal status depends upon a judgment made wholly independently of the later criminal charge. The choice of proof of the legal status is not a choice between concrete and abstract facts, but is between two abstractions. The nature and name of the prior offense is not evidence that has multiple purposes, and is not a proper matter for the jury. The fact of the conviction will not be kept secret, only the exact nature of the offense. However, the nature of the offense is not important to the prosecution's case: it is the fact of the conviction that is important. Proving status without telling the story behind that status does not leave a gap in the story of a defendant's later criminality.

There is no discernable difference between the evidentiary significance of an admission of a prior conviction, and using an official record to prove a conviction. The only distinction between the two is in the risk inherent that the official record will be used to support a conviction on some improper ground, and the lack of such a risk in the admission. The only reasonable conclusion is that the risk of unfair prejudice to Old Chief (D) outweighed the probative value of the evidence. It was therefore an abuse of discretion to admit the evidence when an admission was available.

Old Chief's (D) argument that the record of his prior conviction is not relevant is incorrect. The record of the conviction made that fact more probable than it was without the evidence. Although the nature of the offense was not an ultimate fact, the record is one evidentiary step toward proving an ultimate fact. The availability of alternate proof does not affect the admissibility of the evidence. Exclusion of the record of the conviction does not rest on the availability of the stipulation or admission rendering the record irrelevant, but on the fact that the record is unfairly prejudicial. Reversed.

■ DISSENT

(O'Connor, J.) The majority's opinion misapplies the rules of evidence and upsets longstanding precedent regarding criminal prosecutions. The record of the prior conviction was direct proof of an essential element of the offense with which Old Chief (D) was charged. Old Chief's (D) case may have been damaged when the jury heard what his prior offense was, but it was not unfairly prejudicial.

The majority does not explain why admitting the record of the prior conviction was unfairly prejudicial. The evidence was not admitted to show that Old Chief (D) had a propensity to commit crimes, but to show that he had been convicted of a prior crime. The jury could have been instructed that it was not to consider the nature of the offense as evidence of guilt. The jury would be presumed to have followed such an instruction. Furthermore, there was nothing prejudicial in the record. The record just set out the date and place of the conviction, the name of the offense, the name of the victim, and the sentence Old Chief (D) received.

It is also troubling that the majority is willing to retreat from the settled precedent that a prosecutor is entitled to choose the evidence used in a prosecution. The majority's own arguments do not withstand scrutiny.

Analysis:

Stipulations can be used to blunt the emotional effect of relevant evidence. At the same time, the lack of specific evidence can lead to speculation that could prove equally prejudicial to a defendant. For example, suppose the prior felony conviction was not for a violent crime, but for something akin to the "possession of short lobsters" alluded to by Justice Souter. In such a case, a defendant might prefer that the jury know the precise nature of the felony, rather than let them imagine what potentially heinous offense led to the prior conviction.

CHAPTER TWO

The Specialized Relevance Rules

Tuer v. McDonald

Instant Facts: Tuer (P) claimed it was error to exclude evidence of a change in medical protocol implemented by Dr. McDonald (D) after Tuer's (P) husband's death.

Black Letter Rule: Evidence of remedial measures taken after an allegedly negligent act is not admissible to prove negligence.

Bankcard America, Inc. v. Universal Bancard Systems, Inc.

Instant Facts: Bankcard (P) sued Universal (D) for breach of contract, and Universal (D) tried to introduce evidence of a settlement.

Black Letter Rule: Evidence regarding settlement negotiations is admissible, but only for purposes other than showing liability.

Williams v. McCoy

Instant Facts: McCoy's (D) attorney asked Williams (P) why she saw a chiropractor when she did, and the judge did not allow Williams (P) to explain that she did so after an insurance adjuster spoke with her.

Black Letter Rule: Evidence of liability insurance is inadmissible only when the evidence is offered to show that the insured acted negligently or wrongfully.

United States v. Biaggi

Instant Facts: Mariotta (D) claimed it was error for the court to exclude evidence that he refused an offer of immunity in exchange for his testimony against his co-defendants.

Black Letter Rule: A rejected offer of immunity in exchange for testimony is admissible to show a defendant's innocent state of mind.

Tuer v. McDonald

(Widow) v. *(Surgeon)*

347 Md. 507, 701 A.2d 1101 (1997)

SUBSEQUENT REMEDIAL MEASURES ARE INADMISSIBLE

Good news! Since the jury in my malpractice case won't find out about it, I can treat you better than the guy I just killed.

stus.com

■ **INSTANT FACTS** Tuer (P) claimed it was error to exclude evidence of a change in medical protocol implemented by Dr. McDonald (D) after Tuer's (P) husband's death.

■ **BLACK LETTER RULE** Evidence of remedial measures taken after an allegedly negligent act is not admissible to prove negligence.

■ **PROCEDURAL BASIS**

Appeal from an order of the Maryland Court of Special Appeals affirming a verdict for McDonald (D).

■ **FACTS**

Tuer's (P) husband was scheduled for heart surgery and was admitted to the hospital four days before the surgery due to chest pains. He was given medications for his heart, one of which was Heparin, an anti-coagulant. A few hours before the operation was to begin, the Heparin was discontinued in accordance with hospital protocol and the protocol followed by McDonald (D) and the other surgeon who was to perform the operation. The medication was discontinued so Tuer's (P) husband would not have the medication in his system during the surgery. Shortly before the operation was to begin, McDonald (D) was called away to perform an emergency operation on a patient whose condition was more serious. The surgery on Tuer's (P) husband was postponed for three to four hours. McDonald (D) considered restarting the Heparin, but decided not to do so. Tuer's (P) husband was taken to a unit of the hospital where he could be closely monitored. Nonetheless, Tuer's (P) husband went into cardiac arrest before his surgery, but he was revived and went ahead with the surgery anyhow. He survived the operation, but died the next day. After his death, the hospital and McDonald (D) changed their protocol so that Heparin would be continued until the patient was in the operating room.

Tuer (P) brought an action for malpractice. She sought to introduce evidence of the change in protocol, but the court barred the evidence, holding that the change in protocol was a subsequent remedial measure. The jury returned a verdict for McDonald (D) and the appellate court affirmed.

■ **ISSUE**

Should the court have admitted the evidence of the changed protocol implemented by the doctor charged with malpractice?

■ **DECISION AND RATIONALE**

(Wilner, J.) No. Evidence of remedial measures taken after an allegedly negligent act is not admissible to prove negligence. Courts have held consistently that taking precautions for the future should not be construed as an admission of responsibility for past occurrences. There is also a social policy that steps taken in furtherance of safety should be encouraged, or at least not discouraged. There are limited exceptions to the rule to show that the remedial measures were feasible. And some courts have allowed the evidence to impeach a claim made by a witness. In this case, however, the evidence regarding the change in protocol is not admissible under either theory.

Courts have differed in how claims of feasibility should be analyzed. Some courts have read the term "feasible" narrowly, as meaning physically, technologically, or economically possible. Those courts allow evidence of subsequent remedial measures only when a defendant claims that there was no way the remedial measure could have been taken under the circumstances. Other courts have read the term more broadly, concluding that "feasible" means more than merely possible, and includes actions that are capable of being utilized successfully.

Defendants do not often claim that a remedial measure was not feasible. The issue arises when there is an alternate reason given for failure to take the remedial measure earlier, such as a cost-benefit analysis, a judgment call as to competing values, or a trade-off between competing benefits. Plaintiffs often characterize such a claim as putting feasibility in issue, which is what happened in this case. McDonald (D) and the other defendants did not claim that it was physically impossible to restart the Heparin, but rather that not restarting the Heparin was a judgment call. And McDonald's (D) claim that restarting the Heparin would have been "unsafe" must be read in context. Ordinarily, a physician's claim that a particular course of action would have been unsafe is tantamount to a claim of unfeasibility, but in this case McDonald's (D) testimony leads to the conclusion that "unsafe" should be construed as meaning that the relative safety risks of restarting the medication were not worth taking. The evidence was inadmissible to rebut a claim of feasibility.

The exception for impeachment likewise does not apply here. Almost any claim by a defendant that he or she was not negligent could be rebutted or impeached by proof of a subsequent remedial measure. Allowing the evidence for impeachment depends upon the nature of the contradiction. Courts that have allowed evidence of subsequent remedial measures for impeachment to contradict claims made by witnesses that a product or practice was safe before the measures were taken. The evidence is used to cast doubt on a witness's testimony, not to establish culpability. In this case, there is no showing that McDonald (D) did not believe the protocol was unsafe at the time of Tuer's (P) husband's surgery. The only reasonable interpretation was that McDonald (D) and the other defendants reevaluated the risks of the protocol. The reevaluation is the type of behavior that excluding evidence of subsequent remedial measures was meant to encourage. Affirmed.

Analysis:

The rule against introduction of subsequent remedial measures has more exceptions than the two mentioned in this case. And the three exceptions explicitly set out in Fed. R. Evid. 407—ownership, control, and feasibility—are not the only reasons that such evidence is allowed. It is perhaps most accurate to say that evidence of remedial measures generally *is* admissible, unless used to show negligence or culpability.

■ CASE VOCABULARY

IMPEACHMENT: The act of discrediting a witness, as by catching the witness in a lie or by demonstrating that the witness has been convicted of a criminal offense.

MOTION IN LIMINE: A pretrial request that certain inadmissible evidence not be referred to or offered at trial. Typically, a party makes this motion when it believes that mere mention of the evidence during trial would be highly prejudicial and could not be remedied by an instruction to disregard.

Bankcard America, Inc. v. Universal Bancard Systems, Inc.

(*Independent Sales Organization*) v. (*Contractor*)

203 F.3d 477 (7th Cir. 2000), *cert. denied*, 531 U.S. 877, 121 S.Ct. 186 (2000)

SETTLEMENT NEGOTIATIONS ARE INADMISSIBLE TO SHOW LIABILITY

I know you normally won't consider our settlement talks, but this time it was our "settlement" that caused the misunderstanding.

stus.com

■ **INSTANT FACTS** Bankcard (P) sued Universal (D) for breach of contract, and Universal (D) tried to introduce evidence of a settlement.

■ **BLACK LETTER RULE** Evidence regarding settlement negotiations is admissible, but only for purposes other than showing liability.

■ **PROCEDURAL BASIS**

Appeal from an order overturning a verdict after a retrial.

■ **FACTS**

Bankcard (P) sued Universal (D) for breach of contract. Bankcard (P) claimed that its contract with Universal (D) prohibited Universal (D) from referring customers to competitors. Rothberg, Universal's (D) president, testified that Universal (D) did refer customers to competitors of Bankcard (P), but that it did so because Rothberg thought that a settlement had been reached that allowed such referrals. Rothberg testified that the referrals stopped when he learned that Bankcard had a "change of heart." He also testified that Bankcard (P) had dropped the lawsuit at one point, but reinstated it when no agreement was reached. The trial judge allowed that testimony, but barred any testimony about the terms of the settlement and also disallowed the use of the terms "negotiation" and "settlement."

The jury rendered a verdict for Universal (D). A new trial was granted, and one of the errors cited was the admission of testimony regarding the settlement talks. After the second trial, the judge overturned a second verdict for Universal (D), holding that the evidence of damages was insufficient.

■ **ISSUE**

Is testimony regarding settlement negotiations admissible?

■ **DECISION AND RATIONALE**

(Evans, J.) Yes. Evidence regarding settlement negotiations is admissible, but only for purposes other than showing liability. The purpose of the general prohibition against introducing evidence of offers to compromise is to encourage settlement. The purpose of the rule is not met when a party is led to believe that a settlement has been reached and then is accused of breaching a contract by acting in reliance on the supposed settlement. Universal (D) was correctly allowed to explain the reasons for its actions to counter Bankcard's (P) claim that it breached the contract. It would be unfair to allow Bankcard (P) to invite a breach of contract, and then allow it to block evidence of the invitation. The order granting a new trial is reversed, and the verdict in the original trial is reinstated.

Analysis:

Most settlement agreements state that there is no admission of liability, but the general public often assumes that no one would settle a case unless they were liable. In this case, the judge's order on

---

Rothberg's testimony was very carefully crafted to avoid any inference of an admission. The jury was not told who had initiated the settlement, or what the terms of the agreement were. Such careful limitation was certainly important to the court of appeals in deciding that the evidence was properly admitted.

Williams v. McCoy

(Accident Victim) v. *(Insured)*

550 S.E.2d 796 (N.C. Ct. App. 2001)

EVIDENCE OF INSURANCE IS NOT ADMISSIBLE TO PROVE NEGLIGENCE

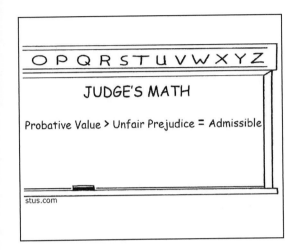

O P Q R S T U V W X Y Z

JUDGE'S MATH

Probative Value > Unfair Prejudice = Admissible

stus.com

■ **INSTANT FACTS** McCoy's (D) attorney asked Williams (P) why she saw a chiropractor when she did, and the judge did not allow Williams (P) to explain that she did so after an insurance adjuster spoke with her.

■ **BLACK LETTER RULE** Evidence of liability insurance is inadmissible only when the evidence is offered to show that the insured acted negligently or wrongfully.

■ **PROCEDURAL BASIS**

Appeal from a judgment entered on a jury verdict.

■ **FACTS**

Williams (P) was injured in an automobile accident and brought a lawsuit against McCoy (D). The trial court made a pre-trial ruling that Williams (P) would not be allowed to testify regarding insurance or any contact or conversation with insurance personnel. Williams (P) objected to the ruling, stating that she retained her attorney after speaking with a claims adjuster for McCoy's (D) insurer. The trial court reserved its ruling.

At trial, Williams (P) testified that she went to see a chiropractor four days after her release from the emergency room, at the urging of her husband. She testified that she waited four days because the doctor would not be available until then. On cross-examination, Williams (P) was asked if she retained her attorney prior to seeing her chiropractor. Williams (P) denied that, and stated that she had been told not to talk about insurance. She was asked the question again, and said she did not remember. The court reminded Williams (P), out of the presence of the jury, that she was not to mention insurance. Her attorney asked that she be allowed to explain that she hired her attorney after being contacted by an adjuster for McCoy's insurer, who told her that she should settle her claim and that she was wasting her time "because [she] had an injury in '76 . . ." Williams's (P) attorney said that McCoy's (D) whole case was built on a claim that Williams (P) was litigious, and that Williams (P) should be allowed to explain why she hired an attorney. The judge denied the request and threatened to hold Williams (P) in contempt and declare a mistrial if she mentioned insurance again. The jury returned a verdict of $3,000 for Williams (P).

■ **ISSUE**

Should Williams (P) have been allowed to testify about the existence of the defendant's liability insurance?

■ **DECISION AND RATIONALE**

(Timmons–Goodson, J.) Yes. Evidence of liability insurance is inadmissible only when the evidence is offered to show that the insured acted negligently or wrongfully. The rules of evidence state that insurance evidence may be admitted to show agency, ownership, control, or the bias or prejudice of a witness. The list of permissible purposes is non-exclusive, and insurance evidence may be admitted as

---

long as it is not used to show negligence. Here, McCoy's (D) attorney knew, based on pre-trial discovery, that Williams (P) would testify that she hired an attorney because of her encounter with the insurance adjuster. He argued during his opening statement that she saw a doctor after hiring an attorney. Williams's (P) explanation did not bear directly on McCoy's (D) negligence, but explained an answer to a question asked by McCoy's attorney.

In considering the admission of relevant evidence, the court must balance the probative value of the evidence against the danger of unfair prejudice to the other party, or the danger of misleading the jury. In this case, the possibility of unfair prejudice in allowing Williams (P) to explain her answer does not outweigh the probative value of the evidence. Most jurors probably assume that drivers carry liability insurance. The possible prejudicial impact of the evidence could have been blunted by a cautionary instruction. Furthermore, the evidence went to one of the major issues of the case and would have allowed Williams (P) to counter the suggestion that she brought her case only for profit. Reversed and remanded.

Analysis:

The court analyzes the admission of the testimony not only in light of the rule regarding admission of insurance evidence, but also in terms of the general rule governing exclusion of otherwise admissible evidence. The court does not merely balance the probative value of the evidence against the chance of unfair prejudice to McCoy (D), but also discusses the unfair prejudice to Williams (P) of excluding the evidence. The unfairness seems especially apparent here, since the whole situation was set up by McCoy's (D) attorney as a part of his trial strategy. Continuing to exclude the testimony about contact with the adjuster would have misled the jury about Williams's (P) motive in bringing her suit.

■ CASE VOCABULARY

DIRECT CONTEMPT: A contempt (such as an assault of a testifying witness) committed in the immediate vicinity of a court; especially, a contempt committed in a judge's presence.

United States v. Biaggi

(Prosecuting Authority) v. *(Congressman)*

909 F.2d 662 (2d Cir. 1990), *cert. denied sub nom. Simon v. United States*, 499 U.S. 904, 111 S.Ct. 1102 (1991)

REJECTED OFFERS OF IMMUNITY ARE ADMISSIBLE TO SHOW CONSCIOUSNESS OF INNOCENCE

■ **INSTANT FACTS** Mariotta (D) claimed it was error for the court to exclude evidence that he refused an offer of immunity in exchange for his testimony against his co-defendants.

■ **BLACK LETTER RULE** A rejected offer of immunity in exchange for testimony is admissible to show a defendant's innocent state of mind.

■ **PROCEDURAL BASIS**

Appeal from convictions entered against six defendants.

■ **FACTS**

Mariotta (D) was chief executive officer of Wedtech and was one of six defendants charged with various crimes relating to government contracts awarded to Wedtech. He sought to offer evidence that the prosecution (P) had offered him immunity in exchange for his testimony against the other five defendants, but he denied any knowledge about the activities of the other defendants, thereby rejecting immunity. Mariotta (D) argued that his rejection of the offer showed a consciousness of innocence. The prosecution (P) claimed that it withdrew its offer of immunity when it concluded that Mariotta's denial of knowledge would not be helpful. The trial court refused to admit the evidence.

■ **ISSUE**

Should the evidence that the offer of immunity was rejected have been admitted?

■ **DECISION AND RATIONALE**

(Newman, J.) Yes. A rejected offer of immunity in exchange for testimony is admissible to show a defendant's innocent state of mind. Rejecting an offer of immunity in exchange for testimony is probative of a state of mind devoid of guilty knowledge. While it is true that there are many reasons a defendant might reject an offer of immunity, such as a fear of retribution from those against whom the defendant testifies, a jury is entitled to believe that most people would accept an opportunity to obtain an assurance of immunity, and to infer that the rejection of the offer means that the defendant did not know about the wrongdoing. The probative force of the rejection of an immunity offer is strong enough to make it relevant. The unfairness of excluding evidence of lack of consciousness of guilt is made especially unfair by the prosecution's (P) introduction of evidence showing a consciousness of guilt. That evidence consisted mostly of actions by Mariotta's (D) wife.

This case presents a different question from that posed by a rejected plea bargain. First, plea negotiations are only inadmissible against the defendant. Second, there are fundamental differences between plea negotiations and offers of immunity. A defendant might reject a plea offer because he or she prefers to take a chance on an outright acquittal by the jury. The admissibility of plea agreements, however, is not at issue in this case. Reversed, and a new trial ordered for Mariotta (D).

Analysis:

The major difference between a plea agreement and an offer of immunity is in the different consequences to the defendant. If a defendant is granted immunity, he or she avoids any criminal punishment and is left, legally, in the same status as if the prosecution had never been instituted in the first place. A plea agreement, by contrast, requires the defendant to admit to some type of criminal conduct and to accept the consequences of that conduct.

■ CASE VOCABULARY

IMMUNITY: Freedom from prosecution granted by the government in exchange for the person's testimony. By granting immunity, the government can compel testimony—despite the Fifth Amendment right against self-incrimination—because that testimony can no longer incriminate the witness.

CHAPTER THREE

Character Evidence

People v. Zackowitz

Instant Facts: Zackowitz (D) was charged with murder, and at trial the prosecution (P) introduced evidence that he possessed several guns.

Black Letter Rule: Evidence of a particular character trait is inadmissible to show that a person acted in conformity with that trait.

United States v. Trenkler

Instant Facts: Trenkler (D) was charged with building a bomb, and at trial the prosecution (P) introduced evidence of another bomb Trenkler (D) had constructed.

Black Letter Rule: Evidence of other criminal acts is admissible to show the identity of the person who committed the acts if there is a high degree of similarity between the other act and the charged crime.

United States v. Stevens

Instant Facts: Stevens (D) was accused of robbery and assault and sought to introduce evidence at his trial that someone else had committed a similar crime.

Black Letter Rule: Evidence that a defendant did not commit similar crimes may be used to show that a defendant did not commit the crime charged.

United States v. DeGeorge

Instant Facts: DeGeorge (D) engaged in a series of transactions that artificially inflated the market value of a yacht prior to intentionally sinking the yacht and collecting the insurance money.

Black Letter Rule: Evidence of prior acts is "inextricably intertwined" with a charged offense, and therefore may be admitted if it constitutes a part of the transaction that serves as the basis for the criminal charge, or when it was necessary to do so in order to permit the prosecutor to offer a coherent and comprehensive story regarding the commission of the crime.

Huddleston v. United States

Instant Facts: Huddleston (D) was charged with selling stolen videotapes, and at trial the prosecution (P) introduced evidence of his other sales of allegedly stolen property.

Black Letter Rule: Evidence of similar acts may be admitted if there is sufficient evidence to support a finding by the jury that the defendant committed the similar acts.

Lannan v. State

Instant Facts: Lannan (D) was convicted of molesting a child after the jury heard evidence that he had molested other girls.

Black Letter Rule: Evidence of prior sexual conduct is inadmissible to prove that a defendant had a tendency to commit a sexual assault.

State v. Kirsch

Instant Facts: Kirsch (D) was charged with molesting three young girls, and testimony that he had molested others was admitted at the trial against him.

Black Letter Rule: Evidence of other acts or crimes is not admissible to show a predilection for committing a certain crime.

United States v. Guardia

Instant Facts: Guardia (D) was accused of sexually assaulting two women during a medical examination, and the prosecutor (P) moved to admit evidence of similar allegations made by other women.

Black Letter Rule: Evidence of a defendant's other sexual conduct will be admitted only if the probative value of the evidence outweighs the danger of undue prejudice, confusion of the issues, misleading the jury, undue delay, waste of time, and the needless presentation of cumulative evidence.

United States v. Mound

Instant Facts: Mound (D) was tried for sexual assault and assault of a child, and the Government (P) introduced evidence that he had pleaded guilty previously to sexual abuse of a child.

Black Letter Rule: Rule 413 of the Federal Rules of Evidence, which does not violate due process or the Equal Protection Clause.

Michelson v. United States

Instant Facts: Michelson (D) called character witnesses to testify on his behalf, and four of them were asked if they had heard about Michelson's (D) arrest for receiving stolen goods.

Black Letter Rule: Character evidence is evidence of a witness's knowledge of a defendant's reputation, not evidence regarding specific acts.

Halloran v. Virginia Chemicals Inc.

Instant Facts: Halloran (P) was injured when a can of Freon exploded, and Virginia Chemicals (D) claimed that it was Halloran's (P) practice to heat the cans.

Black Letter Rule: Evidence of a person's habit is admissible to show that he or she acted according to that habit on a particular occasion.

People v. Zackowitz

(Prosecuting Authority) v. *(Shooter)*

254 N.Y. 192, 172 N.E. 466 (1930)

CHARACTER EVIDENCE IS INADMISSIBLE TO SHOW GUILT

■ **INSTANT FACTS** Zackowitz (D) was charged with murder, and at trial the prosecution (P) introduced evidence that he possessed several guns.

■ **BLACK LETTER RULE** Evidence of a particular character trait is inadmissible to show that a person acted in conformity with that trait.

■ **PROCEDURAL BASIS**

Appeal from a conviction for murder.

■ **FACTS**

Zackowitz (D) and his wife were walking home from a party late one night. After they arrived home, Zackowitz's (D) wife claimed that four young men, one of whom was Coppola, insulted her. Zackowitz (D) went to the place where Coppola and his friends were congregating. Zackowitz (D) had a gun with him at that time, but later gave inconsistent testimony as to whether he had the gun with him the entire evening, or whether he had armed himself at home before he left again. Zackowitz (D) confronted Coppola and his friends, and an altercation ensued. There was testimony that Coppola tried to hit Zackowitz (D) with a wrench. Zackowitz (D) shot once, and Coppola died. Zackowitz (D) and his wife left the area and were arrested approximately two months later.

At trial, Zackowitz (D) did not deny shooting Coppola, but claimed he acted in self-defense and out of a sudden impulse. The prosecution (P) introduced evidence that Zackowitz (D) owned several guns, which he kept in a radio box in his apartment. The prosecutor (P) acknowledged that he introduced the evidence of the other guns solely to show that Zackowitz (D) was a "desperate type of criminal" and a "person criminally inclined." Zackowitz (D) did not bring all of his guns to the scene of the crime, but brought only the gun he used to shoot Coppola. Zackowitz (D) was convicted of murder.

■ **ISSUE**

Was the evidence that Zackowitz (D) owned guns other than the one used to shoot the victim admissible at his murder trial?

■ **DECISION AND RATIONALE**

(Cardozo, J.) No. Evidence of a particular character trait is inadmissible to show that a person acted in conformity with that trait. Character is not an issue in a criminal prosecution unless the defendant raises the issue. The principle of exclusion is based on policy. Although a person of a particular character is more likely to commit a crime than another person, there is a great danger to the innocent if the evidence is allowed. There is a very real danger that the trier of fact will afford excessive weight to the character evidence, or that the evidence will be taken as justification for a conviction regardless of the defendant's guilt of the offense charged.

The evidence in this case was not a passing reference to the ownership of other guns. The weapons were introduced into evidence and were the subject of animated argument. The whole effect was to paint Zackowitz (D) as a criminal, and a man with an evil life. This was especially unfair, in that Zackowitz (D) was not a man of evil life or a professional criminal. He had no criminal record and did not have criminal associates. Apart from the shooting of Coppola, there was nothing criminal in his background. If his testimony is to be believed, he owned the guns as a collection of curios that interested and amused him. Zackowitz (D) should not have been made to answer the inferences raised from his gun ownership as well as the main criminal charge.

The situation would be different of Zackowitz (D) bought the guns in anticipation of his encounter with Coppola. In that case, the other guns would have been evidence of design and preparation. There would likewise be a different question presented if the other guns were connected to the crime so as to identify Zackowitz (D), or if Zackowitz (D) had taken them with him when he left and confronted Coppola. Such evidence would show a preconceived design. There is no such implication from the guns Zackowitz (D) left at home. Reversed and a new trial ordered.

■ DISSENT

(Pound, J.) The guns were not introduced for one of the purposes set out in the rules that disallow introduction of other crimes to show motive, intent, absence of mistake, a common scheme or plan, or identity. The weapons were not a separate incident, but were connected with the crime for which Zackowitz (D) was charged. Zackowitz (D) was not presented to the jury as having a dangerous disposition in general, but as one who had an opportunity to carry out his threats, and did so.

Analysis:

Evidence of a person's character or personality traits is highly probative of the question of whether a person did a particular thing. It is common sense for most people to assume that a person who, for example, has a violent nature is more likely to have committed a violent act. The danger lies in the likelihood of unfair prejudice to the defendant. Juries are more likely to convict a "bad" person than a person they see as generally harmless, regardless of the proof that the defendant actually did what he or she is accused of doing.

■ CASE VOCABULARY

CHARACTER EVIDENCE: Evidence regarding someone's personality traits; evidence of a person's moral standing in a community, based on reputation or opinion.

United States v. Trenkler

(Prosecuting Authority) v. *(Bomber)*

61 F.3d 45 (1st Cir. 1995)

EVIDENCE OF OTHER CRIMINAL ACTS IS ADMISSIBLE TO SHOW IDENTITY

Trademarks are good for businesses, not for criminals.

stus.com

■ **INSTANT FACTS** Trenkler (D) was charged with building a bomb, and at trial the prosecution (P) introduced evidence of another bomb Trenkler (D) had constructed.

■ **BLACK LETTER RULE** Evidence of other criminal acts is admissible to show the identity of the person who committed the acts if there is a high degree of similarity between the other act and the charged crime.

■ **PROCEDURAL BASIS**

Appeal from convictions for receipt of explosive materials, attempted malicious destruction of property by means of explosives, and conspiracy.

■ **FACTS**

Trenkler (D) was charged with building a bomb for Shay (D), to be used against Shay's (D) father. The bomb exploded in the driveway of Shay's (D) father's house, killing a police officer and seriously injuring another officer. Testimony at Trenkler's (D) trial showed that the bomb was a remote-control, radio-activated device that was secured to the bottom of a car by a magnet. Some of the components used in the bomb were purchased at a Radio Shack store near Trenkler's (D) place of work. Shay (D) admitted purchasing many of the items for Trenkler (D).

An expert testifying for the prosecution (P) stated that the bomb was similar to another bomb that had been detonated five years before. Trenkler (D) had admitted earlier that he made that bomb at the request of a friend, and he stipulated to that fact at this trial. That bomb was also a remote-control, radio-activated device attached to the bottom of a truck by a magnet. Many of the components for that bomb were purchased at a Radio Shack store by the nephew of Trenkler's (D) friend. The expert testified that the designs of the bombs, the choice of components, and the method of construction showed that both bombs shared a single maker. The expert testified that he had no doubt that the same person built both bombs. The prosecution (P) bolstered this conclusion by testimony from a law enforcement officer, who stated that a computer analysis of crimes showed only seven that involved a bombing or attempted bombing of a motor vehicle by a remote-control device that used a magnet. One of those incidents was the earlier bomb made by Trenkler (D), and one was the bomb that was used against Shay's (D) father.

Trenkler (D) called an expert to testify on his behalf. His expert testified that there were too many dissimilarities to warrant a conclusion that the same person built both bombs. He also testified that the similarities that did exist did not have sufficient distinguishing qualities to identify them as the handiwork of a specific individual. Trenkler (D) was convicted of all charges against him. On appeal, he claimed that the earlier bomb was not sufficiently similar to the second bomb to be relevant on the issue of the identity of the bomb-maker.

■ **ISSUE**

Was evidence of the prior similar bomb admissible to show the identity of the defendant in a subsequent bombing case?

■ DECISION AND RATIONALE

(Stahl, J.) Yes. Evidence of other criminal acts is admissible to show the identity of the person who committed the acts if there is a high degree of similarity between the other act and the charged crime. It is not enough to show that a defendant committed the same type of commonplace criminal act. The party that seeks to introduce the evidence must show that there are enough distinguishing characteristics to permit an inference of a pattern of activity. An exact match is not necessary. The test focuses on the totality of the comparison and looks for either a conjunction of several identifying traits or the presence of some highly distinctive quality. The court has considerable leeway in deciding whether to admit such evidence, so the decision is reviewed to determine whether there was an abuse of discretion.

In this case, there was sufficient evidence to support an inference that the same person built both bombs. The prosecution's (P) expert testified that he had no doubt that the same individual built both bombs. The two bombs shared many of the same types of components, and there were a number of similarities in the manner in which they were constructed. Trenkler's (D) own expert stated that the method in which the wires were joined in the bombs was unique. He also stated at a pre-trial hearing that there was a probability of a connection between the makers of the two bombs. There is no requirement that the prosecution (P) prove beyond a reasonable doubt that the two bombs were made by the same person. The coalescence of all of the similarities is persuasive of a connection.

Trenkler's (D) expert focused exclusively on the physical evidence regarding the bombs. The test for similarity is not so limited. Similarity looks at all of the evidence presented to the jury. It is significant that both incidents involved bombs, which are fairly distinctive methods of intimidating or killing an individual. Both bombs were remote-control devices placed under motor vehicles. Both bombs were built for friends of Trenkler (D), and someone acting for Trenkler (D) purchased some of the components. In addition, the fact that the bombs were in the same geographic area is also given some weight. The prosecution (P) presented a lengthy list of similarities in design, components, construction, and overall operation. Trenkler (D) offered a lengthy list of reasons that the two bombs were dissimilar. With substantial evidence on either side, and conflicting expert opinions, it cannot be said that the introduction of the evidence was an abuse of discretion.

The evidence must also be reviewed to determine whether its probative value is outweighed by the risk of unfair prejudice. There is always a danger in allowing evidence of prior bad acts that the jury will consider that as evidence of a propensity. In this case, however, the evidence was not unduly inflammatory. The first bomb did not kill or injure anyone and caused only minimal property damage. The jury was instructed not to infer Trenkler's (D) guilt simply because he had built the prior bomb or because building one bomb made it more likely that he built another. The probative value of the earlier bomb evidence was not substantially outweighed by the risk of unfair prejudice. Affirmed.

■ DISSENT

(Torruella, C.J.) The evidence derived from the database focuses only on a few characteristics of the incident. A different result would have been obtained if different characteristics were searched. In addition, the majority misses the point that the central and most important ingredient in the bombs was different. The first bomb used a firecracker-like device, while the second used three sticks of dynamite. The two devices were not equivalent.

Analysis:

The prosecution's (P) task is made much easier by Trenkler's (D) admission and stipulation that he made the prior bomb. Evidence of a prior crime is admissible only when the proponent of the evidence can show that the defendant in fact committed the other crime. It is not enough to show that this is the type of crime the defendant commits. Rather, the crucial point is that the crime was committed in a way unique to the defendant.

■ CASE VOCABULARY

EXPERT WITNESS: A witness qualified by knowledge, skill, experience, training, or education to provide a scientific, technical, or other specialized opinion about the evidence or a fact issue.

MODUS OPERANDI: [Latin, "a manner of operating."] A method of operating or a manner of procedure; especially, a pattern of criminal behavior so distinctive that investigators attribute it to the work of the same person.

United States v. Stevens

(Prosecuting Authority) v. *(Convicted Robber)*

935 F.2d 1380 (3d Cir. 1991)

DEFENDANTS MAY INTRODUCE EVIDENCE THAT THEY DID NOT COMMIT SIMILAR CRIMES

But there's another orange tabby in the neighborhood, and he's the one with an appetite for cockatoos.

stus.com

■ **INSTANT FACTS** Stevens (D) was accused of robbery and assault and sought to introduce evidence at his trial that someone else had committed a similar crime.

■ **BLACK LETTER RULE** Evidence that a defendant did not commit similar crimes may be used to show that a defendant did not commit the crime charged.

■ **PROCEDURAL BASIS**

Appeal from a conviction for robbery and sexual assault.

■ **FACTS**

Two white Air Force police officers, a man and a woman, were robbed at gunpoint at a bus shelter at Fort Dix, New Jersey. The robber was an African–American male. The robber pointed a gun at the male victim's chest and demanded his wallet. The man handed over the wallet, which contained an unsigned money order. The robber frisked the victim to see if he had any more money. The robber then turned to the female victim and asked if she had any money. When she told the robber she did not, he frisked her and then sexually assaulted her. The robber told the victims to leave, and they ran to the nearest building and called the police. They were taken to the military police station. The male victim saw a photograph of Stevens (D) and identified him as the robber. The female victim agreed that the photograph of Stevens (D) resembled the robber, but she thought that the photograph made him look heavier. Five days later, the victims identified Stevens (D) in a lineup at the police station. Each victim viewed the lineup separately and positively identified Stevens (D) as the robber.

Stevens (D) attempted to introduce evidence of a similar robbery committed shortly after the robbery for which he was tried. The victim in that robbery was an African American man who was robbed at gunpoint of several items, including his military identification card. The second robbery took place in the same vicinity as the robbery of which Stevens (D) was accused. Stevens (D) was also a suspect in the second robbery, but the victim stated that Stevens (D) was not the man who robbed him. The identification card taken from the victim of the second robbery was used to cash stolen checks at Fort Meade, Maryland. Someone other than Stevens (D) also cashed the money order stolen from the victim of the *first* robbery at a pharmacy across the street from Fort Meade. Stevens (D) also offered expert testimony on the unreliability of cross-racial identification, but Stevens (D) was not allowed to introduce any evidence relating to his lack of involvement in the later, similar robbery and was convicted of robbery and sexual assault in connection with the first robbery.

■ **ISSUE**

Was evidence that Stevens (D) did not commit another, similar robbery admissible in his trial for robbery?

■ **DECISION AND RATIONALE**

(Becker, J.) Yes. Evidence that a defendant did not commit similar crimes may be used to show that a defendant did not commit the crime charged. Such evidence is especially important when the defendant claims mistaken identification. The standard for introduction of the evidence is solely whether the evidence negates the defendant's guilt, and whether its probative value is not outweighed by considerations of unfair prejudice, confusion of the issues, misleading the jury, or delay or waste of time. Prejudice to the defendant is not a factor to be considered, since the evidence is offered to exculpate the defendant.

The standard for similarity of crimes is lower when the evidence is introduced defensively than when it is introduced to show guilt. When the prosecutor introduces other crimes evidence to prove guilt, there is a high potential for prejudice. When the evidence is used for defensive purposes, there is no such possibility of confusion, so the similarity between the other crimes and the offense charged does not need to be as great. The other crimes, therefore, do not need to be so-called signature crimes, and there does not need to be as many crimes to show a pattern.

The prosecution (P) argued that other crimes evidence could be used defensively only when the government induced the commission of the similar crime, when the defendant was misidentified as the perpetrator of the similar crime, or when the other crimes were sufficiently numerous to show a clear pattern, and Stevens (D) met none of these conditions. The test proposed by the prosecution (D) is too narrow. The only test is whether the evidence is relevant and whether its probative value is not outweighed by the factors set out in the rules.

It is clear that the evidence offered by Stevens (D) met the test of relevance. The case against him rested entirely on the identification of him as the robber. Stevens (D) tried to counter this evidence by showing the unreliability of cross-racial identification, and by showing that an African American failed to identify him as the assailant in a similar crime. The similarities between the two crimes are amply demonstrated. Army CID considered that Stevens (D) committed the second robbery, which happened in the same area, at approximately the same time of day, and was committed against military personnel. The assailant in both cases was an African–American man who was described in similar terms. The items stolen form both victims turned up in Fort Meade. The second robbery did not involve a sexual assault, but there was no female victim in that robbery. There was no real risk that Stevens's (D) trial would become a mini-trial on the issue of who committed the second robbery. The prosecution (P) was willing to stipulate to all of the essential facts about the second robbery, if the evidence were admitted. There was likewise no danger that the jury would be misled or distracted from the real issues in the case. The error was not harmless. The evidence against Stevens (D) was not overwhelming. Reversed.

Analysis:

The type of evidence at issue here poses little, if any, risk of unfair prejudice to a defendant. Evidence of other crimes is allowed to prove guilt under limited circumstances because of the high potential for misuse of the evidence: there is a strong possibility that the jury will see it as evidence of a propensity to commit crimes, and that the defendant is therefore guilty. The reverse evidence does not bear the same possibility of jury misapprehension. The inference that the defendant did not commit a crime charged because he did not have a propensity to commit crimes of that type is not one juries tend to make, especially if there is other evidence of guilt.

■ **CASE VOCABULARY**

HARMLESS ERROR: An error that does not affect a party's substantive rights or the case's outcome.

United States v. DeGeorge

(Prosecuting Authority) v. (Convicted Defendant)

380 F.3d 1203 (9th Cir. 2004)

PRIOR BAD ACTS MAY HELP THE JURY UNDERSTAND THE PROSECUTOR'S CASE

■ **INSTANT FACTS** DeGeorge (D) engaged in a series of transactions that artificially inflated the market value of a yacht prior to intentionally sinking the yacht and collecting the insurance money.

■ **BLACK LETTER RULE** Evidence of prior acts is "inextricably intertwined" with a charged offense, and therefore may be admitted if it constitutes a part of the transaction that serves as the basis for the criminal charge, or when it was necessary to do so in order to permit the prosecutor to offer a coherent and comprehensive story regarding the commission of the crime.

■ **PROCEDURAL BASIS**

On appeal to review the defendant's convictions.

■ **FACTS**

In June 1992, DeGeorge (D) contracted with an Italian firm to construct a yacht for $1.9 million. Shortly thereafter, DeGeorge (D) engaged in a series of transactions with business entities either formed by or closely related to DeGeorge (D). As a result of these transactions, the apparent value of the yacht increased to $3.6 million, although no money ever changed hands. In October 1992, the yacht was insured for $3.5 million. On November 4, DeGeorge (D) and two associates took the yacht on its maiden voyage off the shore of Italy. Two nights later, DeGeorge (D) instructed the others to use power tools to cut holes in the boat, with the intent to sink it. The boat began taking on water, but did not sink before Italian authorities approached. The men told the authorities that three men who had accompanied them on the voyage overpowered them, cut holes in the boat, and sped away in a motor boat. In February 1993, DeGeorge (D) and his associates submitted an insurance claim for the value of the boat. DeGeorge (D) was indicted in 1999 on charges of mail fraud, wire fraud, and perjury and was eventually convicted.

At trial, the Government (P) introduced evidence that DeGeorge (D) had previously lost three boats at sea. While the court did not permit the Government (P) to inform the jury that he had obtained insurance proceeds on each of those boats, it allowed the evidence of the prior losses as "inextricably intertwined" with the charges against DeGeorge (D), ruling that the evidence assisted the jury in understanding why DeGeorge (D) engaged in the series of transactions to distance himself from the boat's ownership.

■ **ISSUE**

Did the court err in allowing evidence of the defendant's prior losses?

■ **DECISION AND RATIONALE**

(Gibson, J.) No. Evidence of prior acts is "inextricably intertwined" with a charged offense, and therefore may be admitted if it "constitutes a part of the transaction that serves as the basis for the

---

criminal charge," or "when it was necessary to do so in order to permit the prosecutor to offer a coherent and comprehensive story regarding the commission of the crime." While the individual prior losses are not part of the same criminal transaction at issue, they are factually connected to the Government's (P) theory of guilt. The Government (P) contends that the series of transactions between DeGeorge (D) and his related business entities was designed to distance himself from ownership of the boat. The relevance of this point may be lost on the jurors without reference to the prior losses and enabling them to understand why DeGeorge (D) could not himself obtain insurance on the yacht. The court correctly determined that the losses were inextricably intertwined with the charged offenses and sufficiently minimized any prejudicial effects of the evidence by preventing any reference to related insurance claims. The probative value of this limited evidence outweighed any prejudice to the defendant. Affirmed.

Analysis:

The fact that DeGeorge (D) had previously lost three boats at sea was not, in itself, damaging to DeGeorge (D). Although one may infer that, based on the facts of this case, that the previous losses involved some wrongdoing, DeGeorge (D) had the opportunity to explain the circumstances of each loss through his testimony at trial. Thus, to the extent that the jury assumed that the losses were intended to reap insurance benefits, that misperception could be corrected. Accordingly, admitting the losses to explain why DeGeorge (D) engaged in the unusual transactions, rather than to establish that he had previously received money for each loss, was not overly prejudicial.

■ CASE VOCABULARY

RELEVANT EVIDENCE: Evidence tending to prove or disprove a matter in issue. Relevant evidence is both probative and material and is admissible unless excluded by a specific statute or rule.

Huddleston v. United States

(*Seller of Tapes*) v. (*Prosecuting Authority*)

485 U.S. 681, 108 S.Ct. 1496 (1988)

THERE MUST BE SUFFICIENT EVIDENCE THAT THE DEFENDANT COMMITTED THE SIMILAR ACTS

■ **INSTANT FACTS** Huddleston (D) was charged with selling stolen videotapes, and at trial the prosecution (P) introduced evidence of his other sales of allegedly stolen property.

■ **BLACK LETTER RULE** Evidence of similar acts may be admitted if there is sufficient evidence to support a finding by the jury that the defendant committed the similar acts.

■ **PROCEDURAL BASIS**

Appeal from an order of the Sixth Circuit Court of Appeals upholding a conviction after a rehearing.

■ **FACTS**

Huddleston (D) was arrested for selling stolen videotapes. He claimed that he did not know that the tapes were stolen, and that he got them from someone named Wesby, to sell on a commission basis. At trial, the prosecution (P) offered evidence that Huddleston (D) sold several television sets to a record store owner approximately one month before selling the tapes. The televisions were sold at a low price, and Huddleston (D) could not provide a bill of sale to show that he owned the televisions. Huddleston (D) claimed that he received the televisions from Wesby, who told him they were legitimate. Approximately one month after he sold the tapes, Huddleston (D) arranged to sell a number of appliances to an undercover FBI agent. When the appliances were delivered, they were found to be a part of a shipment that had been stolen. Wesby delivered the stolen appliances, and Huddleston (D) claimed he had no knowledge that they had been stolen.

Evidence about the sale of the television sets and the appliances was introduced to show that Huddleston (D) knew that the videotapes were stolen. Huddleston (D) did not dispute the admissibility of the evidence regarding the sale of the appliances, but he claimed that the evidence about his sale of the television sets should not have been admitted because the prosecution (P) did not prove by clear and convincing evidence that the television sets had been stolen.

■ **ISSUE**

Was the evidence regarding Huddleston's sale of the stolen television sets admissible in his trial for selling stolen videotapes?

■ **DECISION AND RATIONALE**

(Rehnquist, C.J.) Yes. Evidence of similar acts may be admitted if there is sufficient evidence to support a finding by the jury that the defendant committed the similar acts. The first inquiry the court must make is whether evidence of similar acts is probative of a material issue other than the character of the accused. In this case, the prosecution sought to admit evidence of Huddleston's (D) sale of stolen merchandise that came from a suspicious source. This evidence would be strong proof that Huddleston (D) was aware that all of the items he sold were stolen. But the sale of the television sets is relevant only if the television sets were in fact stolen.

The court was not required to make a preliminary finding that the television sets were stolen before the evidence could be admitted. The Federal Rules of Evidence do not require such a preliminary finding. Relevant evidence generally is admissible unless the rules provide otherwise. Rule 404 (b) of the rules provides that evidence of other acts is inadmissible if used to prove character. The text of the rules does not require any preliminary showing before that evidence may be offered. If the evidence of other acts is offered for a proper purpose, it is subject only to the general rules that limit admissibility. In addition, the legislative history of the rules does not support the contention that a preliminary finding is required. The major concern of Congress was to ensure that undue restrictions would not be placed on the admission of evidence.

The evidence of similar acts must be relevant, however, even if a preliminary finding is not required. Similar act evidence is relevant only if the jury can reasonably conclude that the similar act took place and that the defendant was the one who did it. The admissibility of the evidence is considered according to Fed. R. Evid 104 (b). That rule provides that evidence that is conditionally relevant shall be admitted upon, or subject to, the admission of evidence sufficient to support a finding that the condition has been fulfilled. There is no requirement that the court make a finding that the condition has been proved by a preponderance of the evidence. The trial court must consider *all* of the evidence presented to the jury—both the direct evidence and the indirect evidence. In this case, the court was required to consider not only the facts that the televisions were sold at a suspiciously low price and that there was no bill of sale, but also Huddleston's (D) involvement in the sales of the appliances and videotapes. There was sufficient evidence to conclude that the television sets Huddleston (D) sold were stolen. Affirmed.

Analysis:

The last portion of the Court's opinion contains some circular reasoning. Evidence of the sale of the television sets is relevant to the question of whether Huddleston (D) illegally sold videotapes, which means that it tends to prove the illegal sale. The evidence is relevant because Huddleston (D) was involved in other illegal sales, including the sale of the videotapes. Therefore, the illegal sale of the videotapes helps to establish the illegal sale of the televisions, which helps to prove the illegal sale of the videotapes.

■ CASE VOCABULARY

INDIRECT EVIDENCE: Evidence based on inference and not on personal knowledge or observation; all evidence that is not given by eyewitness testimony.

Lannan v. State

(Accused Molester) v. *(Prosecuting Authority)*

600 N.E.2d 1334 (Ind. 1992)

THE "DEPRAVED SEXUAL INSTINCT" EXCEPTION IS ELIMINATED

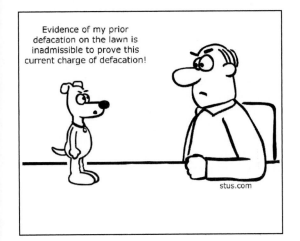

Evidence of my prior defacation on the lawn is inadmissible to prove this current charge of defacation!

stus.com

■ **INSTANT FACTS** Lannan (D) was convicted of molesting a child after the jury heard evidence that he had molested other girls.

■ **BLACK LETTER RULE** Evidence of prior sexual conduct is inadmissible to prove that a defendant had a tendency to commit a sexual assault.

■ **PROCEDURAL BASIS**

Petition for transfer of a conviction for child molestation.

■ **FACTS**

Lannan (D) was charged with molesting a young girl. At his trial, the jury heard testimony from the victim that Lannan (D) had molested her on occasions other than the incident with which he was charged. The jury also heard testimony from another girl, who said that he had molested her several times. The evidence was admitted under the "depraved sexual instinct" rule. On appeal from his conviction, Lannan (D) asked the court to abandon the "depraved sexual instinct" exception.

■ **ISSUE**

Was the evidence of other acts of molestation admissible in the defendant's trial?

■ **DECISION AND RATIONALE**

(Shepard, C.J.) No. Evidence of prior sexual conduct is inadmissible to prove that a defendant had a tendency to commit a sexual assault. The admission of evidence of other sexual acts is to be governed by the usual rules, which provide that the evidence is not admissible to prove that a person acted in conformity with his character. It may, however, be admissible for other purposes permitted by the rules.

It has long been the rule that evidence of prior sexual conduct is admissible in prosecutions for sexual crimes under the "depraved sexual instinct exception" to the general rule of inadmissibility of other bad acts. The justifications presented for the exception are the assumption that sexual offenders repeat their crimes more often than other criminals, and on the need to bolster the testimony of victims that describes acts that would otherwise seem improbable. While both justifications have some merit, there are significant problems with each that outweigh their usefulness.

There is ample evidence for the proposition that sex offenders tend to commit many more crimes than they might ever be charged with committing. The same is true, however, of defendants who face other types of criminal charges. The prosecution may not introduce evidence of other convictions in prosecutions for other crimes, even though such evidence would be highly probative. This exclusionary rule makes character evidence offered solely to show the accused's propensity to commit the crime inadmissible. The prejudicial effect of such character evidence outweighs any probative value it might have. If a high rate of recidivism cannot justify a departure from the propensity rule for all defendants, logic dictates it does not provide justification for departure in sex offense cases.

The rationale that the evidence of other acts is needed to bolster testimony regarding acts that might otherwise seem incredible has its origins in an earlier time, when the idea that an adult male would force himself sexually upon a child may have seemed preposterous. The justification for the need to bolster the testimony is the need to protect children, the most sexually vulnerable people in society. Courts sought to level the playing field to further the desirable social end of convicting child molesters. Accusations of child molestation no longer seem so improbable. This decaying state of affairs in society ironically undercuts the justification for the depraved sexual instinct exception at a time when the need to prosecute is greater.

There is also what might be called the "rationale behind the rationale," the desire to make easier the prosecution of child molesters, who prey on tragically vulnerable victims. The emotional appeal of this argument is powerful; child victims of sexual abuse evoke an especially strong empathy. Even this powerful argument, however, cannot support continued application of an exception that allows a result that the general propensity rule is intended to prevent.

The justifications for maintaining the depraved sexual instinct exception are outweighed by the problems created by the current application of the rule. The rule does not require notice of the prosecution's intention to introduce evidence of a defendant's depraved sexual instinct. The rule also does not require any particular similarity between the prior bad act and the crime charged. Courts have allowed evidence of extremely remote instances of sexual acts, under the theory that remoteness goes to weight and not admissibility.

Abandoning the depraved sexual instinct exception does not mean evidence of prior sexual misconduct will never be admitted in sex crimes prosecutions. It means only that such evidence may not be admitted to show that a defendant acted according to a particular character trait. It will continue to be admitted for other purposes allowed by the evidentiary rules, such as proof of motive, opportunity, intent, preparation, plan, knowledge, identity, and absence of mistake.

In this case, however, admission of the evidence was harmless error, in light of the other evidence of guilt. Conviction affirmed.

■ CONCURRENCE

(Givan, J.) The majority correctly sets out the justifications for the depraved sexual instinct exception. The need to protect children from the harm of molestation justifies the invocation of the rule. In most cases, the evidence of prior conduct probably will come in under accepted evidentiary rules, but this does not justify the abrogation of the exception. A jury is entitled to know that a defendant in a child molestation case has a history of deviate conduct because of the heinous nature of the crime, and because of the possible credibility problems of a child witness.

Analysis:

Both the majority and the concurrence (which was a concurrence only in the result of affirming Lannan's (D) conviction) focus on the use of evidence of other sexual acts in prosecutions of child molesters. The protection of children is a very compelling rationale, and one that is given much weight. As the majority notes, however, such evidence has customarily been allowed in other types of sexual crimes, not just those involving children. The evidence of other acts has also been allowed in cases that do not necessarily require compulsion or a lack of consent, such as sodomy.

■ CASE VOCABULARY

SODOMY: Oral or anal copulation between humans, especially those of the same sex; oral or anal copulation between a human and an animal; bestiality.

State v. Kirsch

(Prosecuting Authority) v. *(Accused Molester)*

139 N.H. 647, 662 A.2d 937 (1995)

EVIDENCE OF OTHER CRIMES IS NOT ADMISSIBLE TO SHOW PROPENSITY

■ **INSTANT FACTS** Kirsch (D) was charged with molesting three young girls, and testimony that he had molested others was admitted at the trial against him.

■ **BLACK LETTER RULE** Evidence of other acts or crimes is not admissible to show a predilection for committing a certain crime.

■ **PROCEDURAL BASIS**

Appeal from a conviction for child molestation.

■ **FACTS**

Kirsch (D) was charged with thirteen counts of sexual assault on three young girls. In addition to the testimony of the three victims, there was testimony from three other young women who claimed Kirsch (D) had molested them when they were younger. All of the victims testified that they became acquainted with Kirsch (D) when they were between seven and ten years of age, and that they met and became close to Kirsch (D) through church activities. The victims all testified regarding similar activities with Kirsch (D). The prosecutor (P) argued that the evidence showed that Kirsch (D) picked victims who were young girls from poor, dysfunctional families who did not have a real father figure. The prosecutor (P) claimed that Kirsch (D) used his role in the church to position himself as a father figure who sometimes fed and clothed the girls. The trial court ruled that the testimony of the other victims was relevant to show "motive, intent, and common plan or scheme." Seven of the indictments against Kirsch (D) were dismissed at the close of the prosecution's (P) case, but Kirsch (D) was convicted of the remaining six charges.

■ **ISSUE**

Was the testimony of the other young victims of sexual assault by the defendant admissible in his trial for sexually assaulting a different child?

■ **DECISION AND RATIONALE**

(Batchelder, J.) No. Evidence of other acts or crimes is not admissible to show a predilection for committing a certain crime. The reasons given by the prosecution (P) for admitting the evidence in this case—intent, motive, common scheme or plan—are indistinguishable from attempting to prove a disposition to molest young girls.

"Motive" refers to the reason a person engages in a particular criminal activity. The desire to engage in sexual activity with a certain type of victim is not a motive, it is a propensity. Similarly, the testimony of other victims does not show Kirsch's (D) intent. In order to be relevant to show intent, evidence of other acts must support an inference that the defendant had the same intent when the uncharged acts were committed as when the charged acts were committed. The testimony of other victims shows that Kirsch (D) purposely selected the same type of victims, which is the same as showing his propensity for a certain type of victim.

The testimony of the other victims does not show a common scheme or plan. In order to show a common scheme or plan, the evidence of other bad acts must show an overall scheme of which each individual crime is a part. A pattern or a systematic course of conduct is not enough to show a plan, and showing that Kirsch (D) gained the trust of young girls from deprived homes in order to seduce them does not demonstrate a common scheme or plan. It is merely proof of Kirsch's (D) penchant or propensity for committing the same offense.

Because the evidence that Kirsch (D) molested other victims was not relevant for a permissible purpose, it should have been excluded and its admission was an abuse of discretion. Reversed.

■ **CONCURRENCE IN PART, DISSENT IN PART**

(Thayer, J.) The prior bad acts show a plan. The rule should not limit the definition of "plan" to a mutually dependent series of events. Kirsch's (D) plan was to use his position of authority in the church to select his victims, using a common set of criteria.

Analysis:

The line between propensity and intent, motive, or plan can be elusive. Clearly, if a defendant committed a certain crime, he or she has a propensity to commit that crime. The inference of propensity is always present behind evidence of other crimes or acts, even if admitted for a proper purpose.

■ **CASE VOCABULARY**

INTENT: The state of mind accompanying an act, especially a forbidden act. While motive is the inducement to do some act, intent is the mental resolution or determination to do it. When the intent to do an act that violates the law exists, motive becomes immaterial.

MOTIVE: Something, especially willful desire, that leads one to act.

United States v. Guardia

(Prosecuting Authority) v. *(Doctor)*

135 F.3d 1326 (10th Cir. 1998)

EVIDENCE OF A DEFENDANT'S PRIOR SEXUAL CONDUCT MAY BE EXCLUDED IF THERE IS A DANGER OF UNFAIR PREJUDICE

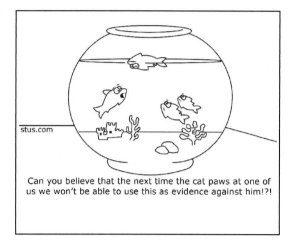

stus.com

Can you believe that the next time the cat paws at one of us we won't be able to use this as evidence against him!?!

■ **INSTANT FACTS** Guardia (D) was accused of sexually assaulting two women during a medical examination, and the prosecutor (P) moved to admit evidence of similar allegations made by other women.

■ **BLACK LETTER RULE** Evidence of a defendant's other sexual conduct will be admitted only if the probative value of the evidence outweighs the danger of undue prejudice, confusion of the issues, misleading the jury, undue delay, waste of time, and the needless presentation of cumulative evidence.

■ **PROCEDURAL BASIS**

Appeal by the prosecution (P) from an order suppressing evidence.

■ **FACTS**

Guardia (D) was charged with sexually abusing two women during medical examinations. The victims alleged that Guardia (D) engaged in contact with them that exceeded the bounds of medically appropriate technique. There were no witnesses to the examinations, other than Guardia (D) and the victims. The prosecution (P) moved to introduce evidence that two other women had made similar allegations against Guardia (D). The trial court held that the risk of jury confusion substantially outweighed the probative value of the evidence. The evidence was excluded.

■ **ISSUE**

Did the trial court err in excluding evidence of allegations of sexual abuse by other patients of the defendant?

■ **DECISION AND RATIONALE**

(Tacha, J.) No. Evidence of a defendant's other sexual conduct will be admitted only if the probative value of the evidence outweighs the danger of undue prejudice, confusion of the issues, misleading the jury, undue delay, waste of time, and the needless presentation of cumulative evidence. The decision to exclude otherwise relevant evidence is within the sound discretion of the trial court and will not be reversed unless there has been an abuse of that discretion.

In cases of sexual assault, Rule 413 of the Federal Rules of Evidence allows the admission of a defendant's other sexual assaults to "be considered for its bearing on any matter to which it is relevant." Evidence offered under the rule must meet three thresholds: the defendant must be accused of a sexual assault, the proffered evidence must show that the defendant committed another sexual assault, and the evidence must be relevant. The first two thresholds are met in this case. The evidence of the prior assaults is also relevant. Evidence that shows a propensity to commit a certain type of crime is relevant. But it may be excluded by other evidentiary rules, despite its acknowledged relevance.

The court is not required to admit the evidence of other assaults solely because evidence of that type is admissible. Rule 413 is not mandatory, but leaves open the possibility of admission. Admission of evidence of other sexual assaults must be analyzed in terms of Rule 403, which provides for the exclusion of otherwise relevant evidence if the probative value of the evidence is outweighed by the enumerated considerations. The court must consider the admission of evidence under Rule 413 by giving careful attention to the probative value of the evidence, as well as to the inherent prejudicial qualities of evidence of other sexual assaults. Rule 413 eliminates the per se exclusion of other crimes evidence, but courts should consider the traditional reasons for the prohibition. There is nothing in rule 413 that leads to the conclusion that Rule 403 has been tempered. The court must evaluate the proffered evidence carefully and make a clear record of the reasoning behind its findings.

In this case, the district court made it clear that the concern was that the probative value of the evidence of other incidents would confuse the issues in the case and mislead the jury. The trial of Guardia (D) will focus on whether his examinations were medically appropriate. Resolution of this issue will depend on expert testimony regarding the propriety of each examination. Introduction of the evidence of other examinations would make it difficult for the jury to separate the evidence of charged conduct from the evidence of uncharged conduct. The proffered evidence is not susceptible of being introduced in a less elaborate manner. The district court did not abuse its discretion in excluding the evidence. Affirmed.

Analysis:

The court does not discuss the standard of proof necessary for the admission of prior sexual assaults. The proffered evidence here is referred to as testimony of four women who "allege" that Guardia (D) abused them during examinations. Rule 413 refers only to "evidence of the defendant's commission of another offense or offenses." Under the analysis of the court here, evidence offered under Rule 413 is to be considered no differently than other evidence of other acts that is admissible under an exception to the general rule barring such evidence.

United States v. Mound

(Prosecuting Authority) v. (Convicted Child Abuser)

157 F.3d 1153 (8th Cir. 1998), *cert. denied*, 525 U.S. 1089, 119 S.Ct. 842 (1999)

ADMISSION OF EVIDENCE OF OTHER SEXUAL ASSAULTS BY THE DEFENDANT IS CONSTITUTIONAL

Who cares if he's guilty THIS time? I'm okay with punishing him again for his prior sexual abuse case.

■ **INSTANT FACTS** Mound (D) was tried for sexual assault and assault of a child, and the Government (P) introduced evidence that he had pleaded guilty previously to sexual abuse of a child.

■ **BLACK LETTER RULE** Rule 413 of the Federal Rules of Evidence, which does not violate due process or the Equal Protection Clause.

■ **PROCEDURAL BASIS**

Dissent from a denial of a motion for a rehearing *en banc*.

■ **FACTS**

The facts of the case are not set out in the excerpt. Essentially, Mound (D) was charged with sexual abuse and assault for the abuse of his daughter. At trial, the Government (P) sought to introduce evidence of Mound's (D) sexual abuse of two young girls approximately ten years earlier. Mound (D) pleaded guilty to abusing one of the girls in exchange for dismissal of the charge that he abused the other. The court allowed the admission of evidence relating to the abuse to which Mound (D) pleaded guilty, but barred the evidence of the other act. Mound (D) was convicted and sentenced to life in prison.

■ **ISSUE**

Did the admission of evidence of the other acts of sexual abuse violate Mound's (D) rights?

■ **DECISION AND RATIONALE**

[Not set out in excerpt.] (Richard S. Arnold, J.) No. Rule 413 does not violate due process, and does not violate the Equal Protection Clause. The district court did not abuse its discretion in admitting the evidence. Affirmed.

■ **DISSENT**

(Morris Sheppard Arnold, J.) The court should rehear the case *en banc* to consider whether Fed. R. Evid. 413 presents such a great risk that a jury will convict a defendant for his past conduct or unsavory character that it violates due process. The common-law rule against propensity evidence is a centuries-old legal tradition. Although it is not embodied in the Constitution, the fact that it has such a long history is some indication that the rule embodies fundamental conceptions of justice. It also must be relevant that members of two committees appointed to examine Rule 413 before its passage unanimously recommended against the adoption of the rule. Committee members were concerned that the new rule would displace essential protections of American jurisprudence that have evolved under long-standing rules and case law. The court should examine the rationale for Rule 413. There is a great deal of evidence that the rate of recidivism for rape is low. While this is a matter that Congress has already considered, reconsideration of such matters is inevitable when fairness is the subject of judicial inquiry.

Analysis:

In its opinion affirming Mound's (D) conviction, the court agreed with the Tenth Circuit, which held that the rule against admission of other acts is not embedded in the Constitution solely because it is a long-standing rule. The court noted that such evidence would be admissible subject to the general rules governing admissibility set out in Rule 403. The court also rejected Mound's (D) equal protection argument, stating that defendants charged with sexual assault are not a suspect class.

■ CASE VOCABULARY

EQUAL PROTECTION: The Fourteenth Amendment guarantee that the government must treat a person or class of persons the same as it treats other persons or classes in like circumstances. In today's constitutional jurisprudence, equal protection means that legislation that discriminates must have a rational basis for doing so. And if the legislation affects a fundamental right (such as the right to vote) or involves a suspect classification (such as race), it is unconstitutional unless it can withstand strict scrutiny.

SUSPECT CLASS: A group identified or defined in a suspect classification.

SUSPECT CLASSIFICATION: A statutory classification based on race, national origin, or alienage, and thereby subject to strict scrutiny under equal-protection analysis.

Michelson v. United States

(Convicted Briber) v. *(Prosecuting Authority)*

335 U.S. 469, 69 S.Ct. 213 (1948)

CHARACTER WITNESSES TESTIFY ABOUT WHAT THEY HAVE HEARD, NOT WHAT THEY KNOW

■ **INSTANT FACTS** Michelson (D) called character witnesses to testify on his behalf, and four of them were asked if they had heard about Michelson's (D) arrest for receiving stolen goods.

■ **BLACK LETTER RULE** Character evidence is evidence of a witness's knowledge of a defendant's reputation, not evidence regarding specific acts.

■ **PROCEDURAL BASIS**

Appeal from an order of the court of appeals affirming a conviction.

■ **FACTS**

Michelson (D) was charged with bribing a federal revenue agent. His defense was that he paid money to the agent in response to the agent's threats and demands. Michelson (D) admitted on direct examination that he had been convicted of a misdemeanor for selling counterfeit watch dials twenty years before his trial on the bribery charges. On cross-examination, it came out that he lied about that conviction on an application three years later. Michelson (D) called five witnesses to testify as to his good reputation. Two of the witnesses testified that they had known Michelson (D) for over thirty years, and the others said that they had known him at least half that long. The witnesses all testified that Michelson (D) had a good reputation for honesty and truthfulness and as a law-abiding citizen.

On cross-examination, four of the witnesses were asked if they had heard of Michelson's (D) conviction for selling counterfeit watch dials. Two of them had heard of the conviction and the other two had not. The four witnesses also were asked if they had heard of Michelson's (D) arrest for receiving stolen property. The prosecutor (P) showed the court a record of the arrest. None of the witnesses had heard of the arrest. The jury was instructed that it was to consider the question about Michelson's (D) arrest only with regard to the witnesses' opinions of Michelson's (D) reputation. Michelson (D) was convicted.

■ **ISSUE**

Was questioning the defense character witnesses regarding knowledge of Michelson's (D) unrelated arrest proper?

■ **DECISION AND RATIONALE**

(Jackson, J.) Yes. Character evidence is evidence of a witness's knowledge of a defendant's reputation, not evidence regarding specific acts. The government is barred from introducing character evidence against a defendant, due to the risk of prejudice to the defendant. But a defendant is allowed to introduce evidence of his or her character to persuade the jury to infer that he or she did not commit the offense charged.

Character evidence encompasses several anomalies. Witnesses who testify regarding character are not only called to testify regarding hearsay, but may testify only to such hearsay. The witnesses are not testifying regarding specific actions, but are testifying to what they have heard about the defendant.

Character is synonymous with reputation. Proof of specific acts would complicate trials, by calling for the introduction of evidence regarding collateral issues. The second anomaly is that lay witnesses are called upon to give their conclusions. At the same time, the witnesses must show that they are acquainted with the defendant and with the defendant's reputation in the community. If a defendant chooses to introduce character evidence, the prosecution may pursue the inquiry by asking the witnesses about damaging rumors, even if those rumors were not well-grounded. A character witness may also be examined as to the contents and extent of the hearsay on which the witness's conclusions are based, and the witness may have to testify about rumors, even of those rumors do not affect his or her conclusions.

The question asked of the character witnesses in this case properly asked for hearsay. Witnesses are asked what they have heard, not what they know. Although arrests are inadmissible to impeach the credibility of a witness, knowledge of an arrest is admissible on the issue of reputation. Reputation is comprised of many different things, so the finality of a conviction is not required to show reputation. The court of appeals thought that the arrest for receiving stolen property was too remote from the bribery charge, but the evidence of the arrest was meant to counter testimony that Michelson (D) had a good reputation for being a law-abiding citizen. The arrest happened many years before the trial in this case, but two of the witnesses who were asked about the arrest dated their acquaintances with Michelson (D) to a time before the arrest. In addition, on direct examination, Michelson (D) testified about a conviction twenty years earlier. The jury was given a proper limiting instruction that was no more difficult to understand than other limiting instructions.

Much of the law on reputation evidence is archaic, paradoxical, and full of compromises and compensations by which an irrational advantage to one side is offset by a poorly reasoned counterprivilege to the other. But the system is workable, since it is moderated by discretionary controls in the hands of the trial court. Affirmed.

Analysis:

The focus of a character witness's testimony is indeed a narrow one. The rule enunciated by the Court here would bar a witness from testifying even as to whether he or she agreed with a defendant's general good reputation. A defendant could have a good reputation based entirely on fabrications or misapprehensions. Questions about those fabrications or misapprehensions are technically limited to the witness's knowledge about them, however, and are not to show that the defendant lied. But this is truly a subtle point: the issue is not whether the defendant lied, but whether the witness has heard that the defendant lied.

■ CASE VOCABULARY

CHARACTER EVIDENCE: Evidence regarding someone's personality traits; evidence of a person's moral standing in a community, based on reputation or opinion.

REPUTATION EVIDENCE: Evidence of what one is thought by others to be. Reputation evidence may be introduced as proof of character when character is in issue or is used circumstantially.

Halloran v. Virginia Chemicals Inc.

(Mechanic) v. *(Freon Seller)*

41 N.Y.2d 386, 361 N.E.2d 991 (1977)

HABIT EVIDENCE MAY BE USED TO SHOW HOW A PARTY ACTED

■ **INSTANT FACTS** Halloran (P) was injured when a can of Freon exploded, and Virginia Chemicals (D) claimed that it was Halloran's (P) practice to heat the cans.

■ **BLACK LETTER RULE** Evidence of a person's habit is admissible to show that he or she acted according to that habit on a particular occasion.

■ **PROCEDURAL BASIS**

Appeal from an order of the appellate division upholding a verdict for Halloran (P).

■ **FACTS**

Halloran (P) was injured when a can of Freon—an air conditioning refrigerant—exploded in his hands. Halloran (P) testified that he had placed the can in some warm water, to make it flow faster. He stated that the water was between ninety and 100 degrees, and that he knew that excessive heat would cause damage. Halloran (P) testified that, over the course of the years, he had serviced "hundreds" of air conditioning units and used "thousands" of cans of Freon. Virginia Chemicals (D) sought to establish that Halloran (P) used an immersion coil to heat the water, which would have made the water too hot, but Halloran (P) denied the use of a coil. Virginia Chemicals (D) offered a witness who was prepared to testify that he had observed Halloran (P) use an immersion coil to heat Freon on several occasions, and that he had warned Halloran (P) of the danger of doing so. The court sustained Halloran's (P) objection to the testimony.

■ **ISSUE**

Was the testimony of Halloran's (P) practice of heating Freon cans admissible in a case involving the explosion of a Freon can?

■ **DECISION AND RATIONALE**

(Breitel, J.) Yes. Evidence of a person's habit is admissible to show that he or she acted according to that habit on a particular occasion. A person who demonstrates a consistent response under a given circumstance is likely to repeat that response when the circumstances arise again. When the issue relates to a deliberate and repetitive practice, a party should be able to obtain an inference of the persistence of that practice and, hence, negligence on a particular occasion. Before such evidence is introduced, the court must be satisfied that there is proof of a sufficient number of instances of the conduct to justify the conclusion that the practice was a habit or regular usage. But it would be preferable if Virginia Chemicals (D) were able to show, at least generally, the times and places of those occurrences. One occurrence of the practice would not be sufficient to show habit. Reversed.

Analysis:

The distinction between habit and propensity is a subtle one. A habit is a specific act that a person does, usually in response to a particular situation or stimulus. Propensity is more generalized, and refers to a person's character, not to specific conduct. Habit does not have any moral connotations, as character and propensity do, but refers only to a person's regular conduct in a precise factual context. Thus, Halloran (P) may have been in the *habit* of heating cans of Freon when they flowed too slowly. Arguably, this could be taken as evidence of a negligent character, or a propensity to behave carelessly.

■ CASE VOCABULARY

HABIT EVIDENCE: Evidence of one's regular response to a repeated specific situation.

CHAPTER FOUR

Impeachment and Character for Truthfulness

United States v. Whitmore

Instant Facts: Whitmore (D) was convicted of firearm and drug charges after the court refused to allow him to introduce character witnesses to challenge the credibility of the Government's (P) primary witness.

Black Letter Rule: Under Rule 608(a), a party may introduce reputation or opinion evidence of a witness's character for truthfulness only if the character witness is acquainted with the witness, his community, and the circles in which he has moved.

United States v. Brewer

Instant Facts: Brewer (D) was charged with kidnapping and transporting a stolen motor vehicle and moved to suppress evidence of prior felony convictions.

Black Letter Rule: Before evidence of prior felony convictions may be admitted for impeachment purposes, the court must determine whether the probative value of admitting the convictions outweighs the prejudicial effect to the defendant.

Luce v. United States

Instant Facts: Luce (D) decided not to testify at his trial after the judge ruled that evidence of his past convictions would be admitted.

Black Letter Rule: A defendant who does not testify may not seek appellate review of a ruling that allows admission of impeachment evidence.

Ohler v. United States

Instant Facts: After the trial court ruled that Ohler's (D) prior convictions would be admissible for impeachment, she took the stand and testified about the prior convictions on direct examination.

Black Letter Rule: A party who introduces evidence waives the right to seek appellate review of the admissibility of that evidence.

United States v. Whitmore

(Prosecuting Authority) v. *(Convicted Defendant)*

359 F.3d 609 (D.C. Cir. 2004)

WITNESSES MUST REALLY KNOW SOMEONE BEFORE TESTIFYING AS TO THEIR CHARACTER

Our angels are well-acquainted with you, your community, and the circles in which you moved.

stus.com

■ **INSTANT FACTS** Whitmore (D) was convicted of firearm and drug charges after the court refused to allow him to introduce character witnesses to challenge the credibility of the Government's (P) primary witness.

■ **BLACK LETTER RULE** Under Rule 608(a), a party may introduce reputation or opinion evidence of a witness's character for truthfulness only if the character witness is acquainted with the witness, his community, and the circles in which he has moved.

■ **PROCEDURAL BASIS**

On appeal to challenge the defendant's conviction.

■ **FACTS**

On November 1, 2001, Officer Russell of the District of Columbia Metropolitan Police Department ordered a crowd to disperse, and everyone with the exception of Whitmore (D) complied. When Russell exited his car, he noticed Whitmore (D) clutching his right jacket pocket while he fled. Russell gave chase and was joined by Officer Soto, who was patrolling the neighborhood. While chasing on foot, Soto also noticed Whitmore (D) clutching his jacket pocket and saw him throw an object against a building as he ran down an alley. After apprehending Whitmore (D), Soto retrieved a gun from a window well in the alley, noting signs that it had recently been thrown against the building. Whitmore (D) was arrested and charged with firearm and drug charges. At trial, Whitmore (D) claimed Soto manufactured the story, and he sought to introduce three character witnesses who would testify that Soto had a reputation for dishonesty. The first witness, Cherkis, was a local reporter who, several years earlier, had investigated and written an article concerning complaints lodged against Soto by residents of the neighborhood in which Whitmore (D) was arrested. A second witness, Cooper, was a local defense attorney who would testify that he and other attorneys considered Soto a liar who provided similar testimony as a government witness in several different cases. Finally, a third witness, Edmonds, was a former acquaintance of Soto who would testify about two specific incidents of dishonesty. The trial court refused to allow the witnesses and further denied Whitmore's (D) attempts to impeach Soto on cross-examination with evidence that he had failed to inform his supervisor of a suspended driver's license as required by police department regulations, as well as evidence of his failure to pay child support. Whitmore (D) was subsequently convicted by a jury.

■ **ISSUE**

Did the court err in refusing to allow the defendant to introduce the testimony of character witnesses to challenge the arresting officer's character?

■ **DECISION AND RATIONALE**

(LeCraft Henderson, J.) No. Under Rule 608(a), a party may introduce reputation or opinion evidence of a witness's character for truthfulness only if the character witness is acquainted with the witness, his

---

community, and the circles in which he has moved. Neither Cherkis nor Edmonds was recently acquainted with Soto such that they could testify to his character with any authority. Likewise, Cooper's testimony represented his conversations with a few criminal defense attorneys, which cannot constitute sufficient acquaintance with Soto's community so as to reliably establish Soto's reputation. Moreover, the foundation required to admit the opinion evidence of these three witnesses was lacking any specific facts upon which to establish a reasonable basis for each witness's opinion. The court correctly excluded the three witnesses.

However, the court abused its discretion in refusing to allow Whitmore (D) to impeach Soto with specific instances of past misconduct under Rule 608(b). Under the rule, Whitmore (D) is allowed to impeach the witness with any past conduct that is probative of the witness's character for truthfulness. The trial court disallowed Whitmore's (D) cross examination because the only support he had for Soto's suspended driver's license was a record from the Maryland Motor Vehicle Administration, which constituted inadmissible hearsay. However, while the record itself may have been inadmissible, counsel need only have some reasonable basis for his questioning on cross-examination. The court apparently presumed that, without admissible proof of the suspension, Soto would simply deny it, leaving the jury nothing to consider. Nonetheless, the court erred in refusing to allow Whitmore (D) to question Soto about his suspended driver's license, his failure to report the suspension to his supervisors, and his failure to pay child support. Because Soto was the Government's (P) primary witness, without whom a conviction appears unlikely, this error was not harmless so as to permit Whitmore's (D) conviction to stand.

Analysis:

In this case, the witnesses' testimony and Soto's past misconduct were all offered for the same purpose—to establish his character (or the lack thereof). Yet, the witnesses' opinions of Soto's reputation and character were inadmissible, while Whitmore (D) should have been able to use Soto's past misconduct against him. The underlying reason for the inadmissibility of the witnesses' opinions was that they were not closely related in time and familiarity to reliably reflect Soto's true, present character. This test is largely a means for the court to weigh the probative value of the evidence against its prejudicial effect to ensure a fair trial. With factual proof of misconduct, which can be tested and discredited by contrary evidence, however, the threat of prejudice is diminished.

■ CASE VOCABULARY

CHARACTER EVIDENCE: Evidence regarding someone's personality traits; evidence of a person's moral standing in the community, based on reputation or opinion.

HARMLESS ERROR: An error that does not affect a party's substantive rights or the case's outcome.

OPINION EVIDENCE: A witness's statement that he or she perceived a fact in issue by one of the five senses, or that the witness was in a particular physical or mental state.

United States v. Brewer

(Prosecuting Authority) v. *(Accused of Kidnapping)*

451 F. Supp. 50 (E.D. Tenn. 1978)

EVIDENCE OF A DEFENDANT'S PRIOR CRIMES IS ADMISSIBLE ONLY IN CERTAIN CIRCUMSTANCES

I weigh the "probative value" vs. the "prejudicial effect" vs. "how I feel". Usually, "how I feel" wins.

stus.com

■ **INSTANT FACTS** Brewer (D) was charged with kidnapping and transporting a stolen motor vehicle and moved to suppress evidence of prior felony convictions.

■ **BLACK LETTER RULE** Before evidence of prior felony convictions may be admitted for impeachment purposes, the court must determine whether the probative value of admitting the convictions outweighs the prejudicial effect to the defendant.

■ **PROCEDURAL BASIS**

Decision on a pretrial motion to suppress evidence.

■ **FACTS**

Brewer (D) was charged with kidnapping and transportation of a stolen motor vehicle. His trial was set for March 15, 1978. Brewer (D) made a motion to suppress evidence of four prior felony convictions. One conviction was an October 1960 conviction in U.S. District Court for kidnapping, for which Brewer (D) was sentenced to ten years in prison. He was released on parole in June 1967. The other convictions were in Ohio state courts; one was for rape, for which Brewer (D) received a sentence of three to twenty years, one was for aggravated assault, which carried a sentence of one to five years, and one was for assault with a deadly weapon, for which he received a sentence of one to fifteen years. The last three convictions were consecutive, and the sentences were imposed on March 22, 1968. After he served time for the state convictions, Brewer's (D) federal parole was revoked and he was not released from federal custody until February 9, 1976, when he was placed on parole again.

■ **ISSUE**

Was any evidence regarding the defendant's prior felony convictions admissible in the defendant's criminal trial for impeachment purposes?

■ **DECISION AND RATIONALE**

(Taylor, J.) Yes. The evidence of the state convictions was admissible, but not that relating to the federal conviction. Before evidence of prior felony convictions may be admitted for impeachment purposes, the court must determine whether the probative value of admitting the convictions outweighs the prejudicial effect to the defendant. All of the convictions meet the threshold requirement for introduction, in that they were punishable by death or imprisonment for more than one year. Brewer (D) argued that the prior convictions were more than ten years old and so should be excluded, unless the court determined that the probative value of the conviction, supported by specific facts and circumstances, substantially outweighed the prejudicial effect of the evidence. In reality, however, none of the convictions is more than ten years old, because the date from which the time begins to run is either the date of the conviction or the date of the final release from custody, whichever is later. The earliest possible release date for the three state convictions was March 1969, which is within the ten-year time limit. Brewer (D) was initially released from custody on the kidnapping charge in 1967; however, he was placed on parole and was not released from parole on that charge until 1976. Brewer's (D) final release from custody was not more than ten years prior to his trial in this case, so the limitation does not apply.

To balance the probative value against the prejudicial effect, the court will look at five factors: the nature of the crime, the time of the conviction and the witness's subsequent history, the similarity between the past crime and the charged crime, the importance of the defendant's testimony, and the centrality of the credibility issue. In this case, the prior convictions were for violent crimes, and crimes of violence have little or no direct bearing on honesty or veracity. This factor weighs against admitting the evidence. But three of the crimes were committed while Brewer (D) was on parole, and Brewer's (D) continued conflict with the law is a factor that supports admission of the conviction for impeachment purposes. The similarity of the prior kidnapping charge is actually a factor *against* its admission into evidence. Admission of evidence of convictions for prior similar offenses could lead the jury to make the impermissible inference that "if he did it once, he probably did it again." The final two factors balance one another out. A defendant's testimony may be important, so that is a factor against admission. On the other hand, credibility may be a central issue in the case, and this factor favors admission.

Overall, the possible prejudicial effect of the kidnapping conviction, even if the jury is given a limiting instruction, outweighs its probative value, so evidence of that conviction may not be admitted. The admission of the other three convictions should serve the purpose of impeaching Brewer's (D) credibility. Motion granted in part and denied in part.

Analysis:

Admission of evidence of other crimes, even for impeachment purposes, is by no means automatic. The probative value on the issue of a witness's capacity for lying depends upon the prior offense. The potential for prejudice, especially when the witness is the defendant, is very high. Note that in his discussion of Brewer's (D) "subsequent history," Judge Taylor mentions that Brewer (D) was convicted of "another crime in Ohio" after he was released from state custody, which led to the revocation of his federal parole. There is no discussion of this other crime, and it appears that there was no attempt to introduce it into evidence.

■ CASE VOCABULARY

IMPEACH: To discredit the veracity of a witness.

IMPEACHMENT: The act of discrediting a witness, as by catching the witness in a lie or by demonstrating that the witness has been convicted of a criminal offense.

PROBATIVE: Tending to prove or disprove. Courts can exclude relevant evidence if its probative value is substantially outweighed by the danger of unfair prejudice.

SUPPRESS: To put a stop to, put down, or prohibit; to prevent (something) from being seen, heard, known, or discussed, as in "the defendant tried to suppress the incriminating evidence."

Luce v. United States

(Non–Testifying Defendant) v. *(Prosecuting Authority)*

469 U.S. 38, 105 S.Ct. 460 (1984)

NON–TESTIFYING DEFENDANTS CANNOT SEEK APPELLATE REVIEW OF CERTAIN EVIDENTIARY RULINGS

■ **INSTANT FACTS** Luce (D) decided not to testify at his trial after the judge ruled that evidence of his past convictions would be admitted.

■ **BLACK LETTER RULE** A defendant who does not testify may not seek appellate review of a ruling that allows admission of impeachment evidence.

■ **PROCEDURAL BASIS**

Appeal from an order of the court of appeals affirming a conviction.

■ **FACTS**

Luce (D) asked the judge in his trial for an advance ruling on the admissibility of evidence of prior convictions. The judge made a tentative ruling that evidence of the convictions would be admissible, and Luce (D) decided not to testify. Luce (D) was convicted.

■ **ISSUE**

Could Luce (D) obtain appellate review of the court's decision to admit evidence of his past convictions when he chose not to testify at his trial?

■ **DECISION AND RATIONALE**

(Burger, C.J.) No. A defendant who does not testify may not seek appellate review of a ruling that allows admission of impeachment evidence. Since Luce (D) did not testify, any possible harm to him flowing from the court's decision is purely speculative. The government (P) may not have attempted to introduce the evidence, or the trial court may have reversed its earlier ruling. In addition, a defendant's decision to testify seldom turns on any one factor. A reviewing court cannot assume that the adverse ruling prompted Luce's (D) decision not to testify. Affirmed.

■ **CONCURRENCE**

(Brennan, J.) The probative value and prejudicial effect of evidence can be evaluated only in the specific factual context of a trial.

Analysis:

It is not unusual for defendants with prior convictions to refrain from testifying. The strong prejudicial effect of prior convictions, even if technically admitted only for impeachment, is a major reason for this decision. In this case, Luce (D) has no argument that the order admitting the evidence harmed him. The evidence was never admitted, since Luce (D) did not testify, so there was no way of knowing if the evidence would have harmed him.

Ohler v. United States

(Testifying Defendant) v. *(Prosecuting Authority)*

529 U.S. 753, 120 S.Ct. 1851 (2000)

THE PARTY WHO INTRODUCES DISPUTED EVIDENCE CANNOT LATER ARGUE AGAINST ITS ADMISSIBILITY

■ **INSTANT FACTS** After the trial court ruled that Ohler's (D) prior convictions would be admissible for impeachment, she took the stand and testified about the prior convictions on direct examination.

■ **BLACK LETTER RULE** A party who introduces evidence waives the right to seek appellate review of the admissibility of that evidence.

■ **PROCEDURAL BASIS**

Appeal from an order of the court of appeals affirming a conviction.

■ **FACTS**

The Government (P) brought a motion to determine whether Ohler's (D) past conviction would be admissible for impeachment purposes, should she decide to testify. The court ruled that it would be admissible. Ohler (D) decided to testify. On direct examination, she admitted to her prior conviction. Ohler (D) was convicted and claimed on appeal that the decision to admit her prior conviction was wrong.

■ **ISSUE**

Was Ohler (D) entitled to appellate review of the judge's decision to admit evidence of her conviction, which she ultimately introduced herself?

■ **DECISION AND RATIONALE**

(Rehnquist, C.J.) No. A party who introduces evidence waives the right to seek appellate review of the admissibility of that evidence. Ohler (D) argues that denying her appellate review is unfair, because such a result would force defendants to forego the tactical advantage of introducing a conviction just to obtain appellate review. The Government (P), on the other hand, argues that jurors may not in actuality perceive a defendant as more credible if the defendant herself introduces evidence of a conviction. The Government (P) also argues that it would actually be an unfair advantage to the defendant if she were viewed as more credible, since the jury would not know that the conviction was disclosed only because a judge did not exclude it. Both arguments obscure the fact that many choices must be made during a trial. Ohler (D) had to decide whether to testify, and, if she had not introduced her prior conviction, the government (P) would have had to make a decision whether it would do so. Ohler (D) may not short-circuit the decisional process and still claim error on appeal. Affirmed.

■ **DISSENT**

(Souter, J.) There is a factual record on which to base a review of Ohler's (D) claim. There is no question that the judge's decision to allow the evidence influenced how Ohler (D) testified. Analysis of her claim is made no more difficult by the fact that the evidence was brought out on direct examination. A jury may well believe that a witness who does not testify about prior convictions has something to hide. Creating that impression is a tactical advantage for the Government (P), but it disserves the search for truth.

Analysis:

The majority's opinion in this case truly is a win for prosecutors. If a judge grants permission to use prior convictions against a defendant, that decision is not reviewable if the defendant tries to blunt the negative effect by admitting to the prior convictions on direct examination. If the defendant does not admit the convictions, the prosecutor may bring them out on cross-examination, with the benefits of all the negative inferences that then arise.

■ CASE VOCABULARY

DIRECT EXAMINATION: The first questioning of a witness in a trial or other proceeding, conducted by the party who called the witness to testify.

CHAPTER FIVE

The Rape Shield Law

People v. Abbot

Instant Facts: Abbot (D) was accused of rape and assault with intent to rape and sought to introduce evidence that the prosecutrix had engaged in prostitution.

Black Letter Rule: Evidence that a prosecutrix in a rape action had prior sexual activities with men is relevant to show consent.

State v. Sibley

Instant Facts: Sibley (D) was accused of rape, and the State (P) introduced evidence of Sibley's (D) bad character.

Black Letter Rule: Evidence of a man's bad character and poor reputation for chastity is inadmissible in a rape prosecution to impeach the character of a witness.

State v. Smith

Instant Facts: Smith (D) was tried for attempted indecent behavior with a juvenile and tried to introduce evidence that the victim had made allegations against others that she later withdrew.

Black Letter Rule: Evidence that a victim has made prior false allegations of sexual assault is not barred by the rape shield law.

Olden v. Kentucky

Instant Facts: Olden (D) was accused of rape and was denied permission to cross-examine the victim regarding her cohabitation with another man.

Black Letter Rule: Shield laws are subject to the defendant's Sixth Amendment right to cross-examine the accuser for bias.

Stephens v. Miller

Instant Facts: Stephens (D) claimed that an attempted rape accusation against him was fabricated because the victim was angry that he asked her about her sexual activity with another man.

Black Letter Rule: A defendant's right to testify in his or her own defense is not absolute and may be limited to protect other legitimate interests.

United States v. Knox

Instant Facts: Knox (D) was accused of rape and attempted to introduce evidence about the victim's prior sexual history to show that he was reasonably mistaken as to her consent.

Black Letter Rule: Evidence of prior sexual behavior is not admissible to show mistake regarding consent if there is no real possibility that there was such a mistake.

People v. Abbot

(Prosecuting Authority) v. *(Accused Rapist)*

19 Wend. (N.Y.) 192 (1838)

EVIDENCE OF A WOMAN'S PRIOR SEXUAL ACTIVITY IS ADMISSIBLE IN A RAPE PROSECUTION

The law used to assume that non-virgins would probably consent to any man.

That was when every lawyer and every judge was a man!

stus.com

■ **INSTANT FACTS** Abbot (D) was accused of rape and assault with intent to rape and sought to introduce evidence that the prosecutrix had engaged in prostitution.

■ **BLACK LETTER RULE** Evidence that a prosecutrix in a rape action had prior sexual activities with men is relevant to show consent.

■ **PROCEDURAL BASIS**

Appeal from a conviction for assault and battery.

■ **FACTS**

Abbot (D) was charged with rape and assault with the intent to commit rape. At trial, he attempted to question the prosecutrix about sexual relations she had with other men. The State's (P) objections to those questions were sustained.

■ **ISSUE**

Should evidence of the prosecutrix's prior sexual relations have been admitted?

■ **DECISION AND RATIONALE**

(Cowen, J.) Yes. Evidence that a prosecutrix in a rape action had prior sexual activities with men is relevant to show consent. Rape, or assault with the intent to rape, is committed in circumstances of utmost privacy. The prosecutrix is usually the sole witness, and the defendant must rely on circumstantial evidence for his defense. Any fact that tends to show that there was not the utmost reluctance and the utmost resistance is to be received. Previous prostitution is one of the circumstances that raises a doubt of assent. Consent is more likely to be inferred from a woman who consents to sexual activity than from a woman who has not. The mind more readily infers assent in the practiced Messalina than in the virtuous Lucretia. The common prostitute and the concubine are entitled to the protection of the law, but the proof of rape in either case is more difficult.

English cases that hold that a woman may not be asked about her sexual experience are anomalies. Other cases have held that it is permissible to prove that a prosecutrix is in fact a common prostitute, or that she has had prior relations with the defendant. Reversed and remanded.

Analysis:

This case exemplifies, if nothing else, the absurdities to which use of propensity evidence can be taken. According to the court, if a woman has consented once, it is hard to believe that she will not consent every time. Messalina, the third wife of the Roman emperor Claudius (10 BCE—54 CE), was executed for her many notorious infidelities. Lucretia (d. 510 BCE), by contrast, was a Roman matron who committed suicide after she was raped so that "no unchaste woman shall henceforth live and plead Lucretia's example."

■ **CASE VOCABULARY**

SHIELD LAW: A statute that restricts or prohibits the use, in rape or sexual-assault cases, of evidence about the past sexual conduct of the victim.

State v. Sibley

(Prosecuting Authority) v. *(Accused Rapist)*
131 Mo. 519 & 132 Mo. 102, 33 S.W. 167 (1895)

THE DEFENDANT'S REPUTATION FOR UNCHASTITY IS INADMISSIBLE IN A RAPE PROSECUTION

■ **INSTANT FACTS** Sibley (D) was accused of rape, and the State (P) introduced evidence of Sibley's (D) bad character.

■ **BLACK LETTER RULE** Evidence of a man's bad character and poor reputation for chastity is inadmissible in a rape prosecution to impeach the character of a witness.

■ **PROCEDURAL BASIS**

Appeal from a conviction for rape.

■ **FACTS**

Sibley (D) was convicted of the rape of his stepdaughter. At his trial, the state (P) introduced evidence that showed that Sibley's (D) character for chastity and virtue was poor. Sibley (D) had not offered any evidence relating to his character as a defendant. Sibley (D) was convicted of the charges against him.

■ **ISSUE**

Was the evidence of Sibley's (D) bad character admissible in his rape trial?

■ **DECISION AND RATIONALE**

(Burgess, J.) No. Evidence of a man's bad character and poor reputation for chastity is inadmissible in a rape prosecution to impeach the character of a witness. It is well known that a man's bad character for chastity does not affect his character for truth as it does a woman's character for truth. A number of great and noble men have been guilty of adultery, and their standing has not been affected by their lack of chastity. Cases that hold a man's character may be impeached by proof of a general reputation for unchastity are reversed. Reversed and remanded.

■ **DISSENT**

(Gantt, J.) Evidence that a woman is unchaste is admitted under the theory that a common prostitute has an impaired moral sense, due to her life of vice. Why should this rule not apply to her companions?

Analysis:

The court seems to wink at sexually licentious behavior by men, noting the high regard in which some men have been held despite their improper behavior. Apparently, boys will be boys, but women must behave themselves. It is hard to imagine a more blatant statement of a sexual double standard.

■ **CASE VOCABULARY**

IMPEACH: To discredit the veracity of (a witness).

State v. Smith

(Prosecuting Authority) v. *(Indecent Behavior Defendant)*
743 So.2d 199 (La. 1999)

PRIOR FALSE ALLEGATIONS OF SEXUAL ASSAULT ARE NOT PRIOR SEXUAL ACTIVITY

Seriously, this time there's a wolf!

stus.com

■ **INSTANT FACTS** Smith (D) was tried for attempted indecent behavior with a juvenile and tried to introduce evidence that the victim had made allegations against others that she later withdrew.

■ **BLACK LETTER RULE** Evidence that a victim has made prior false allegations of sexual assault is not barred by the rape shield law.

■ **PROCEDURAL BASIS**

Appeal from an order of the court of appeals upholding a conviction.

■ **FACTS**

Smith (D) was charged with attempted indecent behavior with a juvenile. At trial, his attorney cross-examined the victim's mother regarding similar accusations the victim made against her cousin, but that she later recanted. The State (P) moved to exclude the evidence, arguing that the evidence was barred by the rape shield law. Smith's (D) attorney stated that the evidence was offered to show the victim's state of mind. The judge held a hearing, pursuant to Rule 412 of the La. Rules of Evidence (similar to Fed. R. Evid. 412), at which the victim's mother denied that the accusations against the cousin were ever recanted. The victim also testified that the allegations were true, and that she had not recanted them. The accused cousin's younger brother testified that the victim told him that the cousin had touched her, but that she later said she was just kidding. The trial court found that there were no prior false allegations of molestation, and that if there were incidents of molestation, they would be inadmissible as prior sexual conduct. Smith (D) was convicted.

■ **ISSUE**

Was the evidence of the victim's prior allegations of sexual misconduct against others admissible?

■ **DECISION AND RATIONALE**

(Traylor, J.) Yes. Evidence that a victim has made prior false allegations of sexual assault is not barred by the rape shield law. The prior false statements are not evidence of past sexual conduct by the victim, but are impeachment evidence, to be used to attack her credibility. Smith (D) was not attempting to prove that the victim had engaged in sexual activity in the past, or that she had an unchaste character, but that she had made false allegations of sexual activity.

No Rule 412 hearing was required, because prior false allegations of sexual conduct are not "past sexual behavior." The question for the court was not whether the allegations were false, but whether reasonable jurors could find, based on the evidence presented by Smith (D), that the victim had made prior false accusations. It was admitted that the victim made false allegations, and there was evidence that she recanted those accusations. There was sufficient evidence to conclude that the victim had made false allegations. As such, the evidence should have been admitted, subject to its meeting the other standards for admissibility. Reversed and remanded.

■ **DISSENT**

(Victory, J.) The evidence of the other complaints should have been excluded as irrelevant.

Analysis:

At trial, Smith (D) probably would have a limited opportunity to use the prior false allegations. The false accusations do not relate to the issue of Smith's (D) guilt or innocence, so they may be used to attack the victim's credibility. If the victim does not call any witnesses to testify as to her good character for truthfulness, Smith (D), under Rule 608 (b), would be able to introduce the evidence of false allegations only by cross-examining the victim. He would not be able to call his own witnesses to testify to the false allegations.

■ **CASE VOCABULARY**

RECANT: To withdraw or renounce (prior statements or testimony) formally or publicly.

Olden v. Kentucky

(Accused Rapist) v. *(Prosecuting Authority)*

488 U.S. 227, 109 S.Ct. 480 (1988)

SHIELD LAWS ARE LIMITED BY THE SIXTH AMENDMENT

■ **INSTANT FACTS** Olden (D) was accused of rape and was denied permission to cross-examine the victim regarding her cohabitation with another man.

■ **BLACK LETTER RULE** Shield laws are subject to the defendant's Sixth Amendment right to cross-examine the accuser for bias.

■ **PROCEDURAL BASIS**

Appeal from a judgment of the Supreme Court of Kentucky affirming a conviction.

■ **FACTS**

Olden (D) was accused of raping Matthews, who lived with another man, Russell. Matthews and Russell were married, but not to each other. Olden (D) admitted engaging in sexual acts with Matthews, but claimed they were consensual. The theory of his defense was that Matthews fabricated the rape allegations, in order to protect her relationship with Russell. The trial court granted the prosecutor's (P) motion *in limine* to exclude all evidence of Matthews's living arrangements. During the trial, when Matthews claimed that she was living with her mother, the court sustained the prosecutor's (P) objection to cross-examination regarding her living arrangements.

■ **ISSUE**

Should the court have allowed the accused rapist to cross-examine his alleged victim about her cohabitation with another man to whom she was not married?

■ **DECISION AND RATIONALE**

(Per Curiam) Yes. Shield laws are subject to the defendant's Sixth Amendment right to cross-examine the accuser for bias. A defendant makes out a Sixth Amendment violation if he or she was prevented from cross-examining a witness in order to present to the jury facts from which the jury could draw inferences about the reliability of a witness. In this case, a reasonable jury might have had a significantly different impression of Matthews's credibility if Olden (D) had been allowed to pursue his proposed line of cross-examination. Matthews's testimony was crucial to the case against Olden (D), and Olden (D) directly contradicted that testimony. Her testimony was corroborated only by Russell, whose impartiality would also have been attacked by evidence of his relationship with Matthews. Reversed.

■ **DISSENT**

(Marshall, J.) The case should not be disposed of in a summary manner.

Analysis:

Rape shield laws are not unconstitutional, but the prohibition against questioning a rape victim about prior sexual history may not be absolute. Olden (D) sought to offer the evidence for a particular purpose, not just as a way of disparaging Matthews's character generally. The evidence that Olden (D) sought to offer is different from what is usually thought of as evidence of a victim's prior sexual conduct, even though it does involve an accusation of adultery. Olden (D) was not accusing Matthews of promiscuity or asking the jury to infer consent from her prior conduct.

■ CASE VOCABULARY

CONFRONTATION CLAUSE: The Sixth Amendment provision guaranteeing a criminal defendant's right to directly confront an accusing witness and to cross-examine that witness.

MOTION IN LIMINE: A pretrial request that certain inadmissible evidence not be referred to or offered at trial. Typically, a party makes this motion when it believes that mere mention of the evidence during trial would be highly prejudicial and could not be remedied by an instruction to disregard. If, after the motion is granted, the opposing party mentions or attempts to offer the evidence in the jury's presence, a mistrial may be ordered. A ruling on a motion in limine does not always preserve evidentiary error for appellate purposes. To raise such an error on appeal, a party may be required to formally object when the evidence is actually admitted or excluded during trial.

Stephens v. Miller

(Convicted Attempted Rapist) v. *(Prison Warden)*

13 F.3d 998 (7th Cir. 1994), *cert. denied,* 513 U.S. 808, 115 S.Ct. 57 (1994)

RAPE SHIELD LAWS MAY LIMIT A DEFENDANT'S RIGHT TO TESTIFY

■ **INSTANT FACTS** Stephens (D) claimed that an attempted rape accusation against him was fabricated because the victim was angry that he asked her about her sexual activity with another man.

■ **BLACK LETTER RULE** A defendant's right to testify in his or her own defense is not absolute and may be limited to protect other legitimate interests.

■ **PROCEDURAL BASIS**

Appeal from an order denying a petition for a writ of habeas corpus.

■ **FACTS**

Wilburn accused Stephens (D) of attempting to rape her. On the day in question, Stephens's (D) friend, Stone, dropped Stephens (D) off at Wilburn's trailer. Wilburn testified that she woke up to find Stephens (D) making advances towards her, but that she screamed and pushed him off. After his encounter with Wilburn, Stephens (D) left her trailer and went to the home of some friends. He told his friends that he had been at a store. Stephens (D) told the same story to the police. At trial, Stone told the same story, too, but then admitted that Stephens (D) had told him to say that. Stone then testified that he dropped Stephens (D) off at Wilburn's trailer.

Stephens (D) claimed that, after his friend Stone dropped him off at Wilburn's trailer, he and Wilburn engaged in consensual intercourse. Stephens (D) offered testimony that he asked Wilburn, "don't you like it like this? . . . . Tim Hall said you did." He also claimed that he asked Wilburn about "switching partners." The court did not allow Stephens (D) to testify as to the details of his statements, but allowed him to testify that Wilburn became angry at something he said, and that led her to fabricate the rape accusation. Stephens (D) was convicted. He claimed that exclusion of the specifics of his statements to Wilburn violated his constitutional right to testify in his own defense. Stephens (D) also claimed that the excluded testimony should have been admitted as the *res gestae* of the attempted rape.

■ **ISSUE**

Did the exclusion of the testimony regarding the defendant's conversation with the victim violate Stephens's (D) right to testify in his own defense?

■ **DECISION AND RATIONALE**

(Bauer, J.) No. A defendant's right to testify in his or her own defense is not absolute, but may be limited to accommodate other legitimate interests. Rape shield statutes are the type of permissible procedural and evidentiary rules that control the presentation of evidence. Rape shield statutes represent a valid legislative determination that victims of rape or attempted rape deserve heightened protection against surprise, harassment, and unnecessary invasions of privacy. The restrictions imposed by the statutes may not, however, be arbitrary or disproportionate to the interests they are designed to serve. In this case, Stephens (D) was allowed to testify that something that he said to

---

Wilburn made her angry and led her to fabricate the attempted rape charge. The court's exclusion of the remainder of his testimony was not arbitrary or disproportionate. The purpose of the rape shield statute is to prevent this type of generalized inquiry into a victim's reputation or past conduct in order to avoid embarrassing the victim and subjecting him or her to possible public denigration. The trial court properly balanced Stephens's (D) right to testify in his own defense with the state's interest in enacting the rape shield law. Stephens (D) and Wilburn told very different stories, and Stephens (D) asked Stone to commit perjury for him. The jury was entitled to believe Wilburn. Admission of the testimony about what Stephens (D) said to Wilburn would have had no purpose other than to humiliate her.

The testimony was not admissible as a part of the *res gestae* of the offense. Accepting that argument would gut the rape shield statutes, as defendants could claim they said something about the victim's past or reputation close to the time and place of the rape. In addition, there is no reason to conclude that *res gestae* has a constitutional basis. The term *res gestae* is largely obsolete in federal law and has no constitutional significance. Affirmed.

■ DISSENT

(Cummings, J.) Stephens (D) has made a colorable claim that the rape shield law has interfered with his right to present a defense. Although the goals of the rape shield law are worthy ones, those goals must sometimes yield to another goal, that of allowing the accused to present a defense. In this case, resolution of the conflicting stories told by Stephens (D) and Wilburn turned in substantial part on whether what Stephens (D) said to Wilburn could have made her angry enough to terminate their encounter and fabricate a rape allegation. Stephens (D) was left to persuade the jury that his story was true, without letting them hear the fragments on which its plausibility turned. Although admission of the evidence would cause Wilburn some embarrassment, the interest in letting her testify free of embarrassment does not outweigh Stephens's (D) interest in receiving a fair trial. Stephens's (D) statements should be admitted because they are crucial to his defense, not because they are a part of the *res gestae.*

Analysis:

The defense offered by Stephens (D) loses a considerable amount of weight when he is denied the opportunity to explain just what it was that offended Wilburn as much as he claimed. The believability of his story depends on just what it was that he said, but the jury was not allowed to consider these details. The trial court may have considered and rested its decision on the fact that Stephens (D) already had changed his story about what he did that night, and that he asked Stone to lie for him.

■ CASE VOCABULARY

RES GESTAE: The events at issue, or other events contemporaneous with them. In evidence law, words and statements about the *res gestae* are usually admissible under a hearsay exception (such as present sense impression or excited utterance). Where the Federal Rules of Evidence or state rules fashioned after them are in effect, the use of *res gestae* is now out of place. *See* Fed. R. Evid. 803 (1), (2).

United States v. Knox

(Prosecuting Authority) v. *(Airman)*

1992 WL 97157 (U.S.A.F. Ct. Mil. Rev. 1992)

EVIDENCE OF PRIOR SEXUAL ACTIVITY MUST BE RELEVANT TO BE ADMISSIBLE

■ **INSTANT FACTS** Knox (D) was accused of rape and attempted to introduce evidence about the victim's prior sexual history to show that he was reasonably mistaken as to her consent.

■ **BLACK LETTER RULE** Evidence of prior sexual behavior is not admissible to show mistake regarding consent if there is no real possibility that there was such a mistake.

■ **PROCEDURAL BASIS**

Appeal from a conviction for rape and conspiracy to commit rape.

■ **FACTS**

Theresa and her boyfriend went to Knox's (D) room. After a time, Knox (D) left the room. Theresa testified that she fell asleep on the bed, but awoke when someone was having sexual intercourse with her. She saw that it was Knox (D) and told Knox (D) and her boyfriend to leave the room. Theresa testified that she did not consent to sexual intercourse with Knox (D). Knox (D) testified that, when he returned to his room, he saw Theresa and her boyfriend engaged in sexual activity. He stated that Theresa looked at him and he interpreted her look as an invitation to participate. Knox (D) admitted having intercourse with Theresa, but claimed she was awake the whole time.

At his court martial, Knox (D) attempted to introduce evidence that Theresa had a reputation for promiscuity, that several people told him that they had contracted a sexually transmitted disease from her, and that Knox (D) had been told that Theresa engaged in various sex acts in the presence of others at a beach party. The trial judge allowed some of Knox's (D) proposed evidence, but did not allow evidence of individual acts or Theresa's reputation. Knox (D) claimed that the evidence was necessary to show that he was mistaken about Theresa's consent.

■ **ISSUE**

Should evidence of an alleged rape victim's past sexual behavior be admitted to show that the defendant made a mistake as to her consent?

■ **DECISION AND RATIONALE**

(Hodgson, J.) No. Evidence of prior sexual behavior is not admissible to show mistake regarding consent if there is no real possibility that there was such a mistake. In this case, there were two distinct possibilities: either Theresa was, as she testified, asleep or she was, as Knox (D) testified, awake. There was no real possibility of mistake. The proposed evidence was not relevant on the issue of consent, and so was properly excluded. Affirmed.

Analysis:

The evidence offered by Knox (D) is little different from propensity evidence, except that he makes it a question of his belief. He is, in essence, basing his defense on the reasoning that he heard Theresa was

---

promiscuous, so he thought she consented to have sex with him. Evidence of prior sexual activity could, however, be relevant to a defense based on mistake regarding consent in some circumstances, such as if the prior acts had been engaged in with the defendant.

■ CASE VOCABULARY

RELEVANT: Logically connected and tending to prove or disprove a matter in issue; having appreciable probative value—that is, rationally tending to persuade people of the probability or possibility of some alleged fact.

CHAPTER SEVEN

The Rule Against Hearsay

Mahlandt v. Wild Canid Survival & Research Center, Inc.

Instant Facts: Mahlandt (P) claimed he was injured by a wolf kept by Poos (D), and he attempted to introduce evidence of statements made by Poos (D) that the wolf had injured Mahlandt (P).

Black Letter Rule: Statements made by an agent or employee that concern a matter within the scope of the agency or employment and that are made during the existence of the relationship are admissible, even if those statements are not made to third parties.

Bourjaily v. United States

Instant Facts: Statements made by an alleged co-conspirator were admitted in Bourjaily's (D) trial for conspiracy, and Bourjaily (D) claimed there was insufficient proof that the statements were made in furtherance of a conspiracy.

Black Letter Rule: Statements made by co-conspirators during the course of the conspiracy are admissible if the existence of the conspiracy is proven by a preponderance of the evidence, which may include the statements themselves.

United States v. Barrett

Instant Facts: Barrett (D) was not allowed to introduce evidence that a witness who implicated him had said earlier that Barrett (D) was not involved in the crime.

Black Letter Rule: Prior inconsistent statements of a witness are admissible to impeach the credibility of that witness.

United States v. Ince

Instant Facts: The Government (P) introduced a statement from a witness that said that Ince (D) confessed to the crime.

Black Letter Rule: Prior inconsistent statements may not be introduced if their only purpose is to circumvent the hearsay rule and admit an otherwise inadmissible confession.

Fletcher v. Weir

Instant Facts: Weir (D) was asked on cross-examination why he did not tell the police officers who arrested him that he acted in self-defense.

Black Letter Rule: A defendant may be cross-examined about his or her post-arrest silence if no *Miranda* warnings were given.

Tome v. United States

Instant Facts: Tome (D) claimed that sexual abuse charges against him were fabricated, and the Government (P) introduced consistent statements made after the motive to fabricate those statements arose.

Black Letter Rule: Prior consistent statements are admissible to rebut a charge of fabrication only if the consistent statements were made before the motive to fabricate arose.

Commonwealth v. Weichell

Instant Facts: Weichell (D) was tried for first-degree murder, and a composite sketch prepared from a witness's description was admitted into evidence.

Black Letter Rule: The record of a witness's out-of-court description of a person is admissible.

United States v. Owens

Instant Facts: Owens (D) was charged with attacking Foster, who could not remember who attacked him but could recall identifying Owens (D) as his attacker some weeks after the attack.

Black Letter Rule: A witness is subject to cross-examination concerning a statement if he or she is placed on the witness stand, under oath, and responds willingly to questions.

United States v. DiNapoli

Instant Facts: At trial, DiNapoli (D) and other defendants sought to introduce grand jury testimony from DeMatteis and Bruno.

Black Letter Rule: The test for whether a party has the same motive in developing evidence is not only whether the questioner was on the same side of the same issue in both proceedings, but also whether the questioner had a substantially similar interest in asserting that side of the issue.

Lloyd v. American Export Lines, Inc.

Instant Facts: Lloyd (P) did not appear in his action, and his testimony at a prior administrative hearing arising out of the same incident was admitted at trial.

Black Letter Rule: Testimony at a prior trial or hearing will be admissible if a party with a like motive to cross-examine the witness as a party in the present proceeding would have been given an adequate opportunity to cross-examine the witness.

Williamson v. United States

Instant Facts: Harris made a statement that incriminated both Harris himself and Williamson (D), but he refused to testify at trial, and his statement was admitted into evidence.

Black Letter Rule: The parts of an out-of-court statement that do not inculpate the declarant are not admissible as statements against interest.

Shepard v. United States

Instant Facts: Shepard's (D) wife asked her nurse about having a bottle of whisky tested for poison, and then said that Shepard (D) poisoned her.

Black Letter Rule: In order to be admissible as a dying declaration, a statement must have been made while the declarant had no hope of recovery and knew that death was imminent.

United States v. Gray

Instant Facts: In the defendant's trial for mail and wire fraud, the Government (P) sought to introduce out-of-court statements made by her late husband, who had been murdered by the defendant.

Black Letter Rule: A defendant who wrongfully and intentionally renders a declarant unavailable as a witness in any proceeding forfeits the right to exclude, on hearsay grounds, the declarant's statements at that proceeding and any subsequent proceeding.

Mutual Life Insurance Co. v. Hillmon

Instant Facts: Hillmon (P) brought suit to recover on three life insurance policies, and Mutual Life Insurance (D) attempted to introduce letters written by the man they claimed was the actual decedent.

Black Letter Rule: Out-of-court statements that express a declarant's present intention are admissible to prove what that intention was.

Shepard v. United States

Instant Facts: Shepard's (D) wife asked her nurse about having a bottle of whisky tested for poison, and then said that Shepard (D) poisoned her.

Black Letter Rule: A declaration of a person's state of mind is inadmissible to prove the actions of someone other than the declarant.

United States v. Iron Shell

Instant Facts: The defendant was prosecuted for assault with intent to commit rape, and the victim's doctor was allowed to testify about what the victim told him had happened.

Black Letter Rule: Admission of an out-of-court statement under the exception for statements made for medical diagnosis or treatment depends on whether the declarant's motive in making the statement was consistent with the purpose of the exception and on whether it was reasonable for the physician to rely on the statement for diagnosis or treatment.

Johnson v. State

Instant Facts: Taylor gave a statement that implicated Johnson (D) in a murder, but he was unable to recall anything about the statement at trial.

Black Letter Rule: In order for a recording of a past recollection to be admissible, the witness whose recollection is refreshed must testify that the recording is accurate.

Palmer v. Hoffman

Instant Facts: Hoffman (P) and his wife were involved in a traffic accident with a train, and the railroad (D) sought to introduce a report of the accident as a business record.

Black Letter Rule: A report of an accident is not made in the regular course of business, and so is not admissible under the business records exception to the hearsay rule.

United States v. Vigneau

Instant Facts: Vigneau (D) was accused of sending money to Crandall (D) for illegal drugs, and records of money transfers with Vigneau's (D) name on them were introduced into evidence at trial.

Black Letter Rule: The business records exception does not include statements in a record that were made by someone not a part of the business if those statements are offered for their truth.

Beech Aircraft Corp. v. Rainey

Instant Facts: Rainey (P) sued Beech (D) for his wife's death in an airplane crash, and Beech (D) introduced the report of an official investigation that said that pilot error was the cause of the crash.

Black Letter Rule: Investigatory reports are not inadmissible solely because they set out a conclusion or opinion.

Dallas County v. Commercial Union Assurance Co.

Instant Facts: Commercial Union (D) introduced into evidence an old newspaper article to show that Dallas County's (P) courthouse had been damaged by fire over fifty years earlier.

Black Letter Rule: Hearsay evidence may be admissible if there is no other way of proving the facts in the hearsay statement and if there are circumstances that show the evidence is trustworthy enough without the need for cross-examination.

United States v. Laster

Instant Facts: Laster (D) was accused of manufacturing methamphetamine and records that showed that he ordered one of the components of the drug were introduced.

Black Letter Rule: The residuary hearsay exception allows the admission of hearsay if there is no indication that the evidence is not reliable, if the hearsay is more probative on the point for which it is offered than any other evidence, and if its admission serves the best interests of justice.

Mahlandt v. Wild Canid Survival & Research Center, Inc.

(Injured Child) v. (Wolf Owner)

588 F.2d 626 (8th Cir. 1978)

DECLARATIONS OF AN AGENT ARE ADMISSIBLE

It says here you like to keep your mouth shut in a crisis. You're hired!

Personnel

stus.com

- **INSTANT FACTS** Mahlandt (P) claimed he was injured by a wolf kept by Poos (D), and he attempted to introduce evidence of statements made by Poos (D) that the wolf had injured Mahlandt (P).

- **BLACK LETTER RULE** Statements made by an agent or employee that concern a matter within the scope of the agency or employment and that are made during the existence of the relationship are admissible, even if those statements are not made to third parties.

■ PROCEDURAL BASIS

Appeal from a judgment for Wild Canid Survival (D) and Poos (D).

■ FACTS

Poos (D) kept a wolf at his home. He used the wolf in his work with Wild Canid Survival (D), presenting educational programs about wolves. The wolf was chained in an enclosure by Poos's (D) home, because she had jumped the fence and attacked a dog.

Mahlandt (P), a child of three, had been sent by his mother to get his brother from a neighbor's house. Another neighbor heard a child screaming and saw a boy lying on his back in the wolf's enclosure, with the wolf straddling him. The neighbor saw Clarke, Poos's (D) son, run and pick the boy up and take him into the house. Clarke stated that he saw Mahlandt (D) in the enclosure, and the wolf standing away from him, wailing. Mahlandt's (D) mother testified that Clarke told her that "a wolf got [Mahlandt (D)] and he is dying." Clarke denied making the statement.

Shortly after the incident, Poos (D) left a note on his superior's door that said that the wolf had bit a child. Poos (D) also spoke to his superior and told him that the wolf bit a child. A few days later, the directors of Wild Canid Survival (D) met and discussed the legal aspects of their wolf biting a child. Poos (D) was not present at that meeting.

At trial, one of the issues was whether the wolf had injured Mahlandt (D). The medical evidence was inconsistent with wolf bites and could have happened when Mahlandt (D) crawled under the fence of the enclosure. There was expert testimony that the howling of the wolf was a call of distress, not aggression, and that if a wolf licks a child's face, it is a sign of care, not attack. Mahlandt (P) offered into evidence the note Poos (D) left on his superior's door, the conversation Poos (D) had with his superior, and an abstract of the minutes of the meeting of the board of Wild Canid Survival (D). The judge excluded all three items. The judge reasoned that all three items were based on hearsay, and the minutes of the board meeting were unreliable because of a lack of personal knowledge.

■ ISSUE

Were the out-of-court statements of an agent of the wolf's owner admissible in evidence?

■ DECISION AND RATIONALE

(Sickle, J.) Yes. Statements made by an agent or employee that concern a matter within the scope of the agency or employment and that are made during the existence of the relationship are admissible, even if those statements are not made to third parties. Such statements are not excluded even if the agent did not have personal knowledge of the facts on which the statements were based. Poos's (D) statements were admissible against him and Wild Canid Survival (D). The minutes of the board meeting, however, were admissible against Wild Canid (D), but not against Poos (D). He did not attend or participate in the meeting. Reversed.

Analysis:

Although the evidence is admissible, it certainly is weak. Poos (D) was reacting to what he was told by those who came on the scene after Mahlandt (D) was injured, and the board's discussion was based on what Poos (D) told them. But the strength of the evidence seldom affects the admissibility. It is up to the parties to argue the strength or weakness of the facts to the jury, and up to the jury to determine which evidence is the more persuasive.

■ CASE VOCABULARY

AGENCY: A fiduciary relationship created by express or implied contract or by law, in which one party (the *agent*) may act on behalf of another party (the *principal*) and bind that other party by words or actions.

AGENT: One who is authorized to act for or in place of another; a representative.

Bourjaily v. United States

(*Convicted Conspirator*) v. (*Prosecuting Authority*)

483 U.S. 171, 107 S.Ct. 2775 (1987)

OUT–OF–COURT STATEMENTS IN FURTHERANCE OF A CONSPIRACY ARE ADMISSIBLE IF A CONSPIRACY IS PROVEN

There would be a chicken and the egg problem, but the rules of evidence don't apply to preliminary questions of fact.

stus.com

Prove Conspiracy   Admit Statements

■ **INSTANT FACTS** Statements made by an alleged co-conspirator were admitted in Bourjaily's (D) trial for conspiracy, and Bourjaily (D) claimed there was insufficient proof that the statements were made in furtherance of a conspiracy.

■ **BLACK LETTER RULE** Statements made by co-conspirators during the course of the conspiracy are admissible if the existence of the conspiracy is proven by a preponderance of the evidence, which may include the statements themselves.

■ **PROCEDURAL BASIS**

Appeal from an order of the court of appeals affirming a conviction.

■ **FACTS**

Bourjaily (D) was charged with conspiracy to distribute cocaine and possession of cocaine with intent to distribute. At his trial, the Government (P) introduced a tape recording of a conversation between an alleged co-conspirator, Lonardo, and an FBI informant. The conversation involved the details of a sale of cocaine to the informant. Lonardo said that he would transfer the cocaine from the informant to a "friend" in a certain parking lot. The transaction took place as planned, and Lonardo and Bourjaily (D) were arrested at the scene.

Bourjaily (D) objected to the introduction of the taped conversation. He argued that the statement did not fall within the hearsay exception for statements made by conspirators during the course of the conspiracy, because there was insufficient evidence that there was a conspiracy. Bourjaily (D) claimed that the conspiracy had to be shown by evidence other than the statements, relying on *Glasser v. United States,* 315 U.S. 60 (1942). Bourjaily (D) was convicted, however, and his conviction was affirmed by the court of appeals.

■ **ISSUE**

Was the evidence of Lonardo's statements to an alleged co-conspirator admissible?

■ **DECISION AND RATIONALE**

(Rehnquist, C.J.) Yes. Statements made by co-conspirators during the course of the conspiracy are admissible if the existence of the conspiracy is proven by a preponderance of the evidence, which may include the statements themselves. The rule that relates to the determination of preliminary questions of fact, Fed. R. Evid. 104(a), provides that the court is not bound in such instances by the rules of evidence, except for those that relate to privilege. The rule in *Glasser* has been replaced by Rule 104(a). The rule is clear that any evidence, except privileged evidence, may be considered.

Bourjaily (D) also argued that out-of-court statements are unreliable and therefore inadmissible, at least until a conspiracy is proven. Out-of-court statements are only presumed unreliable. This presumption may be rebutted by the appropriate proof. In addition, although an individual item of evidence may be insufficient to prove a point by itself, when that item is added to other evidence, the cumulative effect may be sufficient proof. Evidence that is unreliable in isolation may become quite probative when added to other evidence. Even if the out-of-court statements are presumptively unreliable, the courts must be allowed to evaluate the statements for their evidentiary worth as revealed from the circumstances of the case.

A co-conspirator's statements may be probative of the existence of a conspiracy and of the participation of both the declarant and the defendant in that conspiracy. In this case, Lonardo's statements showed that he was involved in a conspiracy with a "friend." The statement went on to provide details about the conspiracy. Each one of the individual statements may have been unreliable when considered in isolation, but taken as a whole, the entire conversation was corroborated by independent evidence.

It is not necessary to determine if the hearsay statements could have been the sole basis for concluding that a conspiracy existed. Affirmed.

Analysis:

The Court's reasoning is circular. The statements are admissible only if they were made in support of a conspiracy. The statements themselves prove a conspiracy. The statements are thus used to lay the foundation for their own admissibility.

The Court does not decide the question of whether the statements would be sufficient to prove the conspiracy without other evidence. There is a strong implication that more evidence would be required. The text of Fed. R. Evid. 801(d)(2), revised after this case was decided, makes it clear that statements alone will not be sufficient proof.

■ CASE VOCABULARY

CONSPIRACY: An agreement by two or more persons to commit an unlawful act; a combination for an unlawful purpose.

United States v. Barrett

(Prosecuting Authority) v. *(Accused Thief)*

539 F.2d 244 (1st Cir. 1976)

PRIOR STATEMENTS THAT CONTRADICT A WITNESS'S TESTIMONY ARE ADMISSIBLE

The defense wasn't permitted to show the government's witness was a big fat liar.

Sounds like a fun time to embarass the trial judge with a reversal!

stus.com

- **INSTANT FACTS** Barrett (D) was not allowed to introduce evidence that a witness who implicated him had said earlier that Barrett (D) was not involved in the crime.

- **BLACK LETTER RULE** Prior inconsistent statements of a witness are admissible to impeach the credibility of that witness.

■ PROCEDURAL BASIS

Appeal from a conviction for theft.

■ FACTS

Barrett (D) was one of eight accused of taking part in the theft of postage stamps. The theft involved disabling the alarm system of a museum. Barrett (D) was the only one of the accused to stand trial. At his trial, Adams, a convicted burglar and thief, testified for the Government (P) in exchange for protection for himself and his family. Adams testified that Barrett (D) discussed alarm systems with him. Adams also stated that Barrett (D) described his involvement in the stamp theft with him. Two other witnesses implicated Barrett (D) in the theft and the disposition of the stolen stamps. Barrett (D) attempted to introduce testimony from yet two other witnesses, each of whom would testify that he or she heard Adams say that he knew that Barrett (D) was not involved. One witness would testify that Adams told him this directly, and the other would say that she overheard the conversation while waiting on Adams in a restaurant. Barrett (D) offered this evidence to impeach Adams's testimony, but the trial court did not allow the evidence to be admitted. The court ruled that the statements were inadmissible hearsay opinions.

■ ISSUE

Should the witnesses have been allowed to testify regarding Adams's prior statements?

■ DECISION AND RATIONALE

(Campbell, J.) Yes. Prior inconsistent statements of a witness are admissible to impeach the credibility of that witness. The statements were clearly inconsistent with Adams's testimony. A prior inconsistent statement is admissible if it gives some indication, either directly or indirectly, that the fact was different from the testimony of the witness. In this case, Adams's testimony had the effect of saying that he learned of Barrett's (D) involvement in the theft. This testimony was different from his later comments.

Although some of the details may be uncertain, that uncertainty is not a sufficient reason to keep the testimony from the jury. It is for the jury to weigh the credibility of the witness. It does not matter that Barrett (D) did not lay the foundation for the evidence by asking Adams about it on cross-examination. Under the Federal Rules of Evidence, it is sufficient that Adams be afforded the opportunity to explain the contradiction. The error was not harmless, in that the credibility of Adams was key to Barrett's (D) defense. Reversed.

Analysis:

The admission of out-of-court statements often depends upon the purpose for which they are offered. In this case, Barrett (D) is careful to note that he is offering the out-of-court statements not to show his innocence, or to show that Adams knew him to be innocent, but to show that Adams was contradicting himself. The distinction is one that may elude many jurors, especially since the prior inconsistent statement is about the central issue of the case. Note that Adams was not one of those involved in the theft. His testimony was that he discussed alarms with Barrett (D), and that Barrett (D) described his involvement in the crime.

■ **CASE VOCABULARY**

CREDIBILITY: The quality that makes something (as a witness or some evidence) worthy of belief.

IMPEACH: To discredit the veracity of (a witness).

PRIOR INCONSISTENT STATEMENT: A witness's earlier statement that conflicts with the witness's testimony at trial. In federal practice, extrinsic evidence of an unsworn prior inconsistent statement is admissible, if the witness is given an opportunity to explain or deny the statement, for impeachment purposes only. Sworn statements may be admitted for all purposes. A prior consistent statement is not hearsay if it is offered to rebut a charge that the testimony was improperly influenced or fabricated.

United States v. Ince

(Prosecuting Authority) v. *(Accused Assailant)*

21 F.3d 576 (4th Cir. 1994)

PRIOR INCONSISTENT STATEMENTS MAY NOT BE USED TO INTRODUCE OTHERWISE INADMISSIBLE EVIDENCE

stus.com

Suzy said that I said I like Kyle?
That's inadmissible hearsay!

■ **INSTANT FACTS** The Government (P) introduced a statement from a witness that said that Ince (D) confessed to the crime.

■ **BLACK LETTER RULE** Prior inconsistent statements may not be introduced if their only purpose is to circumvent the hearsay rule and admit an otherwise inadmissible confession.

■ PROCEDURAL BASIS

Appeal from a conviction for assault with a deadly weapon with intent to do bodily harm.

■ FACTS

A man wearing an orange shirt or jacket fired a pistol at trucks leaving a parking lot after a concert on an army base. The van in which Ince (D) was riding was pulled over, as were other vehicles in the area. A military police officer interviewed Neumann, who was riding with Ince (D). Neumann provided a statement that Ince (D) had said that he fired the shots, but he no longer had the gun. At Ince's (D) trial, Neumann was called to testify. She said that she did not remember what Ince (D) had told her. She was shown a copy of her statement. Neumann repeated that she could not remember what Ince (D) had said. The trial ended with a deadlocked jury.

At Ince's (D) second trial, Neumann was again called to testify. Once again, she claimed she did not remember what Ince (D) had told her. She acknowledged making a statement to the police, but she repeatedly denied any memory of the details of Ince's (D) remarks, even after she was provided with a copy of the statement. The military police officer who took the statement was called to testify, purportedly to impeach Neumann's memory loss. The officer testified that Neumann told him, within hours of the shooting, that Ince (D) had confessed to firing the gun. Ince (D) objected to the officer's testimony, claiming that it was hearsay. Ince's (D) defense was based on mistaken identity. He claimed that Frank Kelly fired the shots. In his closing argument, the prosecutor used Neumann's statement to argue that Ince (D) had said that Kelly didn't shoot the gun, but that Ince (D) did. Ince (D) was convicted.

■ ISSUE

Was the testimony of the military police officer as to the witness's prior inconsistent statement regarding the defendant's confession admissible?

■ DECISION AND RATIONALE

(Murnaghan, J.) No. Prior inconsistent statements may not be introduced if their only purpose is to circumvent the hearsay rule and admit an otherwise inadmissible confession. Although prior inconsistent statements may be admitted to impeach a witness's testimony, there are limits on the prosecution's power to impeach its own witness with such statements. Impeachment by a prior inconsistent statement may not be used as a subterfuge to get otherwise inadmissible evidence before the jury. When the prosecution attempts to impeach its own witness by use of a prior inconsistent statement, the likely prejudicial impact of the statement often outweighs its probative value as impeachment. The jury may ignore limiting instructions and consider the so-called impeachment testimony for substantive purposes. The court should rarely allow such impeachment, especially where, as here, the prior statement contains a defendant's alleged admission of guilt.

In this case, the admission of Neumann's statement must be considered solely with regard to its value for impeaching her testimony or her overall credibility. A review of the record shows that the probative value for impeachment was nil. Neumann's claimed loss of memory at the second trial was no surprise to the Government (P). In addition, her testimony did not affirmatively damage the Government's (P) case. Neumann merely refused to give the testimony the Government (P) hoped she would give. There was no need for the Government (P) to attack her credibility. She was unable to present any evidence either affirming or denying Ince's (D) alleged confession.

The Government (P) claimed that the testimony of the police officer was offered only for impeachment purposes. The jury never heard the Government (P) make that disclaimer, however. In addition, the curative instruction given to the jury, which stated that prior inconsistent statements were admissible only for impeachment purposes, was insufficient to cure the error. Reversed.

Analysis:

The court notes, but does not discuss, the possibility that Neumann's statement could have been admitted as a recorded recollection, pursuant to Fed. R. Evid. 803(5). It may be that the Government (P), knowing at the second trial that Neumann would not testify the way the Government (P) wanted, thought her statement would have more impact if presented through the testimony of the military police officer. The Government (D) may also have been concerned that, if pressed, Neumann would claim that the statement was a fabrication. There is also the possibility that the Government (P) just made a mistake, but it seems unlikely that such a mistake would be made in the second trial, when the issue with Neumann's testimony was already known.

■ CASE VOCABULARY

PAST RECOLLECTION RECORDED: A document concerning events that a witness once knew about but can no longer remember. The document itself is evidence and, despite being hearsay, may be admitted (or read into the record) if it was prepared or adopted by the witness when the events were fresh in the witness's memory. Also termed *recorded recollection*.

Fletcher v. Weir

(*Superintendent of Correctional Facility*) v. (*Manslaughter Defendant*)

455 U.S. 603, 102 S.Ct. 1309 (1982)

POST–ARREST SILENCE MAY BE USED TO IMPEACH

Shouldn't you *Mirandize* me now?

And give up the opportunity to argue that your silence indicates a lack of defense? I think not!

stus.com

■ **INSTANT FACTS** Weir (D) was asked on cross-examination why he did not tell the police officers who arrested him that he acted in self-defense.

■ **BLACK LETTER RULE** A defendant may be cross-examined about his or her post-arrest silence if no *Miranda* warnings were given.

■ PROCEDURAL BASIS

Appeal from an order affirming a grant of habeas corpus relief.

■ FACTS

Weir (D) was charged with intentional murder for stabbing Buchanan during a fight. At his trial, Weir (D) admitted the stabbing, but claimed it was self-defense. On cross-examination, the prosecutor (P) asked him why he did not tell the officers who arrested him that he acted in self-defense, or the location of the knife he used. Weir (D) was found guilty of first-degree manslaughter.

Weir (D) obtained a writ of habeas corpus from the federal district court. The court held that Weir could not be impeached by his post-arrest silence even if no *Miranda* warnings were given. The court rejected the argument that *Doyle v. Ohio*, 426 U.S. 610 (1976), prohibited such impeachment only if *Miranda* warnings were given.

■ ISSUE

Could Weir (D) be impeached by his silence after his arrest if no *Miranda* warnings were given?

■ DECISION AND RATIONALE

(Per curiam.) Yes. A defendant may be cross-examined about his or her post-arrest silence if no *Miranda* warnings were given. When *Miranda* warnings are given, the suspect is told that he or she may remain silent. The implication is that there will be no penalty for doing so. The government has induced silence. An arrest, by itself, does not carry with it any inducement to a person to remain silent. At common-law, witnesses could be impeached by their failure to state facts that would normally have been asserted. It does not violate due process for a state to allow impeachment by post-arrest silence if no *Miranda* warnings are given. Reversed.

Analysis:

The natural impulse most of us have when we think we are accused of wrongdoing is to say something to get out of it. The conclusion drawn from Weir's (D) failure to talk to the arresting officers is that he didn't say anything until he had the time to concoct a good story. The right to remain silent does not depend upon receiving a *Miranda* warning, but whether the exercise of that right may be used to impeach does depend on the giving of the warning.

■ CASE VOCABULARY

HABEAS CORPUS: [Latin, "that you have the body."] A writ employed to bring a person before a court, most frequently to ensure that the party's imprisonment or detention is not illegal (*habeas corpus ad subjiciendum*). In addition to being used to test the legality of an arrest or commitment, the writ may be used to obtain review of (1) the regularity of the extradition process, (2) the right to or amount of bail, or (3) the jurisdiction of a court that has imposed a criminal sentence.

MIRANDA RULE: The doctrine that a criminal suspect in police custody must be informed of certain constitutional rights before being interrogated. The suspect must be advised of the right to remain silent, the right to have an attorney present during questioning, and the right to have an attorney appointed if the suspect cannot afford one. If the suspect is not advised of these rights or does not validly waive them, any evidence obtained during the interrogation cannot be used against the suspect at trial (except for impeachment purposes). *Miranda v. Arizona,* 384 U.S. 436, 86 S. Ct. 1602 (1966).

Tome v. United States

(Convicted Sexual Abuser) v. *(Prosecuting Authority)*

513 U.S. 150, 115 S.Ct. 696 (1995)

PRIOR CONSISTENT STATEMENTS ARE ADMISSIBLE TO REBUT A CHARGE OF FABRICATION

Look, I know you want full custody. But making our puppy claim abuse is abuse of her and of the system.

■ **INSTANT FACTS** Tome (D) claimed that sexual abuse charges against him were fabricated, and the Government (P) introduced consistent statements made after the motive to fabricate those statements arose.

■ **BLACK LETTER RULE** Prior consistent statements are admissible to rebut a charge of fabrication only if the consistent statements were made before the motive to fabricate arose.

■ **PROCEDURAL BASIS**

Appeal from an order of the court of appeals affirming a conviction for sexual abuse of a child.

■ **FACTS**

Tome (D) had primary custody of his daughter. His ex-wife, the child's mother, had custody of her during the summer. In late August 1990, Tome's (D) former wife contacted authorities with the allegation that Tome (D) had sexually abused his daughter. Tome (D) was charged with sexual abuse of his daughter, who was six and one-half years old at the time of the trial. His defense was based on the theory that the allegations were fabricated so the child would not be allowed to return to Tome (D) at the end of the summer. The daughter was reluctant to answer questions about the allegations against Tome (D). After she testified, the Government (P) produced six witnesses who testified about a total of seven statements made by Tome's (D) daughter. The statements were made after the alleged motive to fabricate arose.

The trial court admitted all of the statements pursuant to Fed. R. Evid. 801(d)(1)(B), which allows the admission of prior out-of-court statements that are consistent with a witness's testimony, in order to rebut a charge of fabrication. The Tenth Circuit Court of Appeals affirmed.

■ **ISSUE**

Were the witness's prior consistent statements admissible, even though made after the alleged motive to fabricate arose?

■ **DECISION AND RATIONALE**

(Kennedy, J.) No. Prior consistent statements are admissible to rebut a charge of fabrication only if the consistent statements were made before the motive to fabricate arose. The Federal Rules of Evidence make prior consistent statements of a witness non-hearsay only if the statements are used to rebut a charge of recent fabrication or improper influence or motive. A consistent statement that was made before the motive arose squarely rebuts the charge that the witness's testimony was contrived as a consequence of that motive. The rule, however, explicitly limits the purpose for which the prior statements may be used.

The Government's (P) theory is that the prior statements tend to bolster the testimony of a witness and thus rebut an express or implied charge that the testimony was the result of undue influence. Rule

801(d)(1)(B) does not allow prior consistent statements to be used to support a witness's testimony. Congress, when it adopted the Federal Rules, could have made such a provision, but it did not. Allowing all prior consistent statements could shift the emphasis of trials from the testimony of witnesses to out-of-court statements.

The reading of the rule as allowing only statements made prior to the alleged motive is consistent with common-law practice. Commentators and case law held that prior consistent statements are not relevant unless made before the time of the fact said to indicate bias. Rule 801(d)(1)(B) adopts this common-law principle. The Advisory Committee Notes show an intent to adhere to common-law evidentiary principles unless there is an express provision to the contrary. The Notes do not indicate that the Advisory Committee had any intention to abandon the common-law principles.

The Government (P) argues that exclusion of the statements is inconsistent with the policy of the Federal Rules in favor of broad admissibility of relevant evidence. It is true that hearsay often may be relevant. The language of Rule 801(d)(1)(B), however, rejects such a broad approach to prior consistent statements. Reversed.

■ CONCURRENCE

(Scalia, J.) The case can be resolved by an examination of Rule 801(d)(1)(B). Advisory Committee comments should not be taken as authoritative statements of interpretation.

■ DISSENT

(Breyer, J.) The common-law rule was the majority rule, but it was not the uniform rule. There is no reason for an inflexible rule against the admission of statements made after the motive to fabricate arose. An absolute rule may be easier to administer, but courts certainly would be able to administer a more flexible rule.

Analysis:

Allowing prior consistent statements to bolster a witness's testimony would give greater general credibility to a witness who repeats himself or herself. It is true that "that's my story, and I'm sticking to it" can logically be used to infer truthfulness. After a reason to fabricate the story arises, however, sticking to it may be nothing more than following through on a plan to deceive.

■ CASE VOCABULARY

FABRICATE: To invent, forge, or devise falsely. To fabricate a story is to create a plausible version of events that is advantageous to the person relating those events. The term is softer than *lie*.

Commonwealth v. Weichell

(Prosecuting Authority) v. *(Convicted Murderer)*

390 Mass. 62 (1983), *cert. denied*, 465 U.S. 1032, 104 S.Ct. 1298 (1984)

COMPOSITE DRAWINGS ARE ADMISSIBLE AS IDENTIFICATION

■ **INSTANT FACTS** Weichell (D) was tried for first-degree murder, and a composite sketch prepared from a witness's description was admitted into evidence.

■ **BLACK LETTER RULE** The record of a witness's out-of-court description of a person is admissible.

■ **PROCEDURAL BASIS**

Appeal from a conviction for first-degree murder.

■ **FACTS**

Foley was in a park with some friends. They heard four "bangs," and Foley saw a man run out of the parking lot and head toward a waiting car. One of Foley's friends screamed; the man looked toward them briefly and continued running. Foley had a full-face view of the man for approximately one second as he passed under a streetlight. He gave a description of the man to the police, describing the man's height, weight, clothing, eyebrows, sideburns, and nose. Later that day, Foley assisted a police officer in making a composite drawing of the man he saw. Foley asked for changes to the drawing, made some himself, and declared that the composite "looks like him." Weichell (D) was charged with the murder, and Foley's composite sketch was introduced into evidence. The prosecutor (P) compared Weichell (D) to the picture during his closing argument. Weichell (D) claimed that the sketch was inadmissible hearsay. He was convicted of first-degree murder.

■ **ISSUE**

Was the composite sketch admissible?

■ **DECISION AND RATIONALE**

(Lynch, J.) Yes. The record of a witness's out-of-court description of a person is admissible. Prior decisions have held that a witness's out-of-court identification of a person may be admitted to support that witness's in-court identification of the person. More recent case law has held that the out-of-court identification is admissible as substantive evidence of a defendant's guilt, even if the witness has not made an in-court identification. The requirement that the out-of-court identification corroborate an in-court identification has been eliminated. Foley's statements that described the man he saw are not inadmissible hearsay, so the composite drawing prepared from those statements is not inadmissible, either because it is not a "statement" within the meaning of the rule against hearsay, or because the composite sketch retains the character of the statements that led to its creation. Under either view, the sketch is admissible. There is no logical reason to allow the introduction of a witness's out-of-court identification and to exclude statements that identify the physical characteristics of a person, or the composite of those characteristics.

■ **DISSENT**

(Liacos, J.) Prior out-of-court identifications are regarded as more reliable than an in-court identification. The courtroom is inherently suggestive, and the passage of time also helps diminish the reliability of in-

---

court identification. Composites, however, have not been shown to have a fair degree of reliability, and it cannot be said that they are more reliable than in-court identification. In the absence of proof of their reliability, composite drawings should not be admitted as evidence of guilt.

Analysis:

There is a difference between an identification of a person and a listing of a person's physical characteristics. Consider the distinction between "I saw that man" and "I saw a man who was five feet, nine inches tall, weighed 175 pounds, and had a broken nose and bushy eyebrows." Justice Liacos's concerns for reliability seem particularly well founded in this case. Foley gave his detailed description—including height, weight, clothing, facial hair, and the shape of the perpetrator's nose—after seeing the man for one second as he ran under a streetlight, shortly after midnight.

■ CASE VOCABULARY

IDENTIKIT: A collection of pictures of facial features, used by police to create a composite image of a suspect from witnesses' descriptions.

United States v. Owens

(Prosecuting Authority) v. *(Inmate)*
484 U.S. 554, 108 S.Ct. 838 (1988)

MEMORY LOSS DOES NOT MAKE A WITNESS UNAVAILABLE FOR CROSS–EXAMINATION

Mom was right--Never leave a job unfinished. I was only a couple of blows short of causing the officer to have complete memory loss and therefore to be unable to I.D. me.

stus.com

■ **INSTANT FACTS** Owens (D) was charged with attacking Foster, who could not remember who attacked him but could recall identifying Owens (D) as his attacker some weeks after the attack.

■ **BLACK LETTER RULE** A witness is subject to cross-examination concerning a statement if he or she is placed on the witness stand, under oath, and responds willingly to questions.

■ **PROCEDURAL BASIS**

Appeal from an order of the court of appeals reversing a conviction for assault with intent to commit murder.

■ **FACTS**

Foster, a correctional officer at a federal prison, was severely beaten with a metal pipe. His skull was fractured and he was in the hospital for nearly a month. His injuries left him with an impaired memory. An FBI agent interviewed him while he was in the hospital, but he was unable to remember the name of his assailant. Three weeks later, the FBI agent spoke with Foster again. Foster named Owens (D) as his attacker, and he was able to identify him from an array of photographs. At trial, Foster was able to testify about his activities immediately prior to being attacked. He also testified that he remembered identifying Owens (D) during his second conversation with the FBI agent, but admitted on cross-examination that he did not see who attacked him. Foster also admitted that, although he had several other visitors at the hospital, he could not remember any of them except the FBI agent, and he could not remember if any of his other visitors suggested that someone other than Owens (D) attacked him. Owens's (D) attorney attempted to refresh his recollection with hospital records, including one indicating that Foster blamed someone other than Owens (D) for his attack, but Foster still could not remember anything. The identification was admitted pursuant to Fed. R. Evid. 801(d)(1)(C), which provides for admission of an out-of-court identification if the declarant testifies at trial and is subject to cross-examination concerning the statement.

Owens (D) was convicted of assault with intent to commit murder. The Ninth Circuit Court of Appeals reversed his conviction, holding that Foster's identification was not admissible, because his memory loss prevented him from being subject to cross-examination concerning the statement.

■ **ISSUE**

Was Foster subject to cross-examination regarding his statement made after he was attacked, even though the attack left him with memory loss?

■ **DECISION AND RATIONALE**

(Scalia, J.) Yes. A witness is subject to cross-examination concerning a statement if he or she is placed on the witness stand, under oath, and responds willingly to questions. The trial court may place restrictions on cross-examination, or a witness might assert privilege, so that there is no meaningful cross-examination. That effect is not produced when a witness asserts memory loss. Out-of-court identifications have long been regarded as more reliable than in-court identification. Their use was to be fostered, rather than discouraged, even though they have been traditionally regarded as hearsay. Judging from the legislative history, it seems that the Federal Rule was directed in part toward the problem in this case: memory loss that makes it impossible for a witness to make an identification in-court, or to testify about the details of an earlier identification.

Rule 804(a) of the Federal Rules of Evidence provides that a witness is "unavailable" if he or she testifies to a lack of memory about his or her statement. The definition of "unavailable" in that rule is made for a different purpose. There is no requirement or expectation that the definitions in the two rules should coincide. Reversed.

■ DISSENT

(Brennan, J.) If Foster had died, his identification would not have been admissible. Because he did not die, however, the statement is admitted, but provides no more information than if Foster had died. The Foster who testified at trial was, in effect, different from the person who was attacked and the person who made the identification. He could remember nothing of the attack and could not elaborate on any of the details of his identification of Owens (D). Although the Foster who took the stand could be cross-examined, that questioning could not have elicited any meaningful information that would allow the jury to evaluate the trustworthiness or reliability of the identification. The Confrontation Clause protects more than a defendant's right to question live witnesses. The right guaranteed is the right to an effective cross-examination.

Analysis:

Foster was certainly physically able to testify and, under Justice Scalia's analysis, he was available. He was put under oath and answered questions willingly. Query whether honestly saying "I don't know" is testimony in any real sense. Justice Brennan's inquiry goes beyond the physical presence of the witness and asks if there is any meaningful testimony here. As a practical matter, what was elicited from Foster about his identification was no improvement on what would have been before the court if he had not been present in the courtroom.

■ CASE VOCABULARY

CONFRONTATION CLAUSE: The Sixth Amendment provision guaranteeing a criminal defendant's right to directly confront an accusing witness and to cross-examine that witness.

United States v. DiNapoli

(Prosecuting Authority) v. *(Contractor)*

8 F.3d 909 (2d Cir. 1993)

PROSECUTORS MAY HAVE DIFFERENT MOTIVES BEFORE GRAND JURIES AND AT TRIAL

■ **INSTANT FACTS** At trial, DiNapoli (D) and other defendants sought to introduce grand jury testimony from DeMatteis and Bruno.

■ **BLACK LETTER RULE** The test for whether a party has the same motive in developing evidence is not only whether the questioner was on the same side of the same issue in both proceedings, but also whether the questioner had a substantially similar interest in asserting that side of the issue.

■ **PROCEDURAL BASIS**

Consideration en banc on remand from the U.S. Supreme Court.

■ **FACTS**

DeMatteis and Bruno were called as witnesses in a grand jury investigation of bid-rigging in the concrete construction industry in Manhattan. They both denied any knowledge of a bid-rigging scheme. DeMatteis was asked if he had been instructed not to bid on a project and whether he was aware of an arrangement for the successful bidder to pay money to organized crime figures. DeMatteis denied having been told not to bid and denied knowledge of the payment scheme. The Government (P) cross-examined him about his denials, but refrained from disclosing wiretap information that would have refuted his testimony. Instead, the Government (P) asked about a conversation that already had been made public at another trial.

When Bruno testified before the grand jury, he also denied knowledge of any bid-rigging scheme and arrangement to pay organized crime figures. He also was confronted with the information from the prior trial. Bruno was briefly excused from the grand jury room, and when he returned the prosecutor told him that the grand jury had a strong concern that his testimony had not been truthful. A few days later, Bruno's lawyer wrote to the Government (P) and stated that many of Bruno's answers had been inaccurate. The lawyer offered to answer questions in an affidavit, but the Government (P) declined the offer.

Eleven defendants were tried on racketeering charges. The defendants attempted to call DeMatteis and Bruno to testify, but they invoked their privilege against self-incrimination. The defendants then offered the grand jury testimony of DeMatteis and Bruno as prior testimony under Fed. R. Evid. 804(b)(1), which provides that former testimony of an unavailable witness given in a different proceeding is not excluded as hearsay if "the party against whom the testimony is now offered ... had an opportunity and similar motive to develop the testimony." The trial judge held that the motive of a prosecutor in the investigatory stages of a case is far different from the motive of the prosecutor in conducting the trial, and so denied admission of the testimony.

■ **ISSUE**

Was there a similar motive to develop the testimony during the investigation and at trial?

■ **DECISION AND RATIONALE**

(Newman, C.J.) No. The test for whether a party has the same motive in developing evidence is not only whether the questioner was on the same side of the same issue in both proceedings, but also whether the questioner had a substantially similar interest in asserting that side of the issue. The degree of interest in an issue often depends upon the nature of the proceedings, as well as on the importance of the issue. If both proceedings are trials and the same matter is in dispute at both trials, the motive of a party in developing testimony will normally be the same in both trials.

The situation is not the same when there are significant differences, such as the purposes or the applicable burden of proof, between two types of proceedings. For example, if a prosecutor is using a grand jury to investigate possible crimes and to investigate possible criminals, it may be unrealistic to characterize the prosecutor as an "opponent" of a witness's testimony. Even in cases such as this one, in which the grand jury proceeding has gone beyond a general investigation, the motive to develop testimony contrary to the prosecutor's position is not necessarily the same as the motive the prosecutor would have in presenting that testimony at trial. The prosecutor's task before a grand jury is merely to establish probable cause. If exonerating testimony is given, it may come at a time when probable cause has already been established and there is no chance that the grand jury will not indict. In such a case, the prosecutor will have little motive to develop the testimony. In addition, there may be other reasons that a prosecutor has little interest in developing exonerating evidence. There may be an important interest in not making a premature disclosure of information from an ongoing criminal investigation.

This is not to say that prosecutors will never have the same motive before a grand jury as they do at trial. The inquiry regarding similar motive is fact specific. The availability of alternate ways to challenge testimony that were not used is a relevant factor, but it is not conclusive. The court must consider the nature of the two proceedings, including what is at stake and the burden of proof, as well as the cross-examination at the prior proceeding. In this case, it has been shown conclusively that the Government (P) had no interest in proving that there was no bid-rigging scheme. DiNapoli (D) and the other defendants (D) already were indicted, so the existence of the scheme had been established sufficiently for the purposes of the grand jury. Secondly, the grand jury did not believe the denial of the scheme. The Government (P) had no interest in showing the falsity of testimony the grand jury already disbelieved. In addition, the dissimilarity of the two proceedings is shown by the prosecutor's limitation of his questioning to facts already disclosed. The trial court's ruling that the Government (P) did not have the same motive was correct. Convictions affirmed.

Analysis:

The court is careful to point out that the prosecutor *may* have the same motive at a grand jury hearing and at trial. The court's holding merely was that, in this case, where the investigation had proceeded to a fairly advanced state, the prosecutor did not have the same interest in developing or discrediting testimony at the grand jury level as at trial. Even if the testimony had been introduced, it is hard to see what good it would have done. The denials of the witnesses were unpersuasive to the grand jury, and would be introduced because the witnesses invoked their privileges against self-incrimination. Which would look worse to a jury?

■ **CASE VOCABULARY**

GRAND JURY: A body of (often 23) people who are chosen to sit permanently for at least a month—and sometimes a year—and who, in ex parte proceedings, decide whether to issue indictments. If the grand jury decides that evidence is strong enough to hold a suspect for trial, it returns a bill of indictment (a *true bill*) charging the suspect with a specific crime.

IMMUNITY: Freedom from prosecution granted by the government in exchange for the person's testimony.

RICO: Racketeer Influenced and Corrupt Organizations Act. A law designed to attack organized criminal activity and preserve marketplace integrity by investigating, controlling, and prosecuting persons who participate or conspire to participate in racketeering. Enacted in 1970, the federal RICO statute applies only to activity involving interstate or foreign commerce.

Lloyd v. American Export Lines, Inc.

(Seaman) v. *(Ship Owner)*

580 F.2d 1179 (3d Cir. 1978)

A "PREDECESSOR IN INTEREST" IS DETERMINED ACCORDING TO A PARTY'S MOTIVE IN DEVELOPING TESTIMONY

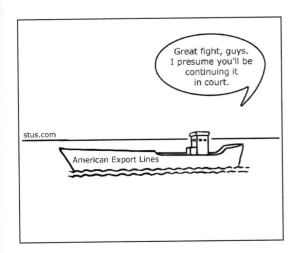

■ **INSTANT FACTS** Lloyd (P) did not appear in his action, and his testimony at a prior administrative hearing arising out of the same incident was admitted at trial.

■ **BLACK LETTER RULE** Testimony at a prior trial or hearing will be admissible if a party with a like motive to cross-examine the witness as a party in the present proceeding would have been given an adequate opportunity to cross-examine the witness.

■ **PROCEDURAL BASIS**

Appeal from a judgment for Alvarez (P).

■ **FACTS**

Lloyd (P) and Alvarez (P) were involved in an altercation aboard a ship owned by American Export (D). Lloyd (P) brought an action against Export (D) for his injuries, alleging unseaworthiness and negligence. Export (D) joined Alvarez (P) as a third-party defendant, and Alvarez (P) counterclaimed against Export (D) for the injuries he sustained in the altercation. Lloyd (P) failed to appear for depositions and did not appear when his case was called for trial. Lloyd's (P) complaint was dismissed and the case went to trial on Alvarez's (P) counterclaim. Alvarez's (P) theory was that Export (D) should have protected him from Lloyd (P) because of Lloyd's (P) known dangerous propensities. Lloyd (P) did not testify at the trial, and his version of what happened was not presented. Export (D) claimed that a transcript of Lloyd's (P) testimony at a Coast Guard hearing, held to determine if his merchant mariner's license should be revoked because of his involvement in the altercation with Alvarez (P), should have been admitted into evidence pursuant to Fed. R. Evid. 804(b)(1). Export (D) argued that Lloyd (P) was unavailable to testify at trial, and that the Coast Guard was Alvarez's (P) predecessor in interest at the license revocation hearing. Both Lloyd (P) and Alvarez (P) testified under oath at that hearing, and both of them were represented by counsel. Lloyd's (P) testimony was that he did not strike Alvarez (P). The transcript was not admitted into evidence, and the jury returned a verdict in favor of Alvarez (P).

■ **ISSUE**

Should the transcript of a prior administrative hearing involving the plaintiff have been admitted into evidence at the trial at which the plaintiff did not appear?

■ **DECISION AND RATIONALE**

(Aldisert, J.) Yes. Testimony at a prior trial or hearing will be admissible if a party with a like motive to cross-examine the witness as a party in the present proceeding would have been given an adequate opportunity to cross-examine the witness. Congress did not define the term "predecessor in interest." The text of Rule 804(b)(1), as drafted by the Supreme Court, provided that a witness's prior testimony would be admissible if the party against whom it was offered had an opportunity to examine the witness. The House Judiciary Committee, when it considered the rule, added the "predecessor in

---

interest" requirement, finding it unfair to impose upon a party against whom evidence is offered the responsibility for another party's manner of handling a witness. The Senate Judiciary Committee concluded that the difference between the two versions was "not great," and so adopted the House version.

In this case, there was sufficient continuity of interest between the Coast Guard at the license revocation hearing and Alvarez (P) at the civil trial to satisfy the requirements of Rule 804(b)(1). The nucleus of operative facts was the same, and the Coast Guard investigating officer sought to establish the same facts that Alvarez (P) sought to establish at the civil trial. The practical and expedient view is that the Coast Guard was the predecessor in interest, and Lloyd's (P) testimony should have been admitted.

Lloyd's (P) unavailability is established by his failure to appear for seven depositions, as well as his failure to appear at trial. Lloyd's (P) attorney represented to the court that numerous attempts had been made to secure his appearance, but all were unsuccessful. Reversed and remanded for a new trial.

■ CONCURRENCE

(Stern, J.) It seems clear the Congress intended the term "predecessor in interest" to be used in a narrow sense, in terms of a privity relationship. Similar motive is a separate prerequisite to admissibility under Rule 804(b)(1). The majority's analysis eliminates entirely the predecessor in interest requirement. In addition, although both proceedings sought to establish Lloyd's (P) fault for the altercation, the goal of the Coast Guard investigator was to do justice, not merely vindicate the rights of the victim. The Coast Guard did not represent Alvarez (P).

Analysis:

The majority seems to consider the "predecessor in interest" language to be superfluous, and focuses exclusively on the motive of the respective parties. As Judge Stern notes in his concurrence, however, the mere fact that two parties attempt to prove the same set of facts does not necessarily mean that they have the same interest. The Coast Guard is neutral in the dispute between Lloyd (P) and Alvarez (P), and its interests would, at least in theory, be vindicated by a finding that Lloyd (P) could keep his license as well as by a finding that his license should be revoked.

■ CASE VOCABULARY

JONES ACT: *Maritime law.* A federal statute that allows a seaman injured during the course of employment to recover damages for the injuries in a negligence action against the employer. If a seaman dies from such injuries, the seaman's personal representative may maintain an action against the employer. 46 U.S.C.A. app. § 688.

UNSEAWORTHY: (Of a vessel.) Unable to withstand the perils of an ordinary voyage.

Williamson v. United States

(Convicted Drug Offender) v. *(Prosecuting Authority)*

512 U.S. 594, 114 S.Ct. 2431 (1994)

ONLY SELF–INCULPATORY PARTS OF OUT–OF–COURT STATEMENTS ARE ADMISSIBLE

■ **INSTANT FACTS** Harris made a statement that incriminated both Harris himself and Williamson (D), but he refused to testify at trial, and his statement was admitted into evidence.

■ **BLACK LETTER RULE** The parts of an out-of-court statement that do not inculpate the declarant are not admissible as statements against interest.

■ **PROCEDURAL BASIS**

Appeal from a judgment of the Eleventh Circuit Court of Appeals affirming convictions.

■ **FACTS**

Harris was arrested when a consensual search of the car he was driving turned up nineteen kilograms of cocaine. He told officers that he obtained the cocaine from a Cuban person in Fort Lauderdale, and that he was told to leave the drugs in a certain dumpster. A Drug Enforcement Administration (DEA) agent took steps to arrange a controlled delivery. Harris then told the agent that he had lied about the Cuban person, and he said that he was transporting the cocaine to Atlanta for Williamson (D). Harris said that Williamson (D) was traveling in front of him in another car and saw Harris's arrest. Harris said that it would be impossible to arrange a controlled delivery of the drugs. Harris also said that he lied because he was afraid of Williamson (D). He refused to sign a written statement or to allow his statement to be recorded. Harris was not promised any benefit for cooperating.

Williamson (D) was tried for possession of cocaine with intent to distribute, conspiring to possess cocaine with intent to distribute, and traveling interstate to promote the distribution of cocaine. Harris refused to testify, even after the court granted him use immunity for his testimony. Harris continued to refuse and was held in contempt. The court then ruled that Harris was unavailable and allowed the DEA agent to repeat Harris's statement as a statement against interest under Fed. R. Evid. 804(b)(3).

■ **ISSUE**

Were Harris's statements implicating Williamson (D) in the crimes admissible as statements against interest when Harris refused to testify?

■ **DECISION AND RATIONALE**

(O'Connor, J.) No. The parts of an out-of-court statement that do not inculpate the declarant are not admissible as statements against interest. Self-inculpatory statements are regarded as particularly trustworthy. The rule that allows the admission of such statements, Fed. R. Evid. 804(b)(3), is founded on the commonsense notion that people who say something that incriminates them would not do so unless they believed their statements to be true. The fact that a person is making a broad confession does not, however, make the parts of his or her statement that are not incriminating more credible. Mixing falsehoods with the truth is an especially effective way to lie. In this case, the parts of Harris's first statement that did not inculpate him were false. When a part of a statement is self-exculpatory, the rationale behind allowing the admission of statements against interest becomes less applicable. Self-exculpatory statements are more likely to be false, and their mere proximity to self-inculpatory statements does not make them more reliable.

There is no support for Justice Kennedy's view that the collateral parts of a statement should be admitted if, overall, the statement was self-inculpatory. The language of the rule leads to the conclusion that only the self-inculpatory part of the statement should be admitted. Whether a statement is self-inculpatory depends upon the context of the statement. The question is whether a statement was sufficiently against a declarant's penal interest that a reasonable person would not have made the statement unless he or she believed it to be true. Vacated and remanded.

■ CONCURRENCE

(O'Connor, J., joined by Scalia, J.) The parts of Harris's confession that implicated him in the crime were admissible. The other parts of the confession did little to implicate him in the crime, and may have been made in an effort to decrease his potential criminal liability.

Analysis:

Harris's so-called confession was largely an effort to shift blame to another person. In fact, the prosecutor offered to join in a motion for a mistrial if it were ruled that Harris's statements about Williamson (D) were admitted in error. The prosecutor agreed there was no way that the jury could distinguish between the parts of the statement that related to Harris and those that incriminated Williamson (D).

■ CASE VOCABULARY

EXCULPATORY EVIDENCE: Evidence tending to establish a criminal defendant's innocence.

INCULPATORY EVIDENCE: Evidence showing or tending to show one's involvement in a crime or wrong.

USE IMMUNITY: Immunity from the use of the compelled testimony (or any information derived from that testimony) in a future prosecution against the witness. After granting use immunity, the government can still prosecute if it shows that its evidence comes from a legitimate independent source.

Shepard v. United States

(Doctor) v. *(Prosecuting Authority)*
290 U.S. 96, 54 S.Ct. 22 (1933)

OUT–OF–COURT STATEMENTS MADE IN ANTICIPATION OF IMMINENT DEATH ARE ADMISSIBLE

Seriously, the dog ate your food.

Would that still be your story if I told you that you are gonna die in the next two minutes?

stus.com

■ **INSTANT FACTS** Shepard's (D) wife asked her nurse about having a bottle of whisky tested for poison, and then said that Shepard (D) poisoned her.

■ **BLACK LETTER RULE** In order to be admissible as a dying declaration, a statement must have been made while the declarant had no hope of recovery and knew that death was imminent.

■ **PROCEDURAL BASIS**

Appeal from an order of the Tenth Circuit Court of Appeals affirming a conviction for murder.

■ **FACTS**

Shepard (D), a doctor, was accused of murdering his wife by poison. The Government (P) offered rebuttal evidence of a conversation Shepard's (D) wife had with her nurse approximately three and one-half weeks before her death. In that conversation, Mrs. Shepard asked her nurse to bring her a bottle of whisky that was in the closet in Shepard's (D) bedroom. When the nurse brought the bottle, Mrs. Shepard identified it as the liquor she had taken just before she collapsed. She asked whether there was enough left in the bottle to be tested for poison, saying that the smell and taste were strange. Mrs. Shepard then added, "Dr. Shepard (D) has poisoned me." When the conversation was first offered into evidence, the Government (P) struck it, but then renewed its offer of the evidence with additional evidence. The additional part of the conversation was the nurse's statement that Mrs. Shepard "said she was not going to get well; she was going to die." Shepard (D) was convicted of murder.

■ **ISSUE**

Was the nurse's conversation with the ailing Mrs. Shepard properly admitted?

■ **DECISION AND RATIONALE**

(Cardozo, J.) No. In order to be admissible as a dying declaration, a statement must have been made while the declarant had no hope of recovery and knew that death was imminent. There has been no proof that Mrs. Shepard spoke without hope of recovery. The evidence showed that she had collapsed two days before the conversation with her nurse, but that she seemed better two days later. None of her physicians thought that she would not recover, and there had been no diagnosis of poisoning when she made her statement. In addition, two weeks later, Mrs. Shepard asked her doctor about the prospects for her recovery. Thus, when she had her conversation with her nurse, she was not speaking with a consciousness that death was imminent. In addition, before a statement will be admitted as a dying declaration, there must be evidence that the declarant knew the facts or had the opportunity to know the facts as declared. A declaration must be excluded if the trial judge concludes that the speaker was merely giving voice to suspicion or conjecture, not to known facts. Reversed on other grounds.

Analysis:

Justice Cardozo seems to make the admission of a dying declaration into a question of conditional relevance. The declaration must be supported by proof that the declarant knew that he or she was dying and that the declarant had a factual basis for the statement. Some commentators think that these issues should go to the weight the jury chooses to give the declaration. The words of the dying are, however, commonly regarded as inherently truthful, in that a person is unlikely to lie when faced with death. Nonetheless, it seems wise to require some preliminary showing that a statement meets the requirements of the rule and that it is based on something more than speculation.

■ CASE VOCABULARY

DYING DECLARATION: A statement by a person who believes that death is imminent, relating to the cause or circumstances of the person's impending death. The statement is admissible in evidence in evidence as an exception to the hearsay rule.

United States v. Gray

(Prosecuting Authority) v. *(Convicted Defendant)*

405 F.3d 227 (4th Cir.), cert. denied, 546 U.S. 912, 126 S.Ct. 275 (2005)

DEFENDANTS MAY NOT KILL WITNESSES TO KEEP THEM FROM TESTIFYING

■ **INSTANT FACTS** In the defendant's trial for mail and wire fraud, the Government (P) sought to introduce out-of-court statements made by her late husband, who had been murdered by the defendant.

■ **BLACK LETTER RULE** A defendant who wrongfully and intentionally renders a declarant unavailable as a witness in any proceeding forfeits the right to exclude, on hearsay grounds, the declarant's statements at that proceeding and any subsequent proceeding.

■ PROCEDURAL BASIS

On appeal to review the defendant's conviction.

■ FACTS

In the summer of 2000, Wilson became friends with Josephine Gray (D). During a visit to Gray's (D) house, Gray (D) confessed to Wilson that she had killed three men. Gray (D) said that she killed he first husband because he was abusive, and made the death appear as a robbery. She also admitted to killing her second husband, Robert Gray, with the help of her cousin and boyfriend, Goode. When Goode demanded money to remain silent about the killing, Gray (D) killed him, too. Gray (D) received life insurance benefits pertaining to each man's death.

Shortly before his death, Robert Gray had filed assault charges against Gray (D) and Goode, alleging that Gray (D) had swung a club at him and lunged at him with a knife, and that Goode had threatened him with a handgun. Robert Gray appeared at the assault trial, only to learn that the case had been continued until a later date. On his way home, Gray (D) and Goode drove up along side his car, whereupon Goode pointed a gun at him. Robert Gray reported the incident to police, and arrest warrants were issued. One week later, Robert Gray was found dead of gun shot wounds.

Based on her admissions to Wilson, Gray (D) was charged with five counts of mail fraud and three counts of wire fraud relating to her receipt of insurance proceeds following the death of the three men. At trial, the Government (P) introduced four out-of-court statements made by Robert Gray in the months preceding his death. Gray (D) was convicted of all counts against her and sought a new trial because of the admission of these statements.

■ ISSUE

Did the court err in admitting the out-of-court testimony of Robert Gray when his unavailability was caused by the actions of the accused?

■ DECISION AND RATIONALE

(Shedd, J.) No. A defendant who wrongfully and intentionally renders a declarant unavailable as a witness in any proceeding forfeits the right to exclude, on hearsay grounds, the declarant's statements at that proceeding and any subsequent proceeding. The common law doctrine of forfeiture by wrongdoing, codified in Fed. R. Evid. 804(b)(6), allows the admission of hearsay evidence when the defendant's own actions caused the declarant's unavailability at trial. To invoke the doctrine, the court must find that (1) the defendant engaged in or acquiesced to wrongdoing; (2) the defendant's actions were intended to render the declarant unavailable as a witness; and (3) that the defendant's actions did, in fact, render the witness unavailable. The court can make this finding from the evidence presented at trial, without a separate hearing.

Gray (D) contends that Rule 804(b)(6) does not apply in this case because there is no evidence to show that she intended to render the witness unavailable for *this* trial. Rule 804(b)(6), by its plain language, requires only that the defendant intend to render the declarant available "as a witness," without further defining in which proceeding the testimony is at issue. Accordingly, Rule 804(b)(6) applies whenever the defendant's wrongdoing was intended to, and did, render the declarant unavailable as a witness against the defendant, without regard to the nature of the charges at trial in which the defendant's statements are offered. Rule 804(b)(6), like the common law doctrine, is to be broadly applied to further its goal of preventing defendants from benefiting from their wrongdoing. Here, the court correctly applied the rule, finding from the evidence that Gray (D) did engage in wrongdoing that intentionally made Robert Gray unavailable to testify as a witness.

Analysis:

Under the majority view, Rule 804(b)(6) requires that the defendant commit wrongdoing with the specific *intent* to make the witness unavailable to testify. It is not enough, generally, that the defendant intended to kill or otherwise harm the witness, which *consequently* made the witness unavailable. A minority view, however, does not allow a defendant to benefit from his misconduct merely because he lacked the specific intent to make his victim unavailable at trial. *See Colorado v. Vasquez*, 155 P.3d 565 (Colo. Ct. App. 2006).

Mutual Life Insurance Co. v. Hillmon

(Insurance Company) v. *(Alleged Widow)*

145 U.S. 285, 12 S.Ct. 909 (1892)

STATEMENTS OF PRESENT INTENT ARE ADMISSIBLE

Hey man, can I borrow your dead body so my wife can claim my life insurance?

stus.com

■ **INSTANT FACTS** Hillmon (P) brought suit to recover on three life insurance policies, and Mutual Life Insurance (D) attempted to introduce letters written by the man they claimed was the actual decedent.

■ **BLACK LETTER RULE** Out-of-court statements that express a declarant's present intention are admissible to prove what that intention was.

■ **PROCEDURAL BASIS**

Appeal from a judgment for Hillmon (P).

■ **FACTS**

Hillmon (P) brought suit on three life insurance policies that covered her husband. She claimed that her husband and a man named Brown left Wichita and traveled through southern Kansas looking for a site for a cattle ranch. Hillmon (P) claimed that, while the men were camped at a place called Crooked Creek, her husband was killed by an accidental gunshot.

Mutual Life (D) claimed that Hillmon's (P) husband was not dead, but that he was alive and in hiding. Mutual (D) introduced evidence to show that the body found at Crooked Creek was not that of Hillmon's (P) husband, but was the body of Frederick Walters. Mutual (D) introduced evidence that showed that Walters left his home in Iowa and went to Kansas. His family received frequent letters from him, the last of which came from Wichita. Walters had not been heard from after his last letter. Mutual (D) also offered the testimony of Walters's sister. She stated that she received a letter from her brother from Wichita, but that she could not find the letter. Mutual (D) asked her what the letter said, but Hillmon's (P) objection to that question was sustained. If the question had been allowed, Walters's sister would have testified that the letter said that Walters expected to leave Wichita in the next few days with "a certain Mr. Hillmon . . . for Colorado or parts unknown to [Walters]." Mutual (D) also offered the testimony of a woman who was engaged to marry Walters. The last letter she received from Walters was placed into evidence, but she was not allowed to testify regarding the contents of the letter. The letter stated that Walters was going to leave Wichita in the next week to go with a man named Hillmon through Kansas, Indian Territory, Colorado, and Mexico.

■ **ISSUE**

Were the contents of the letters setting forth Walters's travel plans admissible?

■ **DECISION AND RATIONALE**

(Gray, J.) Yes. Out-of-court statements that express a declarant's present intention are admissible to prove what that intention was. When the existence of a person's intention is a material fact to be proved, evidence that the person expresses that intention is direct evidence of that fact. The letters would not be proof that Walters actually left Wichita, but they were evidence that he intended to do so and that he intended to travel with Hillmon's (P) husband. Walters's letters made it more probable that he did travel with Hillmon's (P) husband. In light of the conflicting testimony regarding the identity of the body found at Crooked Creek, the contents of the letters might influence the jury's decision on that question. Reversed.

Analysis:

The excerpt is from the Supreme Court's opinion on an appeal from the third trial of the case. The juries in the first two cases heard the contents of the letters and were unable to reach a verdict. The fact to be proved by the letters is the first fact in a chain of inferences that the jury was asked to make. If Walters intended to leave Wichita with a Mr. Hillmon, he did leave with Mr. Hillmon. If he was with Hillmon, the body that was found may have been that of Walters.

■ CASE VOCABULARY

INFERENCE: A conclusion reached by considering other facts and deducing a logical consequence from them.

Shepard v. United States

(Doctor) v. (Prosecuting Authority)

290 U.S. 96, 54 S.Ct. 22 (1933)

DECLARATIONS OF STATE OF MIND CANNOT PROVE WHAT SOMEONE ELSE DID

Before I die, I'd like to make some totally unsubstantiated accusations against my husband.

■ **INSTANT FACTS** Shepard's (D) wife asked her nurse about having a bottle of whisky tested for poison, and then said that Shepard (D) poisoned her.

■ **BLACK LETTER RULE** A declaration of a person's state of mind is inadmissible to prove the actions of someone other than the declarant.

■ **PROCEDURAL BASIS**

Appeal from an order of the Tenth Circuit Court of Appeals affirming a conviction for murder.

■ **FACTS**

Shepard (D), a doctor, was accused of murdering his wife by poison. The Government (P) offered rebuttal evidence of a conversation Shepard's (D) wife had with her nurse approximately three and one-half weeks before her death. In that conversation, Mrs. Shepard asked her nurse to bring her a bottle of whisky that was in the closet in Shepard's (D) bedroom. When the nurse brought the bottle, Mrs. Shepard identified it as the liquor she had taken just before she collapsed. She asked whether there was enough left in the bottle to be tested for poison, saying that the smell and taste were strange. Mrs. Shepard then added, "Dr. Shepard (D) has poisoned me." When the conversation was first offered into evidence, the Government (P) struck it, but then renewed its offer of the evidence with additional evidence. The additional part of the conversation was the nurse's statement that Mrs. Shepard "said she was not going to get well; she was going to die." The Government (P) claimed that the statements were introduced to rebut a claim that Mrs. Shepard committed suicide. Shepard (D) was convicted of murder.

■ **ISSUE**

Was the nurse's conversation with the ailing Mrs. Shepard regarding her suspicions of poisoning admissible?

■ **DECISION AND RATIONALE**

(Cardozo, J.) No. A declaration of a person's state of mind is inadmissible to prove the actions of someone other than the declarant. Shepard's (D) introduction of evidence to show that his wife committed suicide opened the door to evidence consistent with a will to live. The statements that were introduced did not relate to Mrs. Shepard's state of mind at the time she made the statements, but concerned Shepard's (D) actions. The testimony in question faced backward, not forward. A jury would be incapable of separating the accusation of Shepard (D) from the inference that Mrs. Shepard did not want to die.

The testimony was not originally offered to show Mrs. Shepard's state of mind. The original intention was that the evidence should be received as a dying declaration. The evidence was offered and received for an improper, prejudicial purpose. Admission of the statements took Shepard (D) by surprise and made his trial unfair. Reversed.

Analysis:

The Government (P) clearly is clutching at straws to get Mrs. Shepard's accusation admitted. The statement does not meet the criteria for an admissible dying declaration, which would be direct evidence of guilt. Instead, the argument is that the substantive claim in Mrs. Shepard's comment—that her husband poisoned her—is supposedly proof that she was not in a suicidal frame of mind. The fault in such a theory is obvious. The argument that an accusation of another shows a particular state of mind in the declarant is too strained to be credible.

United States v. Iron Shell

(*Prosecuting Authority*) v. (*Accused Assailant*)

633 F.2d 77 (8th Cir. 1980)

STATEMENTS MADE TO A DOCTOR FOR TREATMENT OR DIAGNOSIS ARE ADMISSIBLE

To add insult to injury, anything you tell me about how this happened might be repeated in open court.

■ **INSTANT FACTS** The defendant was prosecuted for assault with intent to commit rape, and the victim's doctor was allowed to testify about what the victim told him had happened.

■ **BLACK LETTER RULE** Admission of an out-of-court statement under the exception for statements made for medical diagnosis or treatment depends on whether the declarant's motive in making the statement was consistent with the purpose of the exception and on whether it was reasonable for the physician to rely on the statement for diagnosis or treatment.

■ **PROCEDURAL BASIS**

Appeal from a conviction for assault with intent to commit rape.

■ **FACTS**

The defendant was charged with assault with intent to commit rape. The victim of the offense was a nine-year old girl named Lucy. The defendant admitted assaulting Lucy, but denied that he intended to rape her. The doctor who examined Lucy shortly after the assault testified, over the defendant's objection, about what Lucy told him when he examined her. The doctor testified that Lucy told him that a man dragged her into some bushes, removed her clothes, and tried to rape her. The doctor also said that Lucy told him she could not scream because the man put his hand over her mouth and neck. He stated that there were injuries to her neck that were consistent with her story, but he could not be absolutely sure what caused the injuries. At trial, Lucy testified that a man pushed her down and threatened to choke her. She gave answers to leading questions from the prosecutor that were consistent with the doctor's account of what she said.

■ **ISSUE**

Was the doctor's testimony about what Lucy told him after her assault admissible?

■ **DECISION AND RATIONALE**

(Stephenson, J.) Yes. Admission of an out-of-court statement under the exception for statements made for medical diagnosis or treatment depends on whether the declarant's motive in making the statement was consistent with the purpose of the exception and on whether it was reasonable for the physician to rely on the statement for diagnosis or treatment. The Federal Rules of Evidence make statements to a physician made for the purpose of diagnosis or treatment admissible as an exception to the rule against hearsay. The rule relies on a patient's strong motive to tell the truth because the patient's diagnosis or treatment depends upon what the patient says. This motive is considered a sufficient indicator of reliability to justify making an exception to the rule against hearsay. In addition, if a statement is considered sufficiently reliable to be the basis of medical diagnosis or treatment, it should be sufficiently reliable to avoid hearsay issues.

In this case, there is no indication that Lucy had any motive other than seeking treatment. Her statements all related to what happened, rather than who did it. Her age also supports the conclusion that she spoke only to obtain treatment. The doctor testified that his questions were meant to provide him with guidelines for his examination. Although his examination would have been similar if Lucy had not answered his questions, the questions enabled him to direct his examination to particular areas. Affirmed.

Analysis:

The court notes that the rule regarding admission of statements made to a physician has been "significantly liberalized." The liberalization was the abolition of the distinction formerly drawn between statements made for diagnosis, which were generally inadmissible, and statements made for treatment, which were admissible. There is some policy justification for the distinction, especially when "diagnosis" is read to include examinations by an expert witness in preparation for litigation. A patient may be tempted to be less than completely honest if aware that the diagnosis will be the basis for the physician's testimony, either for or against the patient.

Johnson v. State

(Accused Murderer) v. *(Prosecuting Authority)*

967 S.W.2d 410 (Tex. Crim. App. 1998)

A WITNESS MUST VOUCH FOR THE ACCURACY OF A RECORDED RECOLLECTION

Evidently, I saw a murder and gave a statement about it. When I couldn't remember anything at trial, the judge excluded my statement. I thought the prosecutor was gonna have a heart attack!

■ **INSTANT FACTS** Taylor gave a statement that implicated Johnson (D) in a murder, but he was unable to recall anything about the statement at trial.

■ **BLACK LETTER RULE** In order for a recording of a past recollection to be admissible, the witness whose recollection is refreshed must testify that the recording is accurate.

■ **PROCEDURAL BASIS**

Appeal from a conviction for capital murder.

■ **FACTS**

Taylor was a witness to the murder of Frank Johnson. Shortly after the killing, he gave a statement to the police that implicated Arnold Johnson (D) in the crime. Johnson (D) was tried for the murder, and Taylor was called as a witness. Taylor testified that he could not recall the crime, and he stated that he did not remember giving a statement to the police. The prosecutor showed Taylor a copy of his written statement, but Taylor testified that he did not remember it, even after reading it. Taylor said that he "guess[ed]" that the incident was fresher in his mind when he gave the statement, and he acknowledged his signature on the statement. The written statement was admitted into evidence. Arnold Johnson (D) was convicted of murder.

■ **ISSUE**

Was the written record of Taylor's statement admissible, even though he could not remember making it?

■ **DECISION AND RATIONALE**

(Mansfield, J.) No. In order for a recording of a past recollection to be admissible, the witness whose recollection is refreshed must testify that the recording is accurate. Generally, the requirements for the admission of a written record of a past recollection are that the record was made by a person with firsthand knowledge of an event at or near the time of the event, and that the witness cannot recall the event when he or she testifies but vouches for the accuracy of the statement. The requirement that the witness vouch for the accuracy is met by an acknowledgement at the time of trial that the statement is accurate. The witness may testify that he or she remembers recording the facts accurately. It has been held sufficient for a witness to testify that he or she recognizes his or her signature on the statement and believes the statement is correct because he or she would not have signed if the witness did not believe the statement was true at the time it was made. The statement may not, however, verify itself. An acknowledgment on the statement is not good enough. The witness must acknowledge the accuracy of the statement while testifying at trial. In this case, there was no proper predicate for admissibility. Reversed.

Analysis:

Under the court's easy standard for admissibility, the prosecutor comes very close to getting the statement admitted. Taylor acknowledged his signature on the statement and conceded that he thought his recollection of the events probably was better when he gave the statement. He does not take the next logical step, however, of saying that he believes his statement was accurate, or even that he would not have signed it if he did not think it was accurate. The value of the boilerplate acknowledgment of accuracy attorneys and investigators routinely include in statements has no evidentiary effect, except perhaps to compel a witness to admit that, at one time, the statement was regarded as accurate.

■ CASE VOCABULARY

CAPITAL OFFENSE: A crime for which the death penalty may be imposed.

Palmer v. Hoffman

(Trustee of Railroad) v. *(Insured in Collision)*

318 U.S. 109, 63 S.Ct. 477 (1943)

ACCIDENT REPORTS ARE NOT BUSINESS RECORDS

■ **INSTANT FACTS** Hoffman (P) and his wife were involved in a traffic accident with a train, and the railroad (D) sought to introduce a report of the accident as a business record.

■ **BLACK LETTER RULE** A report of an accident is not made in the regular course of business, and so is not admissible under the business records exception to the hearsay rule.

■ **PROCEDURAL BASIS**

Appeal from an order of the Second Circuit Court of Appeals affirming a verdict for Hoffman.

■ **FACTS**

Hoffman (P) and his wife were involved in a collision with a train. Hoffman (P) suffered serious injuries, and his wife died from her injuries. After the accident, the engineer of the train was interviewed by a representative of the railroad (D) and the Massachusetts public Utilities Commission. Hoffman (P) brought suit against the railroad (D), claiming that the railroad (D) was negligent in failing to ring a bell or blow a whistle at the crossing and for failure to have a light burning. The engineer of the train died before the case came to trial. The railroad offered his statement, but the court refused to admit it into evidence. The court of appeals affirmed the decision to exclude the statement.

■ **ISSUE**

Was the deceased engineer's statement regarding the railroad accident admissible as a business record?

■ **DECISION AND RATIONALE**

(Douglas, J.) No. A report of an accident is not made in the regular course of business, and so is not admissible under the business records exception to the hearsay rule. Business records are admissible because books and records essential for the conduct of a business are considered trustworthy. The statement of the engineer does not fall into this category of statement. The railroad's (D) normal business is not the payment of tort claims for its employees' negligence. Unlike other types of records, reports of accidents are made for use in court, not in the running of the business.

Congress could have provided for the admission of such reports when it authorized the admission of business records, but it did not do so. There is nothing in either the law or the legislative history of the law to show that Congress intended such a result. If Congress had meant to allow records made in the "regular course of conduct" of a business rather than in the "regular course of a business," it could have done so. It is up to Congress to make such a major change in the evidentiary rules. In fact, some laws require railroads to make investigations and reports of certain accidents. The laws that impose those requirements state that neither the reports nor the investigation may be admitted into evidence in a suit for damages arising out of an accident. Affirmed.

Analysis:

The Court reads the term "regular course of business" narrowly. Tort claims, and the payment of those claims, are a part of doing business, especially in a hazardous business like railroading. If one were to take the Court's reasoning a step further, the only railroad records that would qualify for admission would be those that dealt with the physical operation of a train. Even payroll or accounting records generated by the railroad (D) are arguably not a part of the regular business of railroading.

■ CASE VOCABULARY

BUSINESS RECORDS EXCEPTION: A hearsay exception allowing business records (such as reports or memoranda) to be admitted into evidence if they were prepared in the ordinary course of business. Fed. R. Evid. 803 (6).

United States v. Vigneau

(Prosecuting Authority) v. (Accused Conspirator)

187 F.3d 70 (1st Cir. 1999), *cert. denied*, 528 U.S. 1172, 120 S.Ct. 1200 (2000)

STATEMENTS BY OUTSIDERS TO A BUSINESS ARE NOT ADMISSIBLE AS BUSINESS RECORDS

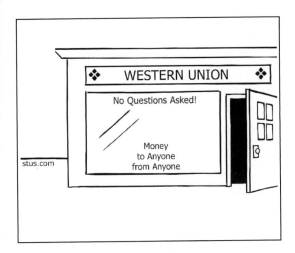

■ **INSTANT FACTS** Vigneau (D) was accused of sending money to Crandall (D) for illegal drugs, and records of money transfers with Vigneau's (D) name on them were introduced into evidence at trial.

■ **BLACK LETTER RULE** The business records exception does not include statements in a record that were made by someone not a part of the business if those statements are offered for their truth.

■ **PROCEDURAL BASIS**

Appeal from convictions for money laundering, conspiracy to launder money, and conspiracy to distribute marijuana.

■ **FACTS**

Vigneau (D) and Crandall (D) were accused of operating a venture to sell marijuana and illegal steroids. At Vigneau's (D) trial, the Government (P) introduced Western Union money transfer forms and computer records to show that Vigneau (D) sent money to Crandall (D). Vigneau's (D) name and address appeared as the sender on twenty-one forms, but Western Union did not require proof of the sender's identity at the time the forms were filled out. Copies of two of the twenty-one forms were found in Vigneau's (D) van, and a witness testified that Crandall (D) told him that Vigneau (D) sent money on one occasion that corresponded to one of the forms. The trial court found that the records were trustworthy and admitted them without redaction, for all purposes. The forms corresponded to the twenty-one counts of money laundering for which Vigneau (D) was convicted. Vigneau (D) claimed on appeal that the forms constituted inadmissible hearsay. The Government (P) claimed that the records were admissible as business records.

■ **ISSUE**

Were the records of the money transfers admissible as business records, when Western Union did not demand proof of the identity of the person identified in the records?

■ **DECISION AND RATIONALE**

(Boudin, J.) No. The business records exception does not include statements in a record that were made by someone not a part of the business if those statements are offered for their truth. Business records are deemed reliable because the regularity of the procedure that generates the record, coupled with the business incentive to keep accurate records, gives some reasonable assurance that the records will be reliable. There are no such safeguards when the record contains a statement by a stranger to the business. Such a statement becomes "hearsay within hearsay."

The outsider statements may have been admissible if offered not for the truth of the statements, but for some other purpose. The forms could have been offered in redacted form, omitting Vigneau's (D) name and address, to show that money was sent to Crandall (D). That was not the purpose for which the statements were offered, however.

Some courts have allowed the admission of outsider statements in business records if there is evidence that the business used some means of verifying identity. The verification is circumstantial evidence of identity. In this case, however, there was no verification of the identity of the sender, and Western Union had no such practice in place.

Three of the forms had some independent evidence to tie them to Vigneau (D). Two were found in Vigneau's (D) van, and one was supported by a witness's testimony. Nevertheless, the error in admitting the records cannot be said to be harmless as to these three records. Convictions vacated.

Analysis:

The court refers to its holding as a "gloss" on Fed. R. Evid. 803(6). The court's broad holding about the admissibility of "outsider" statements probably is unnecessary, in view of the rule's language that allows exclusion of the record if the circumstances "indicate lack of trustworthiness." Note that the copies of the forms found in Vigneau's (D) van seem to be tainted by the same lack of trustworthiness as all the other forms. The court notes that the hearsay problem with respect to these two forms is cured, but still finds that the admission of the statements was not "harmless."

■ CASE VOCABULARY

DOUBLE HEARSAY: A hearsay statement that contains further hearsay statements within it, none of which is admissible unless exceptions to the rule against hearsay can be applied to each level (e.g., the double hearsay was the investigation's report stating that Amy admitted to running the red light). Fed. R. Evid. 805.

LAUNDERING: The federal crime of transferring illegally obtained money through legitimate persons or accounts so that its original source cannot be traced. 18 U.S.C.A. § 1956.

REDACTION: The careful editing of a document, especially to remove confidential references or offensive material; a revised or edited document.

Beech Aircraft Corp. v. Rainey

(Airplane Manufacturer) v. *(Surviving Spouse)*

488 U.S. 153, 109 S.Ct. 439 (1988)

FACTUAL REPORTS MAY INCLUDE CONCLUSIONS OR OPINIONS

The following message is sponsored by the plane's manufacturer. If we go down, it's the pilot's fault.

stus.com

■ **INSTANT FACTS** Rainey (P) sued Beech (D) for his wife's death in an airplane crash, and Beech (D) introduced the report of an official investigation that said that pilot error was the cause of the crash.

■ **BLACK LETTER RULE** Investigatory reports are not inadmissible solely because they set out a conclusion or opinion.

■ **PROCEDURAL BASIS**

Appeal from an order of the Eleventh Circuit Court of Appeals remanding for a new trial.

■ **FACTS**

Rainey's (P) wife was killed in a plane crash during a Navy training exercise. The pilot of the airplane, the only other occupant, also was killed. Rainey (P) brought suit against Beech (D), the manufacturer of the airplane, alleging that the crash was caused by a rollback, or loss of engine power. Rainey (P) claimed that this was due to a defect in the airplane's fuel control system. Beech (D) claimed that the accident was due to pilot error. Beech (D) offered into evidence an investigative report prepared by a Navy investigator on orders of the squadron's commanding officer. The investigator's report was divided into "findings of fact," "opinions," and "recommendations." The trial judge initially allowed the admission of only the factual findings, but not the opinions or conclusions. The judge later reversed the order and ruled that some of the conclusions would be admitted. The court admitted the opinion that it was impossible to determine exactly what happened, and that the most probable cause of the accident was pilot error. Parts of the statement that set out a possible factual scenario for what happened and that stated that rollback could not be ruled out were excluded. The jury returned a verdict for Beech (D). Rainey (P) appealed and the Eleventh Circuit reversed, holding that Fed. R. Evid. 803(8)(C), which allows investigatory reports to be admitted as an exception to the hearsay rule, did not allow the admission of conclusions or opinions.

■ **ISSUE**

Were the conclusions and opinions in the investigatory report admissible?

■ **DECISION AND RATIONALE**

(Brennan, J.) Yes. Investigatory reports are not inadmissible solely because they set out a conclusion or opinion. The language of Rule 803(8)(C) refers to "factual findings resulting from an investigation." It is not apparent from this language that opinions or conclusions are not admissible. Findings of fact may include conclusions drawn from the evidence. Furthermore, the rule does not make "factual findings" admissible, but makes the reports that set out those findings admissible. The rule does not create a distinction between facts and opinions contained in the reports.

The legislative history of the rule does not provide clear guidance. The House Judiciary Committee report on the rule urged a strict construction, so that opinions and evaluations would be excluded. The

Senate Judiciary Committee was of the opposite opinion. The Senate Committee noted that the Advisory Committee that reported on the rule assumed that evaluative reports would be admissible unless the sources of information or other circumstances showed a lack of trustworthiness. The Advisory Committee also does not draw a distinction between facts and opinions. That committee considered only whether evaluative reports should be admitted, and did not limit its consideration to reports that set out only factual findings. The primary safeguard against the admission of unreliable evidence is in the exclusion of evidence the shows a lack of trustworthiness. Neither the language of the rule nor the legislative history lead to the conclusion that opinions in the reports must be excluded. The difference between fact and opinion often is a difference of degree.

A broad approach to the admissibility of investigatory reports is consistent with the general approach in the Federal Rules of Evidence of relaxing the traditional barriers to the admission of opinion testimony. As long as a conclusion is based on a factual investigation and satisfies the requirements of trustworthiness, it should be admissible with the rest of the report. Reversed.

Analysis:

The difference between a fact and an opinion can be a subtle one, as this case illustrates so well. The investigative report contained what factual information the investigator could amass. The report also contained his conclusion that the true cause of the accident could not be known, and that the most likely cause of the crash was pilot error. With no living witnesses to tell what happened in the airplane, there was very little that could be reported that did not have some element of opinion or conclusion attached to it.

Dallas County v. Commercial Union Assurance Co.

(Courthouse Owner) v. *(Insurer)*

286 F.2d 388 (5th Cir. 1961)

HEARSAY MAY BE ADMITTED IF RELIABLE AND NECESSARY

■ **INSTANT FACTS** Commercial Union (D) introduced into evidence an old newspaper article to show that Dallas County's (P) courthouse had been damaged by fire over fifty years earlier.

■ **BLACK LETTER RULE** Hearsay evidence may be admissible if there is no other way of proving the facts in the hearsay statement and if there are circumstances that show the evidence is trustworthy enough without the need for cross-examination.

■ **PROCEDURAL BASIS**

Appeal from a verdict for Commercial Union (D).

■ **FACTS**

The clock tower of the Dallas County (P) courthouse collapsed. The debris from the collapse showed that some of the timbers were charred. There were reports that the tower had been struck by lightning, and a forensic investigation supported that conclusion. Dallas County's (P) insurer, Commercial Union (D), conducted its own investigation. It concluded that the collapse was not due to a lightning strike, but to the general deterioration, structural weakness, and faulty design of the tower. Commercial Union (D) also claimed that the tower had been overloaded by the installation of an air conditioning system. Commercial Union (D) claimed that the charring was caused by a fire that occurred many years before the collapse of the tower.

The cause of the char was disputed at trial. Some witnesses testified that it was fresh and smelled smoky, while others said it was obviously old and had no smoky smell. Commercial Union (D) introduced an unsigned newspaper article that appeared in the local newspaper on June 9, 1901, over fifty years earlier. The article reported that the tower, while still under construction, had been damaged by fire. The editor of the newspaper was called to testify that the newspaper maintained archives of published issues of the newspaper, and that the issue published on June 9, 1901 was in those archives. Dallas County (P) objected that the newspaper article was hearsay, that it was not an ancient record or business document, and that it was not admissible under any exception to the hearsay rule. The article was admitted, however, and the jury returned a verdict for Commercial Union (D).

■ **ISSUE**

Was the fifty-year-old newspaper article admissible?

■ **DECISION AND RATIONALE**

(Wisdom, J.) Yes. Hearsay evidence may be admissible if there is no other way of proving the facts in the hearsay statement and if there are circumstances that show the evidence is trustworthy enough without the need for cross-examination. The fire in the courthouse happened so long before the trial that it is not likely that there are any witnesses alive who were able to understand the event and describe it. If such a witness could be found, his or her recollection probably would not be as accurate as the newspaper account. This is the rationale behind the "ancient documents" exception. Witnesses to the execution of such documents are unavailable, so circumstantial evidence of their authenticity is allowed.

There are three circumstances in which hearsay will be deemed trustworthy enough that cross-examination is not necessary: when a sincere and accurate statement would naturally be uttered and no plan to falsify would have been formed; when other considerations, such as a fear of punishment, would counteract the desire to lie; and when the statement was made under conditions of publicity that mean an error would have been detected and corrected. In this case, there was no motive for the reporter who wrote the story to falsify. Even if there had been such a motive, any false statement would have subjected both the reporter and the newspaper to embarrassment in the community. The usual dangers inherent in hearsay testimony are not present here.

In matters of local interest, when the fact in question is public and would generally have been known throughout the community, and when the fact happened so long ago that a contemporary newspaper account would be more trustworthy than an eye-witness account, a federal court is justified in easing the rules against hearsay to the extent of admitting the newspaper article into evidence. The article is not a business record or an ancient document. It is admitted because it is necessary and trustworthy, relevant and material, and its admission is within the discretion of the trial court judge. Affirmed.

Analysis:

Commentators do not question the admission of the evidence, but question the grounds under which it was admitted. The newspaper article could be deemed to come within the "ancient documents" exception of Fed. R. Evid. 803(16). That rule allows the admission of "statements" in documents in existence twenty years or more. Although the article contains statements that may themselves be hearsay ("[w]hen first seen the fire was in the top of the dome"), but other parts of the article read as if they were from firsthand observation (the dome "was in flames near the top").

■ CASE VOCABULARY

ANCIENT DOCUMENT: A document that is presumed to be authentic because its physical condition strongly suggests authenticity, it has existed for 20 or more years, and it has been maintained in proper custody (as by coming from a place where it is reasonably expected to be found). Fed. R. Evid. 901(b)(8).

United States v. Laster

(Prosecuting Authority) v. *(Accused Drug Manufacturer)*

258 F.3d 525 (6th Cir. 2001)

RELIABLE HEARSAY IS ADMISSIBLE EVEN IF IT DOES NOT COME UNDER A RECOGNIZED EXCEPTION

■ **INSTANT FACTS** Laster (D) was accused of manufacturing methamphetamine and records that showed that he ordered one of the components of the drug were introduced.

■ **BLACK LETTER RULE** The residuary hearsay exception allows the admission of hearsay if there is no indication that the evidence is not reliable, if the hearsay is more probative on the point for which it is offered than any other evidence, and if its admission serves the best interests of justice.

■ **PROCEDURAL BASIS**

Appeal from a conviction for multiple narcotics offenses.

■ **FACTS**

Laster (D) was accused of manufacturing methamphetamine. At trial, the Government (P) introduced records from the Wilson Oil Co. that showed that Laster (D) ordered bottles of hydriodic acid, a component of the drug. Wilson, the sole owner and operator of the Wilson Oil Co., died before Laster (D) went to trial. The records were authenticated by a detective for a state drug task force. The detective was not familiar with the records or recordkeeping of Wilson Oil, and the detective did not ask Wilson when the records of Laster's (D) purchases were compiled. Nonetheless, the trial court held that the records were admissible either under the business records exception to the hearsay rule or under the residual hearsay exception in Fed. R. Evid. 807. Laster (D) was convicted.

■ **ISSUE**

Were the records of the chemical purchases admissible, even if they did not fall within any recognized hearsay exception?

■ **DECISION AND RATIONALE**

(Siler, J.) Yes. The residuary hearsay exception allows the admission of hearsay if there is no indication that the evidence is not reliable, if the hearsay is more probative on the point for which it is offered than any other evidence, and if its admission serves the best interests of justice. If a statement is admissible under a recognized hearsay exception, the court should rely on that exception to admit the evidence. The residual exception should be used only for hearsay that does not fall within one of the recognized exceptions.

The records here did not qualify for admission under one of the specific hearsay exceptions. The district court did not err in admitting the records under the residual exception. Affirmed.

■ **DISSENT**

(Moore, J.) The residual hearsay exception states that it applies to statements "not specifically covered" by a recognized hearsay exception, not to statements "not admissible" under the Rules. The residual exception should apply to those exceptional cases in which a recognized exception does not apply, but in which there are circumstantial guarantees of trustworthiness equivalent to those of the established hearsay exceptions. The legislative history of the rule supports this reading of the exception. The residual exception was intended to provide for new and unanticipated situations.

The reading of the rule that relies on its plain language sometimes is referred to as the "near-miss" theory. A "near-miss" under a specified exception renders evidence inadmissible. The majority seems to be adopting a "close-enough" rule: hearsay is admissible even if it just misses admissibility under an established exception.

The majority's holding appears to make it unnecessary that a sponsoring witness be called to establish the admissibility if there is "no indication" that the records are not reliable. This approach goes against the explicit language of the business records exception. It is unclear that records introduced without the testimony of a sponsoring witness could be said to have circumstantial guarantees of trustworthiness equivalent to those that exist when a witness testifies to the trustworthiness of the records.

Analysis:

It certainly is fair to ask what remains of the exceptions to the hearsay rule after this case. Are the listed exceptions now only examples of the type of hearsay that may be admitted? Note that the majority allows the residual exception to apply if there is "no indication" that the evidence is unreliable. The burden has apparently shifted away from requiring the proponent of hearsay to prove that the evidence is reliable. The party that seeks to keep hearsay out appears to have the burden of showing unreliability.

CHAPTER EIGHT

Confrontation and Compulsory Process

Mattox v. United States

Instant Facts: Mattox's (D) conviction for murder was reversed on appeal, and at his second trial the testimony of two witnesses from his first trial was introduced.

Black Letter Rule: A defendant's rights under the confrontation clause are satisfied if the defendant has once had the opportunity to see a witness face-to-face and subject that witness to cross-examination.

Crawford v. Washington

Instant Facts: Crawford (D) was convicted of assault and attempted murder after his nontestifying wife's tape-recorded statement was admitted into evidence against him.

Black Letter Rule: The Sixth Amendment Confrontation Clause demands that, in order for an out-of-court statement to be admitted into evidence, the witness must be unavailable and the defendant must have had a prior opportunity to cross-examine the declarant.

Davis v. Washington

Hammon v. Indiana

Instant Facts: Out-of-court statements by alleged victims to a 911 operator and a police officer were used as evidence in the domestic violence prosecutions of Davis (D) and Hammon (D), but the victim did not testify in either case.

Black Letter Rule: Statements to the police are non-testimonial if the primary purpose of the interrogation is to enable the police to meet an ongoing emergency, but they are testimonial when there is no ongoing emergency and the primary purpose of the interrogation is to establish or prove past events potentially relevant to a later criminal prosecution.

Bruton v. United States

Instant Facts: A confession from Bruton's (D) co-defendant was admitted into evidence at their joint trial, and the judge instructed the jury that the confession could be considered only against the co-defendant.

Black Letter Rule: Admission of a joint defendant's confession violates the other defendant's rights under the Confrontation Clause, even if a limiting instruction is given to the jury.

Cruz v. New York

Instant Facts: Cruz (D) confessed to a friend that he was involved in a murder, and Cruz's (D) brother and co-defendant made a confession to the police that was introduced at their joint trial.

Black Letter Rule: Confessions of nontestifying co-defendants are inadmissible, even if they interlock with a defendant's own confession.

Gray v. Maryland

Instant Facts: Bell gave a confession to murder that also implicated Gray (D), and when the confession was introduced at trial Gray's (D) name was replaced by "deleted."

Black Letter Rule: A redacted confession of a co-defendant that replaces a defendant's name with an obvious indication of deletion is inadmissible.

Chambers v. Mississippi

Instant Facts: State rules against hearsay prevented Chambers (D) from calling witnesses who would testify that another man confessed to committing the murder with which Chambers (D) was charged.

Black Letter Rule: State evidentiary rules may not be applied in such a manner as to deny a defendant the right to present witnesses in his or her own defense.

Mattox v. United States

(Accused Murderer) v. *(Prosecuting Authority)*

156 U.S. 237, 15 S.Ct. 337 (1895)

THE CONFRONTATION CLAUSE REQUIRES AN OPORTUNITY TO SEE AND CROSS–EXAMINE A WITNESS

■ **INSTANT FACTS** Mattox's (D) conviction for murder was reversed on appeal, and at his second trial the testimony of two witnesses from his first trial was introduced.

■ **BLACK LETTER RULE** A defendant's rights under the confrontation clause are satisfied if the defendant has once had the opportunity to see a witness face-to-face and subject that witness to cross-examination.

■ **PROCEDURAL BASIS**

Appeal from a conviction for murder.

■ **FACTS**

Mattox (D) was convicted of murder. Two of the witnesses against him were Thornton and Whitman. They were fully cross-examined when they testified. Mattox's (D) conviction was reversed by the U.S. Supreme Court and the case was remanded for retrial. Before the case could come to trial a second time, Whitman and Thornton died. A transcript of their testimony was read into evidence. Mattox (D) was convicted, and claimed that his rights under the Confrontation Clause were violated because of the unavailability of the witnesses from his first trial.

■ **ISSUE**

Did the admission of the transcript testimony of two witnesses from the earlier trial who were no longer available to testify violate the Confrontation Clause?

■ **DECISION AND RATIONALE**

(Brown, J.) No. A defendant's rights under the confrontation clause are satisfied if the defendant has once had the opportunity to see a witness face-to-face and subject that witness to cross-examination. The primary objective of the Confrontation Clause is to prevent the use of depositions or affidavits in criminal prosecutions in place of live testimony and cross-examination. This rule allows the defendant to test the witness by making him or her stand in front of the jury, so that the jury can see the witness and judge his or her demeanor. There is some merit to the argument that allowing the prior testimony of Thornton and Whitman to be read into the record deprives Mattox (D) of that right. General rules of law must, however, sometimes give way to considerations of public policy and necessities of the case. Allowing a criminal who was convicted once by the testimony of a witness to go free because that witness died before retrial would be extending the defendant's constitutional protections to an unwarranted degree.

Many constitutional protections are subject to exceptions that were recognized long before the adoption of the Constitution and do not interfere with its spirit. Those exceptions were intended to be afforded respect. The substance of the right to confront witnesses is preserved if the defendant once had an opportunity to see the witness face-to-face and cross-examine that witness. Affirmed.

Analysis:

It has been said that most of what we call constitutional law consists of exceptions to the plain language of the Constitution. The Sixth Amendment starts with the words "[i]n all criminal prosecutions." There are no exceptions or limitations on this very clear command. Use of the prior testimony actually undercuts one of the Court's stated rationales for the Confrontation Clause. The jury at the retrial hears only the questions and answers put to the witnesses, and cannot see how the witness reacts to those questions or evaluate the witness's overall demeanor and credibility, yet the evidence was allowed.

■ CASE VOCABULARY

CONFRONTATION CLAUSE: The Sixth Amendment provision guaranteeing a criminal defendant's right to directly confront an accusing witness and to cross-examine that witness.

Crawford v. Washington

(Convicted Defendant) v. *(Prosecuting Authority)*

541 U.S. 36, 124 S.Ct. 1354 (2004)

OUT–OF–COURT STATEMENTS MAY BE INADMISSIBLE HEARSAY

It was really hot when you stabbed that guy to defend my honor.

Thanks, Baby. Wanna exercise our marital privilege?

stus.com

■ **INSTANT FACTS** Crawford (D) was convicted of assault and attempted murder after his nontestifying wife's tape-recorded statement was admitted into evidence against him.

■ **BLACK LETTER RULE** The Sixth Amendment Confrontation Clause demands that, in order for an out-of-court statement to be admitted into evidence, the witness must be unavailable and the defendant must have had a prior opportunity to cross-examine the declarant.

■ **PROCEDURAL BASIS**

Certiorari to review a decision of the Washington Supreme Court reinstating the defendant's conviction.

■ **FACTS**

Crawford (D) stabbed a man who allegedly tried to rape his wife. After receiving his *Miranda* warnings, Crawford (D) confessed to police that he and his wife went to the man's apartment, where a fight ensued; the man was stabbed in the torso and the wife's hand was cut. Crawford (D) was charged with assault and attempted murder, to which Crawford (D) claimed self-defense. Because of the state marital privilege, Crawford's (D) wife did not testify at trial, but her tape-recorded statement suggesting the fight was not self defense was introduced into evidence without an opportunity for Crawford (D) to cross-examine her. Crawford (D) was convicted. On appeal, the Washington Court of Appeals reversed, reasoning that the statement was untrustworthy and did not satisfy any hearsay exception. The Washington Supreme Court reversed and reinstated the conviction, finding that the statements were sufficiently reliable and trustworthy.

■ **ISSUE**

Does the Confrontation Clause prohibit the admission into evidence of an out-of-court testimonial statement from an unavailable witness when the defendant has no opportunity for cross-examination?

■ **DECISION AND RATIONALE**

(Scalia, J.) Yes. The Sixth Amendment Confrontation Clause demands that, in order for an out-of-court statement to be admitted into evidence, the witness must be unavailable and the defendant must have had a prior opportunity to cross-examine the declarant. In other words, the Confrontation Clause provides that every defendant has the right to confront witnesses against him. Because the constitutional text itself does not clarify exactly what the Sixth Amendment guarantee includes, we must turn to the historical underpinnings of the Confrontation Clause to fully understand its meaning. The Clause has its roots in Roman law, and the issue arose many times throughout the history of the English common law and in the Colonies as well. Cases such as the famous treason trial of Sir Walter Raleigh gave rise to the principle that justice cannot be served if out-of-court statements are used against a defendant without availing him the opportunity to confront his accusers face to face.

The expansive history of the Confrontation Clause supports two inferences. First, the Sixth Amendment is not solely concerned with in-court testimony; rather, its primary concern is "testimonial hearsay," and police interrogations, like that involved here, fall within that class. Second, the Framers of the Constitution would not have allowed admission of testimonial statements from witnesses who did not appear at trial unless they were unavailable *and* the defendant had a prior opportunity for cross-examination. As this body of law developed, the cross-examination requirement became dispositive. Supreme Court precedent is in accord with this history. Testimonial statements of witnesses absent from trial have been held admissible only when the declarant was unavailable and the defendant had a prior opportunity to cross-examine.

The admissibility test set forth in *Ohio v. Roberts*, which requires a firmly established hearsay exception or sufficient indicia of trustworthiness, is both too broad and too narrow, and it departs from historical principles. It both permits admission of some out-of-court statements without the right of confrontation because of some mere indicia of reliability and scrutinizes the reliability of in-court statements with the same analysis as those made out of court. Accordingly, we reject those standards. The Framers would not have wanted the application of constitutional guarantees to hinge on the vagaries of evidence rules, much less on amorphous notions of "reliability." The Constitution demands not merely that evidence is reliable, but that reliability is determined in a prescribed way. "Dispensing with confrontation because the evidence is obviously reliable is akin to dispensing with jury trial because a defendant is obviously guilty. This is not what the Sixth Amendment prescribes."

We could resolve the present case simply by applying the *Roberts* factors and concluding that Sylvia's statement was unreliable, but that would be a failure to interpret the Constitution in a way that secures its intended restraint on judicial discretion. Judges cannot always be relied upon to safeguard the rights of the people. Vague standards, as applied in *Roberts*, are manipulable. Where testimonial statements are at issue, the only true indicium of reliability sufficient to satisfy Constitutional demands is the right to confrontation. Reversed and remanded.

Concurrence in part, Dissent in part: (Rehnquist, C.J.) I concur in the judgment, but I dissent from the majority's decision to overrule *Roberts*. The court's rationale is not any better rooted in history than current doctrine. The Court's jurisprudence has never drawn a line between testimonial and nontestimonial statements, and the Court offers no meaningful means of doing so here. Moreover, the Court need not have overruled *Roberts* in order to find judicial error in the trial court's admission of the statements at issue, for other Court precedent clearly establishes their inadmissibility.

Analysis:

Crawford marks a dramatic shift in the Court's Confrontation Clause jurisprudence. Prior to *Crawford*, the Court consistently emphasized that the purpose of confrontation is to ensure the reliability of the testimony against the defendant. In *Crawford*, the Court insists that cross-examination as a necessary means of ensuring reliability. In so doing, the Court refines not only its view of the admissibility of hearsay statements, but also its analysis of the underlying purpose of the Confrontation Clause.

■ CASE VOCABULARY

CONFRONTATION CLAUSE: The Sixth Amendment provision guaranteeing a criminal defendant's right to directly confront an accusing witness and to cross-examine that witness.

CROSS–EXAMINATION: The questioning of a witness at a trial or hearing by a party opposed to the party who called the witness to testify.

HEARSAY: In federal law, a statement (either a verbal assertion or nonverbal assertive conduct), other than one made by the declarant while testifying at the trial or hearing, offered in evidence to prove the truth of the matter asserted.

Davis v. Washington
Hammon v. Indiana

(Defendant) v. *(Prosecuting Authority)*
547 U.S. 813, 126 S.Ct. 2266 (2006)

THE ADMISSIBILITY OF OUT–OF–COURT STATEMENTS DEPENDS ON WHETHER THEY ARE TESTI-MONIAL OR NON–TESTIMONIAL

■ **INSTANT FACTS** Out-of-court statements by alleged victims to a 911 operator and a police officer were used as evidence in the domestic violence prosecutions of Davis (D) and Hammon (D), but the victim did not testify in either case.

■ **BLACK LETTER RULE** Statements to the police are non-testimonial if the primary purpose of the interrogation is to enable the police to meet an ongoing emergency, but they are testimonial when there is no ongoing emergency and the primary purpose of the interrogation is to establish or prove past events potentially relevant to a later criminal prosecution.

■ **PROCEDURAL BASIS**

Appeals from orders upholding Davis's (D) conviction for violation of a domestic no-contact order, and Hammon's (D) convictions for domestic battery and violating probation.

■ **FACTS**

Davis's (D) former girlfriend, McCottry, spoke to a 911 emergency operator, stating that she was involved in an ongoing domestic disturbance with Davis (D). During the conversation, the operator was told that Davis (D) ran out the door after hitting McCottry, and was leaving in a car with someone else. The operator asked McCottry for more information and learned Davis's (D) full name and birthday, the purpose of his visit, and the context of the assault on McCottry. The police arrived approximately four minutes later and observed McCottry's injuries and her mental state. Davis (D) was charged with felony violation of a domestic no-contact order. The only witnesses for the State (P) were the police officers who responded to the 911 call. The officers testified regarding McCottry's injuries, but could not testify as to the cause of the injuries. McCottry did not appear at the trial. Over Davis's (D) objection based on the Confrontation Clause, the recording of McCottry's 911 conversation was admitted into evidence. Davis (D) was convicted and his conviction was affirmed. The Washington Supreme Court held that the portions of the 911 call in which McCottry identified Davis (D) were not testimonial.

In Hammon's (D) case, the police responded to a report of a domestic disturbance at Hammon's (D) home. When they arrived at the house, Hammon's (D) wife appeared frightened, but told the officers that nothing was the matter. The officers spoke with Hammon (D) and his wife separately. The officer who spoke with Hammon's (D) wife had her fill out and sign a "battery affidavit." In that affidavit, Hammon's (D) wife said that Hammon (D) broke the furnace and shoved her into the broken glass, and that he hit her in the chest and threw her down. She also wrote that Hammon (D) broke lamps, a telephone, and "tore up" her van so that she could not leave. The affidavit also stated that Hammon (D) "attacked" his daughter.

Hammon (D) was charged with domestic battery and violating his probation. His wife was subpoenaed but did not appear at the trial. The State (P) called the officer who spoke with Hammon's (D) wife, and had him repeat what she told him and authenticate the battery affidavit. Hammon's (D) counsel repeatedly objected to the evidence. The trial court admitted the affidavit as a "present sense impression." The Indiana Supreme Court affirmed the conviction, holding that the statements of Hammon's (D) wife were "excited utterances." The court also held that her affidavit was testimonial, in that it was meant to be preserved for potential future use in legal proceedings. Admission of the affidavit was error, but it was harmless beyond a reasonable doubt.

■ ISSUE

Were McCottry's out-of-court statements non-testimonial, such that they were admissible?

■ DECISION AND RATIONALE

(Scalia, J.) Yes. Statements to the police are non-testimonial if the primary purpose of the interrogation is to enable the police to meet an ongoing emergency, but they are testimonial when there is no ongoing emergency and the primary purpose of the interrogation is to establish or prove past events potentially relevant to a later criminal prosecution. The Confrontation Clause refers to "witnesses," or those who bear testimony, against the accused, and so is implicated only by testimonial statements.

The question in Davis's (D) case is whether the interrogation of McCottry by the 911 operator produced testimonial statements. The language in *Crawford v. Washington,* 541 U.S. 36 (2004), that says that "interrogations by law enforcement officers fall squarely within" the class of testimonial hearsay was meant to refer to interrogations solely directed at establishing the facts of a past crime, in order to identify the perpetrator or to provide evidence against the perpetrator. A 911 call, however, and at least the initial questioning in connection with that call, is ordinarily not meant to establish a past fact but to describe current circumstances that require police assistance. McCottry was speaking about events as they were happening. She was not relating past events, but she was making a call for help against a physical threat. The questions McCottry was asked were directed towards resolving a present emergency, not towards learning what happened in the past. McCottry was not acting as a witness or testifying, and what she said was not a "weaker substitute for live testimony" at trial. A witness does not go into court to proclaim an emergency and seek help. This is not to say that a conversation that begins as an interrogation to determine the need for emergency assistance cannot evolve into testimonial statements. Arguably, the emergency for McCottry ended after Davis (D) drove away, and from that point on, her statements were testimonial. This poses no problem, as trial courts will be able to recognize when statements become testimonial.

The statements in Hammon's (D) case, by contrast, are more clearly testimonial. The interrogation was part of an investigation into possibly criminal past conduct. There was no emergency in progress, and Hammon's (D) wife told the office that everything was "fine." The challenged statements were made when the officer questioned her a second time, and when the officer was trying to determine "what happened" rather than "what is happening." The statement of Hammon's (D) wife bears a striking resemblance to civil-law *ex parte* examinations. Her statement deliberately recounted, in response to police questioning, how potentially criminal past events began and progressed. Her statement was also made some time after the events she described were over. Her statement was an obvious substitute for live testimony, meant to do what a witness does on direct examination.

The statements made by Hammon's (D) wife cannot be compared to the statements made by McCrotty in the case against Davis (D). McCrotty spoke when she was alone, unprotected by police and apparently in immediate danger from Davis (D). She was seeking aid, and describing an immediate situation. In contrast, Hammon's wife spoke at some point in time removed from the events she described. Her affidavit was made to establish events that occurred previously. While the implication that virtually any initial inquiries at a crime scene will be non-testimonial is rejected, the notion that no questions at the scene will be non-testimonial is also rejected. In cases such as Hammon's (D), however, the fact that the statements were given at a crime scene is immaterial.

The offense involved in these cases—domestic violence—is notoriously susceptible to witness intimidation or coercion of the victim to ensure that she does not testify. When this happens, the Confrontation Clause gives the defendant a windfall. Constitutional guarantees will not be made ineffective because they will allow the guilty to go free. If a defendant does try to undermine the judicial process by procuring or coercing silence from a victim, the Sixth Amendment does not require the courts to acquiesce. The rule of forfeiture by wrongdoing extinguishes confrontation claims on equitable grounds, and a defendant who obtains the absence of a witness by wrongdoing forfeits the constitutional right to confrontation. The standard for proof at a hearing on a forfeiture is generally held to be a preponderance-of-the-evidence standard. Absent such a finding, the statement by Hammon's (D) wife is excluded. Judgment affirmed as to Davis (D); reversed and remanded as to Hammon (D).

Concurrence in part, Dissent in part: (Thomas, J.) The majority has adopted an unpredictable test, in which courts are charged with deciding the "primary purpose" of police interrogations. In addition, the statements that are considered testimonial, and that are therefore inadmissible, bear little resemblance to the evidence targeted by the Confrontation Clause. The history of the Confrontation Clause shows that it was directed in particular against the use of *ex parte* examinations as evidence. This history could be squared with the Clause by defining "witness" as "one who bears testimony." "Testimony" is a solemn affirmation or declaration used to prove a fact. Exclusion of the evidence against Hammon (D) extends the Confrontation Clause far beyond the abuses it was intended to prevent. The fact that the officer was investigating Hammon's (D) past conduct does not preclude the possibility that the officer was trying to determine whether Hammon (D) remained a danger to his wife.

Analysis:

At first glance, the question of whether a statement is testimonial or non-testimonial seems as though it could be easily answered by asking whether the statement refers to past or ongoing events, with statements about past events being testimonial, and statements about ongoing events being non-testimonial. The difference between the two, as noted by Justice Thomas, may be elusive. In Hammon's (D) case, for example, the majority notes that everything was quiet when they arrived, and Hammon's (D) wife said that everything was alright. It may be difficult for an officer on the scene to know if she is asking about past events, or if she has merely stepped into a lull in a dangerous situation, but the court, with the advantage of hindsight, will be making that decision after the fact.

Bruton v. United States

(Accused Robber) v. *(Prosecuting Authority)*

391 U.S. 123, 88 S.Ct. 1620 (1968)

CONFESSIONS OF ONE CO–DEFENDANT ARE INADMISSIBLE IN A JOINT TRIAL

■ **INSTANT FACTS** A confession from Bruton's (D) co-defendant was admitted into evidence at their joint trial, and the judge instructed the jury that the confession could be considered only against the co-defendant.

■ **BLACK LETTER RULE** Admission of a joint defendant's confession violates the other defendant's rights under the Confrontation Clause, even if a limiting instruction is given to the jury.

■ **PROCEDURAL BASIS**

Appeal from an order of the Eighth Circuit Court of Appeals affirming a conviction for armed postal robbery.

■ **FACTS**

Bruton (D) and Evans were tried jointly for armed postal robbery. At the trial, a postal inspector testified that Evans told him that he and Bruton (D) committed the robbery. Evans also made another confession, in which he admitted to the robbery but refused to name an accomplice. Evans did not testify at trial. The jury was instructed that the confessions were to be considered only as evidence against Evans, but that they were inadmissible hearsay against Bruton (D) and should be disregarded when determining his guilt. Bruton (D) was convicted. Evans's conviction was reversed on the ground that his confession should not have been admitted into evidence against him. Bruton's (D) conviction, however, was affirmed. The court of appeals relied on the case of *Delli Paoli v. United States,* 352 U.S. 232 (1957), and held that the jury was properly instructed that the confessions should not be considered against Bruton (D).

■ **ISSUE**

Did the admission of Evans's confession violate his co-defendant's right of cross-examination?

■ **DECISION AND RATIONALE**

(Brennan, J.) Yes. Admission of a joint defendant's confession violates the other defendant's rights under the Confrontation Clause, even if a limiting instruction is given to the jury. The testimony of the postal inspector in this case was legitimate evidence against Evans and was properly before the jury in the case against him. There was a strong likelihood that the jury believed that Evans made the statements, and that they were entirely true—not only the parts that implicated Evans, but the parts that implicated Bruton (D) as well. *Delli Paoli* assumed that a limiting instruction that directs the jury to disregard the hearsay would avoid the infringement on a co-defendant's right of cross-examination. That assumption has been repudiated by the case of *Jackson v. Denno,* 378 U.S. 368 (1964). In that case, the Court held that a jury is not to be relied upon to determine whether a confession was voluntary. Admonitions against the misuse of testimony are regarded as intrinsically ineffective and futile. The Government (P) should not be given the advantage of having the jury consider evidence that is not properly admitted against the defendant, but that cannot be put out of the minds of the jurors. A jury cannot effectively ignore evidence against one defendant, while considering the evidence against another defendant. *Delli* Paoli is overruled.

One of the justifications for *Delli Paoli* is that the benefits of joint trials, such as economy, diminished inconvenience, and avoidance of delays, should not be sacrificed by requiring separate trials. These advantages cannot be secured at the price of a defendant's constitutional rights. The price is too high. In addition, the reasoning of *Delli Paoli* was tied to faith in the jury system. There are many circumstances in which this faith is justified. Not every evidentiary error will amount to reversible error, and limiting instructions may be used to cure those errors. There are, however, contexts in which the risk that the jury cannot or will not follow instructions is so great, and the consequences of failure so vital to the defendant, that the limitations of the jury system cannot be ignored. Such a circumstance exists in this case. The incriminating statements are devastating, and their credibility is suspect. Reversed.

■ DISSENT

(White, J.) Evans's confession was admitted only against Evans, not Bruton (D). There is nothing in the record to suggest that the jury did not follow the limiting instruction and ignore the confessions when considering Bruton's (D) guilt.

This case poses a different situation than *Jackson v. Denno,* in which the Court held that a jury may not determine if a confession was voluntary. A defendant's own confession is probably the most probative evidence that can be admitted. In addition, a coerced confession is not excluded because it is unreliable, but because the Constitution demands it. The jury may have great difficulty understanding and applying that rule. The same cannot be said of the confession of a co-defendant. A jury will be able to disregard the portion of a co-defendant's confession that implicates another defendant if instructed to do so.

The rule announced by the majority will severely limit the circumstances in which defendants may be tried jointly. Joint trials are far more economical and minimize the burdens on all concerned. The majority should have spelled out how the federal courts may comply with the ruling. It probably will be necessary to exclude all out-of-court confessions, unless the parts that deal with other defendants are deleted.

Analysis:

Courts traditionally assume that a jury followed, or is capable of following, a judge's instructions. Limiting instructions are favored and regarded as an effective curative for many testimonial errors. In most cases, there is a minimal risk of harm if the jury disregards the instruction. The majority in this case is careful to note that, in most cases, limiting instructions will suffice, but the risk in this case is too great to tolerate the possibility of error.

■ CASE VOCABULARY

CAUTIONARY INSTRUCTION: A judge's instruction to the jurors to disregard certain evidence or consider it for specific purposes only.

Cruz v. New York

(Accused Murderer) v. *(Prosecuting Authority)*

481 U.S. 186, 107 S.Ct. 1714 (1987)

INTERLOCKING CONFESSIONS OF CO–DEFENDANTS ARE INADMISSIBLE

I'm instructing you to ignore the co-defendant's confession, even though I know you won't.

stus.com

■ **INSTANT FACTS** Cruz (D) confessed to a friend that he was involved in a murder, and Cruz's (D) brother and co-defendant made a confession to the police that was introduced at their joint trial.

■ **BLACK LETTER RULE** Confessions of nontestifying co-defendants are inadmissible, even if they interlock with a defendant's own confession.

■ **PROCEDURAL BASIS**

Appeal from an order of the New York Court of Appeals affirming a conviction for murder.

■ **FACTS**

During the course of a murder investigation, the police spoke with the victim's brother, Norberto. Norberto told them that, a few months earlier, Cruz (D) told him that he and his brother, Benjamin, killed a gas station attendant during a robbery. Norberto also said that Benjamin gave him a similar account. The police questioned Benjamin about the murder of Norberto's brother. Benjamin denied involvement in that murder, but spontaneously confessed to the murder of the gas station attendant. Later, he gave a detailed videotaped confession in which he admitted that he, Cruz (D), Norberto's brother, and a fourth man robbed the gas station, and that Benjamin shot and killed the attendant. Benjamin and Cruz (D) were tried jointly. The prosecutor (P) was allowed to introduce Benjamin's videotaped confession. The jury was instructed that the confession was to be considered only as evidence against Benjamin. Norberto testified about his conversation with Cruz (D), and his testimony was the only admissible evidence that linked Cruz (D) to the crime. Cruz (D) argued that Norberto fabricated his testimony to get revenge on Cruz (D), whom he suspected of killing his brother. Both Benjamin and Cruz (D) were convicted. The New York Court of Appeals upheld Cruz's (D) conviction. The court held that Benjamin's confession did not have to be excluded because Cruz (D) had confessed to Norberto, and his confession interlocked with Benjamin's.

■ **ISSUE**

Did the admission of Benjamin's confession violate Cruz's (D) rights under the Confrontation Clause?

■ **DECISION AND RATIONALE**

(Scalia, J.) Yes. Confessions of nontestifying co-defendants are inadmissible, even if they interlock with a defendant's own confession. The plurality opinion in the case of *Parker v. Randolph,* 442 U.S. 62 (1979), held that the Confrontation Clause is violated only when the introduction of a co-defendant's statement is "devastating" to a defendant's case. The devastating effect of a confession is not something that is assessed on a case-by-case basis. Instead, that factor was one of the justifications relied on by the Court in *Bruton v. United States,* 391 U.S. 123 (1968), for excepting confessions of a co-defendant from the general rule that jury instructions suffice to exclude improper testimony. There is no reason that interlocking confessions should not be similarly excluded. In fact, interlocking confessions probably are more devastating to a defendant than non-interlocking confessions. A co-defendant's confession will be relatively harmless if it is different from the story told by the defendant, but damaging if it confirms the defendant's alleged confession. It is illogical to believe that co-defendant confessions are less likely to be taken into account the more they are corroborated by the defendant's own admissions. Reversed.

■ DISSENT

(White, J.) Cruz (D) admitted the crime, and this fact was before the jury. It is not likely that every jury in an interlocking confession case will ignore instructions not to consider a co-defendant's confession against the defendant. It also is not possible that, in every case that involves an interlocking confession, the admission of the interlocking confession of a co-defendant will have a devastating effect. Common sense should prevail, even when logic may seem to justify the extension of what otherwise might be a sound constitutional rule.

Analysis:

Justice White's dissent regards this case as an extension of the *Bruton* rule. Arguably, the Court is not extending the rule of that case so much as it is declining to create exceptions to the rule. Although prosecutors and judges may not, as Justice White writes, be "comforted" by the Court's opinion, the rules that must be followed are nonetheless clear. There is less chance of an evidentiary decision being second-guessed on appeal than if the trial court were required to consider "factors" before deciding on the admissibility of a co-defendant's confession.

Gray v. Maryland

(Accused Murderer) v. *(Prosecuting Authority)*

523 U.S. 185, 118 S.Ct. 1151 (1998)

REDACTED CONFESSIONS OF CO–DEFENDANTS ARE NOT ADMISSIBLE

The defendant's confession reads, "<Deleted> and I killed her".

I bet <deleted> is the co-defendant!

stus.com

■ **INSTANT FACTS** Bell gave a confession to murder that also implicated Gray (D), and when the confession was introduced at trial Gray's (D) name was replaced by "deleted."

■ **BLACK LETTER RULE** A redacted confession of a co-defendant that replaces a defendant's name with an obvious indication of deletion is inadmissible.

■ **PROCEDURAL BASIS**

Appeal from an order of the Court of Appeals of Maryland affirming a conviction for murder.

■ **FACTS**

Gray (D) and Bell were charged with the murder of Williams. Bell gave the police a confession that named Gray (D) as a participant in the murder. Gray (D) and Bell were tried together, but Bell did not testify. His confession was introduced into evidence with the names of Gray (D) and the other alleged participant in the murder deleted. The witness who read Bell's confession to the jury—the arresting officer—used the word "deleted" or "deletion" whenever Gray's (D) name appeared. A written copy of the confession was introduced, and that copy had blank spaces wherever the names of Gray (D) and the other participant appeared. After the confession was read into evidence, the prosecutor (P) asked, "after he gave you that information, you subsequently were able to arrest [Gray (D)]; is that correct?" The officer replied that it was correct. Gray (D) testified, denying that he participated in the murder. He was convicted, however, and his conviction was upheld by the state appellate courts.

■ **ISSUE**

Did the admission of the redacted confession of his co-defendant violate Gray's (D) rights under the Confrontation Clause?

■ **DECISION AND RATIONALE**

(Breyer, J.) Yes. A redacted confession of a co-defendant that replaces a defendant's name with an obvious indication of deletion is inadmissible. Bell's confession originally implicated Gray (D). The redaction here was such an obvious alteration that it resembles an unredacted statement. The follow-up question asked by the prosecutor (P) eliminated any doubt as to the identity of the person to whom the redacted parts of the confession referred.

A jury generally will react to an unredacted confession in the same manner as it would to a confession redacted in this manner. Jurors will make the inference that the omission refers to the non-confessing defendant. A judge's instruction that the confession is not to be considered against the defendant provides an obvious reason for the blank. A sophisticated juror might wonder how the confession could not refer to the other defendant, since the prosecutor has argued for the guilt of both defendants. The obvious deletion also could call attention to the deleted name. By encouraging the jury to speculate, the redaction may overemphasize the importance of the accusation in the confession. Statements redacted to leave a blank or a symbol also are obviously accusatory.

This case is distinguishable from *Richardson v. Marsh,* 481 U.S. 200 (1987), which also involved a redacted confession. In that case, however, the confession was carefully redacted to remove any indication that anyone other than the confessing defendant and a third-party were involved in the crime. The non-confessing defendant later testified that she was present when the crime was discussed. From that testimony, the jury could have inferred that she was involved in the crime. The confession in that case required linkage, and was incriminating only because of the other evidence at trial. The redacted confession itself made no reference to the non-confessing defendant's existence. That was not the situation in the present case. Reversed.

■ DISSENT

(Scalia, J.) *Bruton v. United States,* 391 U.S. 123 (1968), recognized a narrow exception to the rule that jurors are assumed to follow instructions. The rule in *Bruton* has never been applied to statements that are not facially incriminating. When incrimination is only inferential, it is less likely that the jury will not follow an instruction to disregard the evidence. It is true that confessions redacted to omit a defendant's name are more likely to incriminate than confessions redacted to omit any reference to a defendant's existence. It also is true that confessions redacted to omit a name are less likely to incriminate than confessions that expressly state a defendant's name. The issue is not whether a confession incriminates a defendant, but whether the incrimination is so powerful that the courts must depart from the normal presumption that a jury will follow instructions.

Analysis:

Gray (D) and Bell were tried together, and a confession by Bell stating that he, along with "deleted," committed the murder was admitted into evidence. The jury was told that they were not to consider this confession as evidence against Gray (D), the other person on trial for the same murder. In this scenario, the omitted name in Bell's confession was so obviously Gray's (D) that the redaction was pointless. As the Court points out, however, if a redaction carefully omits any reference to a co-defendant at all, the redacted confession should not incriminate the co-defendant.

■ CASE VOCABULARY

REDACTION: The careful editing of a document, especially to remove confidential references or offensive material; a revised or edited document.

Chambers v. Mississippi

(Accused Murderer) v. *(Prosecuting Authority)*

410 U.S. 284, 93 S.Ct. 1038 (1973)

EXCLUSION OF TRUSTWORTHY HEARSAY MAY BE A DUE PROCESS VIOLATION

■ **INSTANT FACTS** State rules against hearsay prevented Chambers (D) from calling witnesses who would testify that another man confessed to committing the murder with which Chambers (D) was charged.

■ **BLACK LETTER RULE** State evidentiary rules may not be applied in such a manner as to deny a defendant the right to present witnesses in his or her own defense.

■ **PROCEDURAL BASIS**

Appeal from an order of the Mississippi Supreme Court affirming a conviction for murder.

■ **FACTS**

Chambers (D) was accused of the murder of a police officer. He used two lines of defense at his trial. The first was that he did not commit the murder, and the second was that another man, McDonald, was the one who killed the officer. Chambers (D) introduced the testimony of two witnesses who said that they saw McDonald shoot the officer. He also attempted to introduce evidence that McDonald had confessed to the murder. A few months after the murder, McDonald gave a sworn statement to Chambers's (D) attorneys in which he admitted to the killing. After he gave the statement, McDonald was turned over to the police. He repudiated his confession at a preliminary hearing, saying that he had been promised that he would not be arrested and that he would share in the proceeds of a lawsuit Chambers (D) would bring. McDonald also said that he was drinking beer with a friend, Turner, when the officer was shot. McDonald claimed that he did not possess a gun at the time of the shooting.

At his trial, Chambers (D) called McDonald to testify. McDonald repeated his repudiation of his confession. Chambers (D) requested permission to treat McDonald as an adverse witness, but his request was denied. Chambers (D) then attempted to call witnesses to discredit McDonald's (D) testimony. Two witnesses would have testified that McDonald had told them that he committed the murder. Another witness was Turner, the man with whom McDonald claimed he was drinking at the time of the shooting. Turner would have testified that he was not in the café as McDonald claimed, and that he was not drinking with McDonald that day. Turner also would have testified that McDonald said that he shot the officer, and that he owned a .22 caliber pistol, the same type that was used to shoot the officer. The court sustained the State's (P) objection to all three witnesses, however, on the ground that their testimony was hearsay.

■ **ISSUE**

Was Chambers (D) denied due process when the court did not allow the three witnesses to testify as to their conversations with the man who was possibly the actual murderer?

■ **DECISION AND RATIONALE**

(Powell, J.) Yes. State evidentiary rules may not be applied in such a manner as to deny a defendant the right to present witnesses in his or her own defense. Rules against hearsay are based on the notion that untrustworthy evidence should not be presented to the jury. Exceptions have developed that allow the admission of hearsay statements made under circumstances that assure reliability, thus compensating for the lack of an oath and the lack of cross-examination. One of the most common exceptions is for a statement made against the declarant's interest. Mississippi recognizes such an exception, but only for statements against pecuniary interest. Statements against penal interest are not allowed.

The hearsay statements here were made under circumstances that provided considerable assurance of their reliability. All of McDonald's confessions were made spontaneously, to a close acquaintance, shortly after the murder occurred. Each statement was corroborated by other evidence. In addition, each statement was self-incriminating and unquestionably against McDonald's interest. He stood to gain nothing and must have been aware that he could be subjecting himself to criminal prosecution. If there were any doubt about any of the statements, McDonald could have been cross-examined under oath. The excluded testimony was also crucial to Chambers's (D) defense. In these circumstances, when constitutional rights that directly affect the ascertainment of guilt are implicated, the hearsay rules may not be mechanically applied to defeat a defendant's right to present a defense. Reversed.

Analysis:

The holding in this case is crafted so narrowly that it is questionable whether it is precedent for any proposition. Arguably, the case could be taken as holding that exceptions to hearsay rules may be constitutionally required in some circumstances. The Court does not say that these exceptions must be codified or formalized in any way. It appears to be enough that trial courts may admit some hearsay evidence when it is crucial to a defendant's defense. Note that the Mississippi Rules of Evidence now include a hearsay exception for statements against a declarant's penal interest that is virtually identical to the exception in the Federal Rules of Evidence. *See* Miss. R. Evid. 804(b)(3).

CHAPTER NINE

Lay Opinions and Expert Testimony

United States v. Ganier

Instant Facts: Ganier (D) moved to exclude testimony about a report analyzing searches run on his computers because it was expert testimony that had not been summarized in writing.

Black Letter Rule: Testimony is expert testimony if it is based on knowledge of a field that goes beyond the knowledge of the average layperson.

United States v. Johnson

Instant Facts: A witness gave his opinion to the geographic origin of some marijuana, and his opinion was based on knowledge he gained as a user and seller of marijuana.

Black Letter Rule: A witness may qualify as an expert if the witness's expertise is derived entirely from experience in a particular area.

Jinro America Inc. v. Secure Investments, Inc.

Instant Facts: Secure Investments (D) called an expert witness to testify on the general practices and ethics of Korean businesses.

Black Letter Rule: Expert testimony must be confined to the area of the witness's expertise.

Hygh v. Jacobs

Instant Facts: An expert witness gave testimony that a police officer's actions constituted force that was not justified and totally improper.

Black Letter Rule: Expert testimony is not allowed on legal conclusions that are to be reached by the jury.

State v. Batangan

Instant Facts: An expert witness testified that Batangan's (D) daughter behaved in a manner consistent with being sexually abused.

Black Letter Rule: An expert may not offer an opinion that a witness is telling the truth.

United States v. Hines

Instant Facts: Hines (D) was identified by an eyewitness as the man who robbed a bank, and he introduced evidence on the reliability of the eyewitness identification.

Black Letter Rule: Expert testimony may be introduced on matters ordinarily within the understanding of the jury if the inferences the jury may draw on the subject could be erroneous.

Frye v. United States

Instant Facts: At his trial for murder, Frye (D) offered the testimony of an expert on the results of a lie detector test Frye (D) took, and the testimony was ruled inadmissible.

Black Letter Rule: An expert opinion that is based on a scientific principle will be admitted only if the scientific principle is sufficiently established so that it has gained general acceptance in its particular field.

Daubert v. Merrell Dow Pharmaceuticals, Inc.

Instant Facts: Daubert (P) opposed Merrell Dow's (D) summary judgment motion with scientific evidence, but the trial court did not consider that evidence on the ground that it was of a type not generally accepted by the scientific community.

Black Letter Rule: General acceptance is not a precondition to the admissibility of scientific evidence as long as an expert's testimony rests on a reliable foundation and is relevant to the issues in the case.

Daubert v. Merrell Dow Pharmaceuticals, Inc.

Instant Facts: The U.S. Supreme Court reversed the grant of summary judgment on Daubert's (P) products liability claim and remanded for the consideration of the admissibility of expert opinions.

Black Letter Rule: Expert testimony must reflect scientific knowledge and must be relevant to the proposing party's case.

United States v. Crumby

Instant Facts: Crumby (D) passed a polygraph examination and moved to introduce the results of the examination at his trial for bank robbery.

Black Letter Rule: Polygraph evidence will be admitted for the limited purpose of impeaching or corroborating the credibility of a defendant who testifies.

Kumho Tire Company v. Carmichael

Instant Facts: An expert witness for Carmichael (P) offered testimony that a defect in the manufacture or design of a tire was the cause of the blowout that injured Carmichael (P).

Black Letter Rule: All expert testimony must be evaluated to determine if it has a connection to the relevant inquiry and a reliable basis in the knowledge and experience of the relevant discipline.

State v. Kinney

Instant Facts: At Kinney's (D) trial for rape, the Government (P) introduced evidence regarding rape trauma syndrome.

Black Letter Rule: Trial courts may admit expert testimony if the reliability of the evidence equals that of other technical evidence held to be admissible and the evaluation of other courts allowing admission of the evidence is complete and persuasive.

United States v. Ganier

(Prosecuting Authority) v. *(CEO)*

468 F.3d 920 (6th Cir. 2006)

SPECIALIZED KNOWLEDGE OF COMPUTER SOFTWARE IS THE BASIS FOR EXPERT, NOT LAY, TESTIMONY

Here's the written summary of the "expert" testimony. We used small words to help the moronic defense attorney.

JURY

stus.com

■ **INSTANT FACTS** Ganier (D) moved to exclude testimony about a report analyzing searches run on his computers because it was expert testimony that had not been summarized in writing.

■ **BLACK LETTER RULE** Testimony is expert testimony if it is based on knowledge of a field that goes beyond the knowledge of the average layperson.

■ **PROCEDURAL BASIS**

Appeal from an order of the district court excluding evidence.

■ **FACTS**

Ganier (D) was CEO of a company that was under investigation for improprieties regarding state contracts. After grand jury subpoenas were issued, Ganier (D) allegedly tried to implement an e-mail policy at his company that would delete employee e-mail after six months, and he also allegedly deleted files relevant to the investigation from his computers and the computer of an employee.

Ganier (D) was indicted for obstruction of justice and for altering, destroying, or concealing documents with intent to impede a federal investigation. Ganier (D) filed a summary of expected expert testimony in which he indicated that he would offer evidence that the allegedly deleted files were transferred to the recycle bin and not deleted, and that duplicates and similar drafts of the documents remained on the computers. Ganier (D) also indicated that he would offer evidence that the computers each possessed search functions that would have located the duplicates and similar drafts, thus permitting a user intent on concealment to delete all or substantially all of the copies of particular documents on those computers.

Special Agent Drueck, a forensic computer specialist for the government (P), used forensic software to determine what searches had been run on the computers. The day before trial, Drueck determined from reports generated by the software that searches had been run using search terms relevant to the grand jury investigation and the allegedly deleted files. The next morning, before the jury was impaneled, Ganier (D) moved to exclude the reports and related testimony, claiming that the evidence was expert testimony that was required to be summarized in writing. The government (P) contended that the reports generated by the software were not expert reports but were lay testimony, produced by running commercially available software. The government (P) further argued that this testimony was the same as facts that could be observed by any person reasonably proficient in commonly used software. The district court granted the motion, however, and excluded the evidence.

■ **ISSUE**

Was the proposed testimony regarding the results of the computer search "expert testimony"?

■ DECISION AND RATIONALE

(Moore, J.) Yes. Testimony is expert testimony if it is based on knowledge of a field that goes beyond the knowledge of the average layperson. Some software may be as commonly used as home thermometers, but the tests Drueck ran are more like specialized medical tests run by physicians. Although the average layperson may be able to interpret the output of popular software programs, Drueck needed to apply specialized knowledge, akin to the specialized knowledge law enforcement officers use to interpret slang and code words used by drug dealers.

The 2000 amendments to the Federal Rules of Evidence provide that lay opinions or inferences cannot be based on scientific, technical, or other specialized knowledge that comes within Rule 702. Even before the amendment, witnesses who performed after-the-fact investigations were generally not allowed to use specialized knowledge in giving lay testimony. The trial court correctly concluded that Drueck's testimony was expert testimony, and the government (P) should have provided a written summary to Ganier (D).

Exclusion of the testimony was too severe. Sanctions for failure to comply with the disclosure rules include an order to permit discovery, a continuance, exclusion of the evidence, or any other just remedy. When fashioning a sanction, the court should consider the reasons for the government's (P) delay in producing the evidence, including whether the government (P) was acting in bad faith, the prejudice, if any, to the defendant, and the possibility that the prejudice could be cured by some other device, such as a continuance or a recess. The sanction imposed should be the least severe sanction possible, and exclusion of evidence should be ordered only when exclusion is necessary to serve some remedial objective. In this case, there is no evidence of bad faith. The government (P) turned over the reports almost as soon as it had them. The government (P) did not act in bad faith when it argued that Drueck would provide only factual testimony, and the district court's order was appealed immediately. The government (P) may have been negligent, but negligence does not, by itself, warrant suppression. In addition, the record does not show any prejudice to Ganier (D) that could not be cured by some lesser sanction. Order vacated and remanded to determine the appropriate remedy.

Analysis:

Although the court's opinion characterizes Drueck's evidence as expert testimony, the court is opening the door to the admission of lay testimony about most of the usual functions and uses of a computer. This is a departure from the approaches of the several courts that still require detailed expert testimony to describe how any electronic evidence may have been created. The key factor for the court here seems to be the ubiquity of a particular program, and not its complexity. The court did not discuss the difficulty of using the forensic software, but looked instead at how uncommon it was.

United States v. Johnson

(Prosecuting Authority) v. *(Marijuana Smuggler)*

575 F.2d 1347 (5th Cir. 1978), *cert. denied sub nom. Harelson v. United States,* 440 U.S. 907, 99 S.Ct. 1213 (1979)

EXPERIENCE MAY MAKE A WITNESS AN EXPERT

Your Honor, he admitted smoking marijuana over 1,000 times and dealing it at least 20 times. Please do the right thing.

Okay, I'll qualify him as an expert.

stus.com

■ **INSTANT FACTS** A witness gave his opinion to the geographic origin of some marijuana, and his opinion was based on knowledge he gained as a user and seller of marijuana.

■ **BLACK LETTER RULE** A witness may qualify as an expert if the witness's expertise is derived entirely from experience in a particular area.

■ **PROCEDURAL BASIS**

Appeal from a conviction for smuggling marijuana.

■ **FACTS**

Johnson (D) and five co-defendants were charged with smuggling marijuana into the United States. Johnson (D) and the others admitted that they were dealing in marijuana. They claimed that, since the marijuana was never seized, there was no evidence that the marijuana came from outside the United States. The Government (P) called de Pianelli to testify as to the origin of the marijuana. De Pianelli identified the marijuana as coming from Colombia. He based his testimony on the appearance of the marijuana, as well as on the smell and the effect he felt when he smoked it. De Pianelli also testified that he had smoked marijuana over a thousand times and had dealt in it as many as twenty times. He said that he had been asked to identify marijuana over a hundred times, and had always done so without making a mistake. De Pianelli had no special training or education, but gained his qualifications entirely from being around and smoking marijuana. Johnson (D) countered de Pianelli's testimony with the testimony of a professor of biological sciences, who testified that the origin of marijuana could not be determined by inspecting its physical characteristics. The witness based his testimony on the lack of scientific tests that demonstrate the difference between marijuana grown in Colombia and marijuana grown elsewhere. The witness also admitted that tests had shown that marijuana grown in Canada was different from marijuana grown elsewhere.

■ **ISSUE**

Was de Pianelli properly qualified as a marijuana expert based on his experience with using and dealing the drug?

■ **DECISION AND RATIONALE**

(Clark, J.) Yes. A witness may qualify as an expert if the witness's expertise is derived entirely from experience in a particular area. The subject of de Pianelli's opinion is something that is not likely to be within the knowledge of an average juror. It was within the trial court's discretion to consider de Pianelli's qualifications for giving that opinion. Rule 702 of the Federal Rules of Evidence provides that a witness's expertise may be obtained by experience, as well as by formal education or training. De Pianelli's substantial experience with marijuana included identifying marijuana from Colombia. The trial court was within its discretion when it decided to admit de Pianelli's testimony.

Expert testimony does not foreclose jury consideration of an issue. The jury is free to disregard the testimony of the expert. A defendant is free to call an expert to counter the testimony of the Government's (P) expert, and that is what Johnson (D) did. The conflict between the experts was properly before the jury. Affirmed, except as to Johnson (D) only, who was not proved to have engaged in the conspiracy.

Analysis:

The Federal Rules of Evidence acknowledge that an expert could become such partly or entirely through experience. Expert testimony is not conclusive, and the jury is free to reject the testimony, or to credit the testimony of a different expert. In this case, the jury apparently chose to credit the testimony of the frequent drug user over that of the more respectable professor of biological sciences. The validity of an expert's opinion, once it is admitted, is a question solely for the jury.

■ CASE VOCABULARY

VOIR DIRE: [French, "to speak the truth."] A preliminary examination of a prospective juror by a judge or lawyer to decide whether the prospect is qualified and suitable to serve on a jury (loosely, the term refers to the jury-selection phase of a trial); a preliminary examination to test the competence of a witness or evidence.

Jinro America Inc. v. Secure Investments, Inc.

(*Chicken Importer*) v. (*Chicken Seller*)

266 F.3d 993 (9th Cir. 2001)

EXPERT OPINIONS MUST RELATE TO THE WITNESS'S FIELD OF EXPERTISE

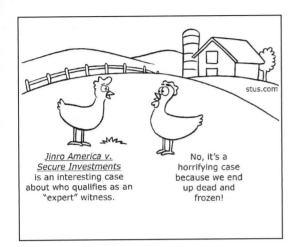

Jinro America v. Secure Investments is an interesting case about who qualifies as an "expert" witness.

No, it's a horrifying case because we end up dead and frozen!

stus.com

■ **INSTANT FACTS** Secure Investments (D) called an expert witness to testify on the general practices and ethics of Korean businesses.

■ **BLACK LETTER RULE** Expert testimony must be confined to the area of the witness's expertise.

■ **PROCEDURAL BASIS**

Appeal from an order entering summary judgment after trial against Jinro America (P).

■ **FACTS**

Jinro (P) sued Secure (D) for breach of contract, racketeering, and fraud. The action arose out of a business deal relating to the sale of frozen chicken. Secure (D) claimed that the transaction was a sham. To support its claim, Secure (D) called Pelham to testify as an expert witness. Pelham was the general manager of a business that provided commercial security to foreign businesses doing business in Korea. Pelham was trained as an investigator by the United States Air Force, and in the past commanded the office that investigated Korean companies doing business with the Air Force. His other qualifications were that he served five tours of duty in Korea, had lived in Korea for about twelve years, and was married to a Korean woman. Pelham had no formal training in law, in business, or as a cultural expert. He claimed that he had familiarized himself with Korean business practices as a hobby. Pelham testified regarding an alleged propensity on the part of Korean companies to engage in fraudulent activities, including the avoidance of Korean currency laws. He stated that it was not safe to enter into oral contracts with Korean businesses, "because of the culture." Pelham testified that his opinion was based on newspaper articles and unspecified information from his office staff. The jury found for Secure (D), and the trial court *sua sponte* entered summary judgment against Jinro (P) on all of its claims.

■ **ISSUE**

Was Pelham's testimony properly admitted as expert testimony?

■ **DECISION AND RATIONALE**

(Fisher, J.) No. Expert testimony must be confined to the area of the witness's expertise. Pelham was not qualified to offer testimony about Korean business practices generally. He did not have the legal, business, or financial expertise to evaluate the substance of the transaction at issue here. Pelham offered only his generalized impressions about Korean businesses. His testimony was based on his personal investigative experience, input from his office staff, his hobby of studying Korean business, and his marriage to a Korean woman. Pelham did not provide any evidence to support his conclusions, except for newspaper articles and anecdotal examples. Pelham did not base his testimony on personal knowledge of Jinro (P) or its affiliates.

Pelham's expertise qualified him to testify about other matters, such as the structure of the Korean governmental and banking systems, but his testimony did not concern these matters. Pelham's testimony culturally stereotyped Korean businesses generally. Reversed and remanded.

■ CONCURRENCE

(Wallace, J.) Pelham had many years' experience as an investigator of Korean businesses. It was not an abuse of discretion to determine that Pelham had the necessary qualifications to offer his opinion. Pelham's testimony was irrelevant, but that should not be used to determine retroactively that he was not qualified to testify.

Analysis:

The transactions at issue in this case involved a number of complex deals to speculate on the market price of frozen chicken. Secure (D) claimed that the transactions were actually a cover for a high-risk scheme to invest in foreign commercial paper that was illegal under Korean law. The trial court bifurcated the breach of contract claims from the fraud and racketeering claims. Once the jury found for Secure (D) on the contract claim, summary judgment was entered on the remaining claims.

■ CASE VOCABULARY

BIFURCATED TRIAL: A trial that is divided into two stages, such as for guilt and punishment or for liability and damages.

Hygh v. Jacobs

(Brutality Victim) v. *(Police Officer)*
961 F.2d 359 (2d Cir. 1992)

EXPERTS MAY NOT TESTIFY AS TO LEGAL CONCLUSIONS

Your expert testimony about excessive force is, ironically, excessive.

stus.com

■ **INSTANT FACTS** An expert witness gave testimony that a police officer's actions constituted force that was not justified and totally improper.

■ **BLACK LETTER RULE** Expert testimony is not allowed on legal conclusions that are to be reached by the jury.

■ **PROCEDURAL BASIS**

Appeal from a judgment entered for Hygh (P).

■ **FACTS**

Hygh (P) was involved in an altercation with Jacobs (D), a police officer who was trying to arrest him. Jacobs (D) struck Hygh (P) and fractured his cheekbones. Jacobs (D) claimed that he acted in self-defense, but Hygh (P) claimed he was struck from behind. The surgeon who performed reconstructive surgery on Hygh's (P) face testified that Hygh's (P) injuries were of a type caused by a blunt instrument. Jacobs (D) admitted he was carrying a flashlight when he arrested Hygh (P). Hygh (P) brought an action against Jacobs (D) under 42 U.S.C.A. § 1983, claiming that Jacobs (D) used excessive force.

At trial, Hygh (P) introduced the testimony of a Professor Cox, an expert on law enforcement. Cox testified that the use of a flashlight as a weapon greatly increased the risk of injury. He also testified that the use of a flashlight to strike a person in the head constituted deadly physical force that would not be justified in the circumstances. Accepting Hygh's (P) account of his arrest, Cox further testified that there was no legitimate reason for the use of any force by Jacobs (D). When asked if Jacobs's (D) actions were reasonable, assuming the incident happened the way Jacobs (D) claimed, Cox replied that Jacobs (D) had used deadly force that was not warranted under the circumstances. He defined "deadly force" as "using force in such a way that it has the potential to kill someone." Cox further testified that Jacobs's (D) conduct in the circumstances was totally improper.

■ **ISSUE**

Did Cox's testimony as to the improper police conduct invade the province of the jury?

■ **DECISION AND RATIONALE**

(Mahoney, J.) Yes. Expert testimony is not allowed on legal conclusions that are to be reached by the jury. Opinion testimony is not barred solely because it embraces issues or questions to be determined by the jury, but the testimony may not merely tell the jury what result to reach. Instructing the jury is the role of the judge, not of the witness. Allowing experts to testify regarding conclusions of law creates the risk that the jury will think the expert knows more than the judge.

Cox provided a definition of "deadly force" that was different from the statutory definition to be followed. The difference was minimal, and any error was cured by the court's instruction to the jury. Cox also testified that Jacobs's (D) conduct was not justified and was totally improper. This testimony went beyond the permissible limits of expert opinion. Cox was testifying regarding the ultimate legal conclusion to be reached by the jury. It was error to admit this testimony, but the error was harmless. It was expressed within a larger body of unobjectionable testimony concerning police procedure. This evidence could have let the jury draw the same conclusions that Cox did. In addition, the evidence that Jacobs (D) used excessive force was strong, and the judge instructed the jury on the use of force. The judge also instructed the jury that it could reject expert testimony. Affirmed.

Analysis:

The fault in Cox's testimony amounts to not knowing when to stop. He was allowed to testify as to proper police procedures, and the proper procedures to be followed when dealing with violent arrestees. He should not have been allowed to take that testimony one step further and reach the conclusion that what happened to Hygh (P) was unjustified. Applying standards to the facts of the case is the role of the jury.

■ CASE VOCABULARY

DEADLY FORCE: Violent action known to create a substantial risk of causing death or serious bodily harm. A person may use deadly force in self-defense only if retaliating against another's deadly force.

EXCESSIVE FORCE: Unreasonable or unnecessary force under the circumstances.

LEGAL CONCLUSION: A statement that expresses a legal duty or result but omits the facts creating or supporting the duty or result.

State v. Batangan

(Prosecuting Authority) v. *(Accused Sexual Abuser)*

71 Hawaii 552 (1990)

EXPERTS CANNOT TESTIFY AS TO CREDIBILITY

I'll skip the boring scientific stuff, and just start speculating about who's telling the truth.

stus.com

■ **INSTANT FACTS** An expert witness testified that Batangan's (D) daughter behaved in a manner consistent with being sexually abused.

■ **BLACK LETTER RULE** An expert may not offer an opinion that a witness is telling the truth.

■ **PROCEDURAL BASIS**

Appeal from a conviction for first-degree sexual abuse.

■ **FACTS**

Batangan (D) was accused of having sexual contact with his daughter. The alleged contact was not reported until several months after it took place. Batangan's (D) daughter initially said that Batangan (D) had physically abused her, then admitted that she lied about the physical abuse but accused Batangan (D) of sexually abusing her. Batangan (D) was charged with second-degree rape and first-degree sexual abuse. He was acquitted of the rape charge, but the jury was deadlocked on the sexual abuse charge.

At Batangan's (D) second trial, the state (P) called an expert on the treatment of sexually abused children, Dr. Bond, to testify. Bond testified about his evaluation of Batangan's (D) daughter and what she told him. Bond also testified about the behavior of sexually abused children and how he evaluates whether a child is telling the truth about being abused. Bond implicitly testified that Batangan's (D) daughter was believable and that she was telling the truth. Batangan (D) was convicted of first-degree sexual abuse.

■ **ISSUE**

Was Bond's opinion testimony that the victim was telling the truth a proper expert opinion?

■ **DECISION AND RATIONALE**

(Wakatsuki, J.) No. An expert may not offer an opinion that a witness is telling the truth. Expert testimony is meant to assist the jury in understanding an issue that is outside the knowledge of laypeople. In most cases, the common experience of a jury will provide a sufficient basis for evaluation of a witness's credibility. Scientific and expert testimony presents the danger that the jury will abdicate its role of evaluating the truthfulness of a witness. Expert testimony on a witness's credibility is, therefore, generally inappropriate.

The sexual abuse of children presents a different issue. The common experience of the jury may not provide an adequate foundation for assessing the credibility of a child who complains of sexual abuse. Children who are victims of sexual abuse may exhibit behaviors that are seemingly inconsistent with the victims of other types of assault. Some of these behaviors—such as delayed reporting or recantation of abuse allegations—may normally be put down to inaccuracy or prevarication. In this type of situation, it is helpful for the jury to know that many child sexual abuse victims behave in the same manner. Expert testimony that tells jurors of the unique dynamics involved in intrafamily sexual abuse cases may be helpful in letting the jury evaluate the evidence free from popular myths. This evidence may bolster a witness's credibility, but that does not make the evidence inadmissible. The inadmissible evidence is expert testimony that concludes that the abuse did occur and that the victim's testimony is truthful and believable.

In most child sexual abuse cases, the only evidence is the victim's accusation and the defendant's denial. Expert testimony on whom to believe is nothing more than advice to jurors on how the case should be decided. In this case, Bond did not give much testimony on the general behavior of victims of child sexual abuse. He asked the jurors several times to recall their own childhoods, and suggested that Batangan's (D) daughter behaved as a normal child would under the circumstances. He testified that he lacked data on the subject of retraction of abuse allegations. Bond did not explicitly sate that Batangan's (D) daughter was truthful, but there is no doubt that the jury was left with the impression that that was his conclusion. Conviction vacated; case remanded for a new trial.

Analysis:

Bond's testimony was improper, even though he never testified directly that Batangan's (D) daughter was believable. Courts assume that jurors will give expert testimony special weight, and so even this indirect evidence of credibility is not allowed. Bond, an acknowledged expert on child sexual abuse, apparently devoted little time to testifying generally about the behavior of sexual abuse victims. The court suggests strongly that such testimony would have been proper.

■ CASE VOCABULARY

CREDIBILITY: The quality that makes something (as a witness or some evidence) worthy of belief.

United States v. Hines

(Prosecuting Authority) v. *(Accused Bank Robber)*

55 F. Supp. 2d 62 (D. Mass. 1999)

EXPERT TESTIMONY MAY BE USED TO COUNTER ERRONEOUS INFERENCES

It's definitely the one in the middle.

stus.com

■ **INSTANT FACTS** Hines (D) was identified by an eyewitness as the man who robbed a bank, and he introduced evidence on the reliability of the eyewitness identification.

■ **BLACK LETTER RULE** Expert testimony may be introduced on matters ordinarily within the understanding of the jury if the inferences the jury may draw on the subject could be erroneous.

■ **PROCEDURAL BASIS**

Memorandum on evidentiary issues likely to arise at a second trial.

■ **FACTS**

Dunne, a white female bank teller, was an eyewitness to a bank robbery. She described the robber as a black man with dark skin, a wide nose, and a medium build. Dunne was not able to identify the robber from photographs. She picked out a few pictures, but said that none of the subjects was as dark as the robber. A police artist worked with her and made a sketch of the robber. After Dunne made that sketch, she was shown photographs and she said that the photograph of Hines (D) resembled the robber, but she could not be sure. Some months later, she picked Hines (D) out of a lineup.

At trial, Hines (D) offered the testimony of Kassin, a psychologist who studies human perception. Kassin's testimony was offered to show the relative inaccuracy of cross-racial identification as opposed to same-race identification, the effect of stress and time on identification, the absence of a relationship between confidence expressed in a witness's memory and the accuracy of that memory, the suggestiveness of aspects of the identification process, and transference (meaning a witness is able to recognize a face, but is unable to say where that recognition comes from). Kassin testified to various factors that could have affected the accuracy of Dunne's identification. The Government (D) introduced testimony from its own expert, Ebbesen. Ebbesen did not agree that the conclusions from Kassin's experimental studies could be applied to real life settings.

■ **ISSUE**

Was the testimony of Kassin on the inaccuracy of cross-racial identification properly admitted?

■ **DECISION AND RATIONALE**

(Gertner, J.) Yes. Expert testimony may be introduced on matters ordinarily within the understanding of the jury if the inferences the jury may draw on the subject could be erroneous. While jurors may be confident about their abilities to draw the proper inferences about eyewitness identification, that confidence may be misplaced, especially regarding cross-racial identifications. Common sense inferences may well be off the mark.

The testimony does not take away the function of the jury. Kassin's testimony did not tell the jury whether to believe Dunne. All his testimony did was to provide the jury with more information the jury could use to make an informed decision. Only the expert can provide that information. The fact that Kassin did not interview Dunne makes it less likely that his testimony will be accepted by the jury and more likely that the testimony will be given the proper consideration. The science behind Kassin's testimony does not attempt to predict whether a particular witness is accurate or mistaken. Testimony on eyewitness identification is allowed, along with the testimony of the Government's (P) witness.

Analysis:

The decision to admit the testimony of Hines's (D) expert may have been made easier by the presence of the Government's (P) expert, to counter that testimony. A "battle of the experts" makes it less likely the jury will regard one expert's testimony as conclusive and keeps the jury as the final finder of disputed facts.

The procedural posture of this case is unique. Hines (D) was tried on the bank robbery charge, but the jury deadlocked. The judge who presided at that trial anticipated that many of the same evidentiary issues from the first trial would recur during the second trial. This opinion was written to outline some of those issues and to give the court's reasons for reaching the decisions that it did.

■ CASE VOCABULARY

DEADLOCK: A state of inaction resulting from opposition, a lack of compromise or resolution, or a failure of election.

Frye v. United States

(Accused Murderer) v. *(Prosecuting Authority)*

293 F. 1013 (D.C. Cir. 1923)

EXPERT OPINION MUST BE BASED ON GENERALLY ACCEPTED SCIENTIFIC PRINCIPLES

Your science sure looks impressive, but the word on the street is that you're kind of a quack.

stus.com

■ **INSTANT FACTS** At his trial for murder, Frye (D) offered the testimony of an expert on the results of a lie detector test Frye (D) took, and the testimony was ruled inadmissible.

■ **BLACK LETTER RULE** An expert opinion that is based on a scientific principle will be admitted only if the scientific principle is sufficiently established so that it has gained general acceptance in its particular field.

■ **PROCEDURAL BASIS**

Appeal from a conviction for murder.

■ **FACTS**

Before his trial for murder, Frye (D) took a systolic blood pressure deception test, also known as a "lie detector" test. The theory behind the test was that it measured the changes in blood pressure brought about by the test subject's reactions to deception or concealment of a crime. At trial, Frye (D) offered the testimony of the scientist who conducted the test on him. The court sustained the Government's (P) objection to the testimony. Frye (D) offered to conduct a test in the presence of the jury, but his offer was refused.

■ **ISSUE**

Were the lie detector test results admissible?

■ **DECISION AND RATIONALE**

(Van Orsdel, J.) No. An expert opinion that is based on a scientific principle will be admitted only if the scientific principle is sufficiently established so that it has gained general acceptance in its particular field. It is difficult to define when a scientific principle crosses the line between experimental and demonstrable. The systolic blood pressure deception test has not yet gained the standing and scientific recognition that would justify admitting the results of the test into evidence. Affirmed.

Analysis:

Although they are in widespread use, lie detector tests have yet to be universally accepted by either the legal or scientific community. The National Academy of Sciences issued a study in 2002 that concluded that lie detector tests are "reliable" in the sense that the results are consistent, but they are not "valid," in that they do not actually measure what they purport to measure. Lie detector tests are used now more as a means to extract information from the person being examined, rather than as a means of measuring the truthfulness of a subject's answers.

■ CASE VOCABULARY

FRYE TEST: The now-defunct federal common law rule of evidence on the admissibility of scientific evidence. It required that the tests or procedures must have gained general acceptance in their particular field.

POLYGRAPH: A device used to evaluate veracity by measuring and recording involuntary physiological changes in the human body during interrogation.

Daubert v. Merrell Dow Pharmaceuticals, Inc.

(*Children with Birth Defects*) v. (*Drug Manufacturer*)

509 U.S. 579, 113 S.Ct. 2786 (1993)

THE FRYE TEST IS REJECTED

My theories aren't generally accepted yet.

It's okay if your peers don't respect you, as long as the judge and jury do.

stus.com

■ **INSTANT FACTS** Daubert (P) opposed Merrell Dow's (D) summary judgment motion with scientific evidence, but the trial court did not consider that evidence on the ground that it was of a type not generally accepted by the scientific community.

■ **BLACK LETTER RULE** General acceptance is not a precondition to the admissibility of scientific evidence as long as an expert's testimony rests on a reliable foundation and is relevant to the issues in the case.

■ **PROCEDURAL BASIS**

Appeal from an order of the Ninth Circuit Court of Appeals affirming a grant of summary judgment.

■ **FACTS**

Daubert (P) brought a products liability action against Merrell Dow (D). Daubert (P) claimed that Bendectin, an anti-nausea medication manufactured by Merrell Dow (D) and taken by his mother during her pregnancy, caused him to suffer serious birth defects. Merrell Dow (D) moved for summary judgment, alleging that its drug did not cause Daubert's (P) birth defects. In support of its motion, Merrell Dow (D) submitted an affidavit of Lamm, a physician and epidemiologist. The affidavit stated that Lamm had reviewed all the available literature on Bendectin and birth defects. None of the studies had found that Bendectin was a substance capable of causing birth defects, and so Lamm concluded that Bendectin did not create a risk of birth defects. Daubert (P) responded by presenting the testimony of eight experts, all of whom concluded that Bendectin can cause birth defects. The experts' conclusions were based on laboratory studies that found a link between Bendectin and birth defects, pharmacological studies that compared the chemical structure of Bendectin to substances known to cause birth defects, and the reanalysis of previously published human statistical studies.

The district court granted Merrell Dow's (D) motion for summary judgment, and the court of appeals affirmed. The court relied on the standard of *Frye v. United States,* 293 F. 1013 (D.C. Cir. 1923), and held that an expert opinion based on a scientific technique is inadmissible unless the technique is generally accepted as reliable in the relevant scientific community. The reanalysis offered by Daubert (P) was criticized as unpublished, not subjected to peer review, and generated solely for use in litigation. The court ruled that Daubert (P) had not provided a sufficient foundation for the admission of the evidence.

■ **ISSUE**

Can expert evidence meet the standards for admissibility even though it fails the Frye test?

■ **DECISION AND RATIONALE**

(Blackmun, J.) Yes. General acceptance is not a precondition to the admissibility of scientific evidence, but the trial judge must ensure that an expert's testimony rests on a reliable foundation and is relevant to the issues in the case. The rule set out in *Frye* has been superseded by Fed. R. Evid. 702, which provides that scientific, technical, or specialized information will be admitted if it will assist the trier of fact in understanding the evidence or determining a fact in issue. The rule does not incorporate a "general acceptance" standard. A rigid "general acceptance" standard would be at odds with the liberal thrust of the Rules and their general approach of relaxing the barriers to the introduction of opinion testimony.

Although the *Frye* test has been displaced, judges still must ensure that scientific evidence is both relevant and reliable. The requirement that an expert's testimony pertain to "scientific knowledge" is a standard of evidentiary reliability. "Scientific" connotes a grounding in scientific methods and procedures. "Knowledge" means something more than subjective belief or unsupported opinion. The evidence or testimony must also assist the trier of fact. This condition relates to the relevance of the evidence. There must be a "fit" between the evidence and an issue in the case.

Determining whether the evidence meets the standards of admissibility requires the court to make a preliminary assessment of whether the reasoning or methodology underlying the testimony is scientifically valid and of whether that reasoning or methodology can be applied to the facts at issue. A key question to be answered in this assessment is whether the theory or technique has been, or can be, tested. Another consideration is whether the theory or technique has been subject to peer review or publication. While publication is not essential, submission to scrutiny by the scientific community increases the chance that substantial flaws in methodology will be detected. The general acceptance of a technique or theory also may have a bearing on the inquiry. A theory or technique that has attracted only minimal support may properly be viewed with skepticism.

The inquiry envisioned by Rule 702 is a flexible one. The focus must be on the principles and their validity, not on the conclusions they generate. The judge must be mindful of other evidentiary rules, such as Fed. R. Evid. 703, which states that hearsay may be the basis of an admissible opinion only if the hearsay is of a type reasonably relied upon by experts in the field. Rule 706 allows the court to procure an expert of its own choosing, and Rule 403 permits the exclusion of relevant evidence if its probative value is substantially outweighed by the danger of unfair prejudice, confusion, or misleading the jury. Expert evidence has a great potential to mislead, so the judge has more control over experts than over lay witnesses.

The abandonment of the "general acceptance" standard will not result in a "free-for-all" that will confuse juries. Cross-examination, presentation of contrary evidence, and instruction on the burden of proof are the traditional means of attacking shaky but admissible evidence. Similarly, recognizing a screening role on the part of the judge will not stifle scientific progress. The inquiry in a courtroom is of a different type than the inquiry in the laboratory. Scientific theories that probably are wrong have no place in a trial. Reversed.

■ CONCURRENCE IN PART, DISSENT IN PART

(Rehnquist, C.J.) The majority was correct in concluding that *Frye* was superseded by the Federal Rules of Evidence. Beyond that, the majority's "general observations" are not necessary to the decision of the case. They are of a vague and general nature and raise many questions. Does the Court's opinion apply only to "scientific" knowledge? What is the difference between "scientific" and "technical" knowledge? Rule 702 does not impose a requirement that judges become amateur scientists when deciding questions that relate to proffered expert testimony.

Analysis:

The majority's opinion seems to impose a great burden on judges who must decide if expert testimony is admissible. The author of the opinion, Justice Blackmun, was conversant and comfortable with complex scientific concepts—his undergraduate training was in mathematics, and he worked for many years as counsel to the Mayo Clinic. Few judges will have such knowledge or inclinations. It is likely that many judges will continue to rely on some type of *Frye* analysis in deciding these questions.

Daubert v. Merrell Dow Pharmaceuticals, Inc.

(Children with Birth Defects) v. *(Drug Manufacturer)*

43 F.3d 1311 (9th Cir. 1995), *cert. denied*, 516 U.S. 869, 116 S.Ct. 189 (1995)

THE DAUBERT TEST IS ENUNCIATED

Before we get started, can I take a closer look at your credentials?

stus.com

■ **INSTANT FACTS** The U.S. Supreme Court reversed the grant of summary judgment on Daubert's (P) products liability claim and remanded for the consideration of the admissibility of expert opinions.

■ **BLACK LETTER RULE** Expert testimony must reflect scientific knowledge and must be relevant to the proposing party's case.

■ **PROCEDURAL BASIS**

On remand from the U.S. Supreme Court.

■ **FACTS**

Daubert (P) brought a products liability action against Merrell Dow (D). Daubert (P) claimed that Bendectin, an anti-nausea medication manufactured by Merrell Dow (D) and taken by his mother during her pregnancy, caused him to suffer serious birth defects. Merrell Dow (D) moved for summary judgment, alleging that its drug did not cause Daubert's (P) birth defects. In response to the motion, Daubert (P) submitted the testimony of eight experts, all of whom concluded that Bendectin can cause birth defects. The experts' conclusions were based on laboratory studies that found a statistical link between Bendectin and birth defects, pharmacological studies that compared the chemical structure of Bendectin to substances known to cause birth defects, and the reanalysis of previously published human statistical studies. The studies all were done in order to prepare for litigation in Bendectin cases. None of the experts had published their studies or submitted them for peer review.

The district court granted Merrell Dow's (D) motion for summary judgment, and the court of appeals affirmed. The court relied on the standard of *Frye v. United States,* 293 F. 1013 (D.C. Cir. 1923), and held that an expert opinion based on a scientific technique is inadmissible unless the technique is generally accepted as reliable in the relevant scientific community. The U.S Supreme Court remanded, holding that the proper test under Fed. R. Evid. 702 is whether an expert's testimony rests on a reliable foundation and is relevant to the issues in the case.

■ **ISSUE**

Is scientific testimony based on unpublished studies not subjected to peer review admissible?

■ **DECISION AND RATIONALE**

(Kozinski, J.) No. Expert testimony must reflect scientific knowledge and must be relevant to the proposing party's case. The Supreme Court's opinion remanding this case requires the court to resolve disputes among scientists about matters within their area of expertise, in areas in which there is no scientific consensus, and reject testimony if it is not derived by the scientific method.

There is no set list of factors to be considered in deciding this question. One very significant fact to be considered is whether the experts will testify about matters that grow out of independent research, or whether they have developed their opinions expressly for the purpose of testifying. If research was conducted independent of litigation, there is objective proof that the research comports with the dictates of good science. If the proffered expert testimony is not based on independent research, the party who proffers it must come forward with objective, verifiable evidence that the testimony is based on scientifically valid principles. One manner of demonstrating this is by showing that the conclusions have been subjected to normal scientific scrutiny through peer review and publication.

The testimony proffered by Daubert (P) is not the product of independent research. In addition, none of the research has been published in a scientific journal or subjected to formal review. The only review the research has received has been in courtrooms. The controversy regarding Bendectin has been going on for many years, and no one in the scientific community, with the exception of Merrell Dow's (D) experts, has deemed the research worthy of comment, verification, or refutation. When an expert's research was not produced independently and has not been published or the subject of peer review, testimony of the expert may still in some cases be used to show that the expert's testimony reflects "scientific knowledge." The expert must explain precisely how conclusions were reached and point to some objective source, such as a scientific journal, to show that the scientific method was followed. Daubert (P) has not made such a showing. His experts have presented only their credentials, their conclusions, and their assurances of reliability. That is not enough.

The second test for admissibility—the "fit" of the evidence—also is not satisfied here. The pertinent inquiry in this case is causation, specifically, whether Bendectin caused Daubert's (P) birth defects. Daubert's (P) experts do not show causation directly. Instead, they show circumstantial proof of causation. The expert testimony consists of chemical studies that show that Bendectin has a structure similar to known causes of birth defects, and statistical studies that show that Bendectin increases the risk of birth defects. This evidence is not the same as showing that Bendectin was the cause of Daubert's (P) birth defects. Daubert (P) must show not only that Bendectin increased the likelihood of his injury, but that it more likely than not caused his injury. Daubert (P) must show that Bendectin more than doubled the risk of birth defects, and the expert opinions offered do not do so. None of Daubert's (P) experts was willing to testify that Bendectin caused his injuries. Instead, they testified that it was capable of doing so, which is not the same as saying that it did cause Daubert's (P) birth defects. The possibility is not quantified. This defect in the expert testimony could not be cured on remand, as it would force the experts to revise their conclusions. Summary judgment affirmed.

Analysis:

There is no question that the court here is not happy with the standards imposed by the Supreme Court. The advantage of the superseded test enunciated in *Frye v. United States,* 293 F. 1013 (D.C. Cir. 1923), was that the resolution of the type of question addressed here was left to scientists, not judges. In this case, the court reaches the same conclusions that it did using a *Frye* analysis. The path the court used to reach that conclusion arguably is just an expansion of *Frye,* with a more detailed recitation of what acceptance by the scientific community truly means.

■ CASE VOCABULARY

DAUBERT TEST: A method that federal district courts use to determine whether expert testimony is admissible under Federal Rule of Evidence 702, which generally requires that expert testimony consist of scientific, technical, or other specialized knowledge that will assist the fact-finder in understanding the evidence or determining a fact in issue. In its role as "gatekeeper" of the evidence, the trial court must decide whether the proposed expert testimony meets the requirements of relevance and reliability. The court applies the test outside the jury's presence, usually during a pretrial *Daubert* hearing. At the hearing, the proponent must show that the expert's underlying reasoning or methodology and its application to the facts are scientifically valid. In ruling on admissibility, the court considers a flexible list of factors, including (1) whether the theory can be or has been tested, (2) whether the theory has been subjected to peer review or publication, (3) the theory's known or potential rate of error and whether there are standards that control its operation, and (4) the degree to which the relevant scientific community has accepted the theory.

United States v. Crumby

(*Prosecuting Authority*) v. (*Accused Bank Robber*)

895 F. Supp. 1354 (D. Ariz. 1995)

POLYGRAPH EVIDENCE IS ADMISSIBLE ON THE ISSUE OF CREDIBILITY

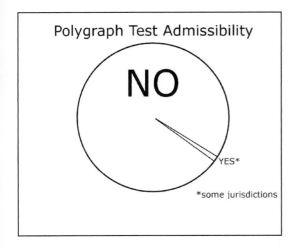

Polygraph Test Admissibility

NO

YES*

*some jurisdictions

■ **INSTANT FACTS** Crumby (D) passed a polygraph examination and moved to introduce the results of the examination at his trial for bank robbery.

■ **BLACK LETTER RULE** Polygraph evidence will be admitted for the limited purpose of impeaching or corroborating the credibility of a defendant who testifies.

■ **PROCEDURAL BASIS**

Trial court decision on a motion to introduce polygraph evidence.

■ **FACTS**

Crumby (D) was accused of participating in a bank robbery. He claimed he was innocent. Crumby (D) moved the court for permission to introduce the results of a polygraph test that he took. The results of the test showed that Crumby (D) was telling the truth when he stated that he did not participate in the robbery.

■ **ISSUE**

Were the results of the polygraph examination admissible for any purpose?

■ **DECISION AND RATIONALE**

(Strand, J.) Yes. Polygraph evidence will be admitted for the limited purpose of impeaching or corroborating the credibility of a defendant who testifies. The Ninth Circuit has traditionally held that, absent a stipulation, polygraph evidence is *per se* inadmissible. The rationale for the rule was that polygraph results were of questionable reliability and presented a great potential for prejudice from inaccurate evidence. The rule will be re-examined in this case. Here, the defendant seeks to introduce the test results as exculpatory evidence, and the Supreme Court's decision in *Daubert v. Merrell Dow Pharmaceuticals, Inc.*, 509 U.S. 579 (1993), requires that courts reconsider the traditional approaches to the admissibility of scientific evidence. In addition, the reliability of polygraph evidence has increased significantly in recent years.

Analysis of polygraph evidence using the factors set out in *Daubert* leads to the conclusion that the evidence should be admitted. Polygraphy has been subjected to vigorous scientific testing, and the assumptions that underpin the science have been deeply analyzed. The science has been subjected to extensive peer review and publication. The known error rates for polygraph tests are low, especially when compared to more inexact forensic sciences. It is also more likely that a polygraph will erroneously show a truthful witness to be lying than a deceptive person to be truthful. A test result that shows a person to be truthful is thus more likely to be accurate than one that shows him or her to be deceptive. Polygraph evidence has widespread acceptance in the scientific community of psychophysiologists. Finally, the research on which polygraphy is based has no relation to the litigation in this

---

case and was not developed for the purposes of litigation. Polygraphy evidence is therefore sufficiently reliable to justify admission of the evidence under Fed. R. Evid. 702.

Before polygraph results are admitted, however, the evidence must be considered under Fed. R. Evid. 403 to determine if its probative value is outweighed by the dangers of unfair prejudice, confusion of the issues, misleading the jury, undue delay, waste of time, or needless presentation of cumulative evidence. The probative value here is unquestionable, but the potential prejudicial effects are enormous as well. Many of the arguments concerning prejudice are either overstated or unfounded. The prejudice arguments in this case are used to prevent a self-proclaimed innocent man from using scientific evidence to prove his innocence. The argument that the evidence will waste time has little merit in a criminal trial when the evidence is extremely probative, and the amount of time required for the evidence will decrease as more courts develop an approach to admitting the evidence and establish the purposes for which the evidence may be used. The stronger argument is that polygraph tests have an "aura of infallibility" about them. The counter-arguments are that polygraph evidence is admitted by stipulation, the evidence is subject to cross-examination and the presentation of counter-evidence to show how a test may be flawed, and a proper limiting instruction may be given to explain to the jury the proper use of the evidence. If the evidence is used in a limited manner, the jury's role in determining credibility will be maintained.

The court must be careful to ensure that the polygrapher's ability to determine the credibility of a witness is not confused with the jury's obligation to determine the ultimate issues in the case. The use of polygraph evidence must be narrowly tailored to the circumstances circumscribed to limit its potentially prejudicial effects. The main concern in this case is that the jury will confuse the polygrapher's testimony about the credibility of the witness with an opinion about whether Crumby (D) committed the crime in question. The polygraph evidence may therefore be used only to impeach or corroborate the credibility of Crumby (D). If Crumby (D) testifies and the Government (P) impeaches his credibility, he may support his credibility. Motion to allow polygraph evidence is granted, subject to the requirement that Crumby (D) provide adequate notice to the Government (P) and the Government's (P) opportunity to administer a similar test to Crumby (D), and further subject to the requirement that the evidence be used only to impeach or corroborate Crumby's (D) testimony if he should decide to testify.

Analysis:

The rule in this case remains the minority rule. Courts seem to have a lingering disbelief in polygraph evidence that makes them reluctant to allow its admission. There also is the argument that polygraph evidence amounts to an expert's declaration that a witness is telling the truth, which is traditionally a matter for the jury's determination. For some, polygraph evidence raises the specter of "trial by machine," in which the jury must evaluate a witness according to the analysis of measured physical reactions.

■ CASE VOCABULARY

POLYGRAPH: A device used to evaluate truthfulness by measuring and recording involuntary physiological changes in the human body during interrogation. Polygraph results are inadmissible as evidence in most states but are commonly used by the police as an investigative tool.

Kumho Tire Company v. Carmichael

(Tire Manufacturer) v. *(Driver)*

526 U.S. 137, 119 S.Ct. 1167 (1999)

THE DAUBERT ANALYSIS APPLIES TO ALL EXPERT TESTIMONY

Ta-da! Here's my opinion.

Daubert liberalized the admission of expert opinions, but that doesn't mean you can pull your opinion out of thin air.

stus.com

■ **INSTANT FACTS** An expert witness for Carmichael (P) offered testimony that a defect in the manufacture or design of a tire was the cause of the blowout that injured Carmichael (P).

■ **BLACK LETTER RULE** All expert testimony must be evaluated to determine if it has a connection to the relevant inquiry and a reliable basis in the knowledge and experience of the relevant discipline.

■ **PROCEDURAL BASIS**

Appeal from an order of the Eleventh Circuit Court of Appeals reversing a grant of summary judgment.

■ **FACTS**

Carmichael (P) and several others were injured when a tire on the minivan Carmichael (P) was driving blew out. Carmichael brought an action against Kumho (D), the manufacturer and distributor of the tire. Carmichael (P) based his case on the testimony of Carlson, an expert in tire failure analysis. Carlson concluded that the failure of the tire was due to a defect in manufacturing or design. His conclusion rested in part on certain findings that were in dispute. First, Carlson said that if tire failure is not caused by a type of misuse known as overdeflection, the cause ordinarily is a defect. Carlson also stated that, if there has been overdeflection, the tire should show certain physical symptoms. Carlson said that when he does not find at least two of the physical signs of overdeflection, he concludes that the failure was due to a manufacturing or design defect.

Kumho (D) moved to exclude Carlson's testimony on the ground that his methodology failed to meet the requirements of Fed. R. Evid. 702. The trial court used the analysis of *Daubert v. Merrell Dow Pharmaceuticals, Inc.,* 509 U.S. 579 (1993), and found that there were insufficient indications of the reliability of the methods used by Carlson. The court excluded Carlson's proffered testimony and entered summary judgment for Kumho (D). The court of appeals reversed, holding that Carlson's testimony was about technical, rather than scientific, matters, so the *Daubert* analysis should not have been used.

■ **ISSUE**

Do the factors for evaluating expert testimony listed in *Daubert* apply to expert testimony regarding non-scientific matters?

■ **DECISION AND RATIONALE**

(Breyer, J.) Yes. All expert testimony must be evaluated to determine if it has a connection to the relevant inquiry and a reliable basis in the knowledge and experience of the relevant discipline. Rule 702 itself makes no distinction between scientific and technical or other specialized knowledge. It is the knowledge, not the fact that it is scientific, that establishes a standard of evidentiary reliability. The Federal Rules of Evidence grant testimonial latitude to expert witnesses on the assumption that an expert's opinions will have a reliable basis in knowledge and experience. That leeway is granted to all experts, not just scientific ones. It would prove difficult, if not impossible, for judges to distinguish between scientific and technical or other specialized knowledge. Furthermore, there is no convincing need for them to do so.

Daubert set out a list of factors that the court may consider in determining questions of the admissibility of expert opinions. The factors include whether a theory or technique can be and has been tested, whether it has been subjected to peer review and publication, whether there is a high known or potential rate of error for a particular technique and standards controlling the technique's operation, and whether the theory or technique enjoys general acceptance within a relevant scientific community. This list of factors is not an exclusive list. The inquiry regarding expert testimony is fact-specific, and much depends on the facts and circumstances of the individual case. There may be some cases in which not all of the factors will apply. The types of questions mentioned in *Daubert* may be asked when an expert relies on observation based on skill or experience, not just when the expert relies on scientific principles. The trial court is given latitude in deciding how to evaluate an expert's reliability, and decisions of this type will be reviewed according to an abuse of discretion standard.

In this case, the trial court excluded Carlson's testimony because it doubted the reliability of the methodology used in analyzing the data. The court also doubted the scientific basis for the analysis. The court determined that Carlson's testimony fell outside the range where experts might reasonably differ and where the jury must decide among conflicting views of different experts. The issue before the court was the reasonableness of Carlson's use of a visual and tactile inspection to determine whether overdeflection caused the blowout, and the reasonableness of the method of analyzing the data obtained by that inspection, to draw a conclusion regarding the particular matter. The relevant issue was whether Carlson could determine the cause of the tire failure that injured Michaelson (P). Carlson's conclusion depended upon the assumption that, in the absence of certain signs of abuse, the tire failure was caused by a design or manufacturing defect. His conclusion also depended upon the assumption that his visual and tactile inspection could determine that the tire had not been abused, despite some signs of abuse. In addition, the transcripts of Carlson's testimony cast considerable doubt on the reliability of the theories he relied upon. His conclusions were highly subjective, and he had only inspected the tire itself on the morning of the deposition, and then only for a few hours. There was no defense of Carlson's methodology.

Applying the *Daubert* factors, the trial court properly concluded that Carlson's testimony was unreliable. There is no indication that other experts in the tire industry use the tests Carlson did, and there is no reference to articles or papers that validate his approach. The conclusion that Carlson's testimony should be excluded was within the district court's discretion. Reversed.

Analysis:

The majority's opinion could serve as a guide for the trial lawyer on discrediting an expert witness on cross-examination. Expert testimony is subject to special, very intense scrutiny not applied to other witnesses. The justification for such scrutiny is that an expert usually has no first-hand knowledge of what took place, but is only giving his or her opinion regarding the case. This fact-opinion dichotomy gives rise to the suspicion of experts.

State v. Kinney

(Prosecuting Authority) v. *(Accused Rapist)*

171 Vt. 239 (2000)

COURTS MAY RELY ON OTHER COURT DECISIONS TO DECIDE IF EVIDENCE IS RELIABLE

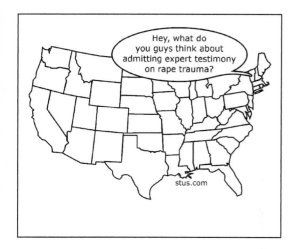

■ **INSTANT FACTS** At Kinney's (D) trial for rape, the Government (P) introduced evidence regarding rape trauma syndrome.

■ **BLACK LETTER RULE** Trial courts may admit expert testimony if the reliability of the evidence equals that of other technical evidence held to be admissible and the evaluation of other courts allowing admission of the evidence is complete and persuasive.

■ **PROCEDURAL BASIS**

Appeal from convictions for kidnapping, aggravated sexual assault, and lewd and lascivious behavior.

■ **FACTS**

Kinney (D) was charge with kidnapping and rape. He admitted carrying the victim out of her home and placing her in a car, but he claimed that she was giggling and went in the car voluntarily. The victim said that she resisted Kinney (D), repeatedly told him she did not want to go with him, and asked repeatedly to be let out of the car. Kinney (D) and some friends then took the victim to a house. Kinney (D) and one of his friends claimed that the victim went into the house voluntarily, while the victim and another friend said she was dragged into the house. While in the house, everyone, including the victim, drank beer and smoked marijuana. The victim claimed that she drank and smoked because she did not want Kinney (D) and his friends to think she was afraid. After the party broke up, the victim went to Kinney's (D) house with him. The victim testified that Kinney (D) took her up to his room and raped her. Kinney (D) claimed that he was going to ask his parents to drive the victim home, but decided it was too late. Kinney (D) claimed that he and the victim had consensual sex. The victim said that after Kinney (D) raped her, she fell asleep. In the morning, Kinney (D) arranged for a friend to drive her home.

At trial, the State (P) called a Dr. Tyler to testify about rape trauma syndrome and the characteristics and conduct of rape victims. The State (P) noted that Tyler would have no contact with the victim and would offer no opinion on whether the victim was raped by Kinney (D). Kinney (D) challenged Tyler's testimony as inadmissible under *Daubert v. Merrell Dow Pharmaceuticals, Inc.,* 509 U.S. 579 (1993). The trial court overruled the objection and allowed the testimony. Tyler testified regarding the behaviors and symptoms associated with rape trauma syndrome. Tyler also testified that that rape victims are more likely to resist their attackers by making verbal protests than by struggling or screaming. She testified that it would not be unusual for a victim to fall asleep after a rape. Tyler also testified to statistics regarding the low rate of false reporting of rape. Kinney (D) was convicted.

■ **ISSUE**

Was the testimony regarding rape trauma syndrome admissible?

■ **DECISION AND RATIONALE**

(Dooley, J.) Yes. Trial courts may determine that expert testimony is admissible if the reliability of the evidence equals that of other technical evidence held to be admissible and the evaluation of other courts allowing admission of the evidence is complete and persuasive. Most of Tyler's testimony was of the type that has been found admissible in cases of child sexual abuse. Trial courts may take judicial notice of the admissibility of such evidence. *Daubert* and *Kumho Tire Co. v. Carmichael,* 526 U.S. 137 (1999), emphasize the gatekeeper role of the trial court in determining the admissibility of novel scientific and technical testimony. This is nothing more than an example of the traditional role of the court to determine that evidence presented to the jury is admissible. In many cases, the issue is whether a certain category of evidence is admissible, and this issue is often a recurring one. Decisions of other appellate courts may provide a basis for evaluating the reliability of a particular category of expert testimony.

The Vermont courts have not ruled on the admissibility of evidence of rape trauma syndrome. The trial court was obligated to evaluate the admissibility of Tyler's testimony, but it was not required to make findings of fact on each of the *Daubert* factors. It is enough that the trial court analyzed the testimony to determine that its reliability equaled that of other evidence that has been found admissible. The evidence of a low rate of false reporting of rape was not, however, admissible. Such testimony was tantamount to expert testimony on the victim's credibility. The error was prejudicial. But Kinney (D) made no specific objection to the testimony, and it was not plain error, so Kinney's (D) conviction will be affirmed.

Analysis:

The U.S. Supreme Court in *Daubert* and *Kumho Tire* noted that the question of the admissibility of expert opinion is a fact-specific inquiry, but that does not necessarily mean that a new hearing should be conducted every time an issue comes up. Evidentiary issues do recur, and there is no reason why trial courts should not be guided by precedent in this area. Why re-invent the wheel? The court in this case goes still further and allows trial courts to avoid conducting a *Daubert*-type analysis if the court decides a particular type of expert testimony is just as reliable, even though not identical to, evidence that has been approved by some other court, even a court of another jurisdiction.

■ CASE VOCABULARY

JUDICIAL NOTICE: A court's acceptance, for purposes of convenience and without requiring a party's proof, of a well-known and indisputable fact; the court's power to accept such a fact. Fed. R. Evid. 201.

PLAIN ERROR: An error that is so obvious and prejudicial that an appellate court should address it despite the parties' failure to raise a proper objection.

CHAPTER TEN

Authentication, Identification, and the "Best Evidence" Rule

<hr>

United States v. Stelmokas

Instant Facts: Documents from Germany and Lithuania that showed that Stelmokas (D) participated in the murder of Jews during the Second World War were introduced in a proceeding to revoke Stelmokas's (D) citizenship.

Black Letter Rule: The requirement that a document be authenticated before it may be admitted into evidence is satisfied by evidence sufficient to support a finding that the document is what its proponent claims it to be.

State v. Small

Instant Facts: Evidence of a telephone call was introduced at Small's (D) trial on the basis of testimony that the person who answered had an accent like Small's (D), identified himself by a name Small (D) used, and spoke about a debt owed to Small (D).

Black Letter Rule: A voice over the telephone may be identified as being that of a particular person if there is evidence that shows the person identified is the only one who could have uttered the speech under the circumstances.

Simms v. Dixon

Instant Facts: Simms (P) was not allowed to introduce photographs of her car taken after a collision with Dixon (D).

Black Letter Rule: A photograph is authenticated for evidentiary purposes if a witness with knowledge of the facts is able to testify that the photograph is a correct portrayal of those facts.

Wagner v. State

Instant Facts: A videotape of Wagner (D) selling drugs to an informant was introduced at Wagner's (D) trial.

Black Letter Rule: Pictorial evidence is admissible if there is an adequate foundation attesting to the accuracy of the process that produced the image.

Seiler v. Lucasfilm

Instant Facts: Seiler (P) claimed that Lucasfilm (D) infringed his copyright in characters he created, but he was unable to produce originals of the characters that were allegedly the subject of the infringement.

Black Letter Rule: When the contents of a written document or the equivalent are at issue, the contents must be proved by the original document unless the original is unavailable for some reason that is not the fault of the proponent.

United States v. Jackson

Instant Facts: Jackson (D) moved to bar introduction of copy-and-paste notes that allegedly recorded parts of online chats he participated in.

Black Letter Rule: In order to prove the contents of a writing or recording, the best evidence rule requires the introduction of either the original or an accurate duplicate of the original.

<hr>

United States v. Stelmokas

(Prosecuting Authority) v. *(Alleged War Criminal)*

100 F.3d 302 (3d Cir. 1996), *cert. denied*, 520 U.S. 1242, 117 S.Ct. 1847 (1997)

PHYSICAL EVIDENCE MUST BE AUTHENTICATED BY SUFFICIENT PROOF

■ **INSTANT FACTS** Documents from Germany and Lithuania that showed that Stelmokas (D) participated in the murder of Jews during the Second World War were introduced in a proceeding to revoke Stelmokas's (D) citizenship.

■ **BLACK LETTER RULE** The requirement that a document be authenticated before it may be admitted into evidence is satisfied by evidence sufficient to support a finding that the document is what its proponent claims it to be.

■ **PROCEDURAL BASIS**

Appeal from a judgment revoking citizenship.

■ **FACTS**

Stelmokas (D) was admitted into the United States in 1949 as a displaced person. When he applied for displaced person status, he told the investigator that he had been a teacher in Lithuania and a laborer in Germany during the Second World War. Several years later, the Government (P) brought an action to revoke Stelmokas's (D) citizenship, and to order him to surrender his certificate of naturalization. The Government (P) alleged that Stelmokas (D) had voluntarily joined a Lithuanian unit of the German armed forces during the war, the Schutzmannschaft, and that he assisted the Germans in confining and murdering Jews. The government (P) also alleged that Stelmokas (D) went to Germany when the German occupation of Lithuania ended and joined the German Air Force. After the war, the Schutzmannschaft was deemed inimical to the United States. Stelmokas (D) did not disclose his military service when he applied for admission to the United States.

At trial, the government (P) introduced records from archives in Lithuania and Germany that traced Stelmokas's (D) service in the German military. One record showed that Stelmokas (D) was in a military hospital in Germany. Court opinions showed that the record keeping of the German units was consistent with the German practice at the time. The trial court found that Stelmokas (D) had served as the commander of the guard at the Jewish ghetto. Records also showed that Stelmokas's (D) unit participated in a particular massacre, and that Stelmokas (D) was on duty at the time. Eyewitnesses testified as to the participation of Lithuanian units, but did not identify Stelmokas (D). The trial court ordered revocation of Stelmokas's (D) citizenship. Stelmokas (D) argued that the records showing his military service had not been properly authenticated. He argued that the Government (P) had not shown how the records arrived in the archives in Lithuania. He also claimed that the documents were suspicious because the Germans preserved the records of Lithuanian misconduct, while destroying the evidence of their own crimes. Stelmokas (D) also claimed that the documents from Soviet sources were suspect, because the Soviet government had a policy of discrediting the Baltic states.

■ **ISSUE**

Was the documentary evidence properly authenticated?

■ DECISION AND RATIONALE

(Greenberg, J.) Yes. The requirement that a document be authenticated before it may be admitted into evidence is satisfied by evidence sufficient to support a finding that the document is what its proponent claims it to be. Competent archival personnel in Lithuania certified the documents as accurate. Experts on European Holocaust records also testified regarding the authenticity of the documents and stated that records from Soviet sources were as reliable as records form western countries An expert also testified that the documents were genuine and not forgeries. Another expert testified that the documents were found in a place where they would be expected to be found. Stelmokas (D) introduced no evidence to discredit the authenticity of the records. It is inconceivable that the documents were created as a part of a plot to incriminate Stelmokas (D). Affirmed.

Analysis:

Proving the authenticity of physical evidence once entailed an elaborate ritual of testimony by anyone who had possession of the item up until the trial. Such testimony often accomplished little beyond the satisfaction of the technical requirement. Witnesses who testified rarely were subjected to cross-examination, unless there was some reason to question the authenticity of the item. The Federal Rules of Evidence have replaced strict, formal requirements for authentication with a more commonsensical approach. The proponent of the evidence must offer sufficient proof of authenticity, without specific requirements as to what that proof might be.

■ CASE VOCABULARY

AUTHENTICATION: Broadly, the act of proving that something (as a document) is true or genuine, especially so that it may be admitted as evidence; the condition of being so proved. Specifically, the assent to or adoption of a writing as one's own.

CHAIN OF CUSTODY: The movement and location of real evidence from the time it is obtained to the time it is presented in court; the history of a chattel's possession.

State v. Small

(Prosecuting Authority) v. (Accused Murderer)

2007 Ohio 6771 (Ohio App. 2007)

THE CONTENT OF TELEPHONE CALLS MAY BE ADMISSIBLE EVIDENCE

How do I know it's you? Because I called you.

stus.com

■ **INSTANT FACTS** Evidence of a telephone call was introduced at Small's (D) trial on the basis of testimony that the person who answered had an accent like Small's (D), identified himself by a name Small (D) used, and spoke about a debt owed to Small (D).

■ **BLACK LETTER RULE** A voice over the telephone may be identified as being that of a particular person if there is evidence that shows the person identified is the only one who could have uttered the speech under the circumstances.

■ **PROCEDURAL BASIS**

Appeal from a conviction for aggravated murder.

■ **FACTS**

Small (D) was charged with the murder of Medhin. Small's (D) wife testified that Small (D) was angry with Medhin because Medhin owed Small (D) money. Ellos, a friend of Medhin, testified that Medhin so believed his life was so in danger over a $900 debt that he asked Ellos for a gun. Ellos did not know the name of the person to whom Medhin owed the money.

On the night of the murder, Medhin made a call on Ellos's phone. He told the person who answered the call that he did not have the money. After he learned of the murder, Ellos retrieved the phone number Medhin called and called it. The person who answered had a Jamaican accent and said his name was Dominique. Ellos and Dominique discussed repayment of Medhin's debt. Small (D), too, had a Jamaican accent, and his wife testified that he used the name Dominique. Small (D) objected to the introduction of evidence of the telephone call, however, claiming it was hearsay. The state (P) claimed the telephone call was an admission of a party opponent.

■ **ISSUE**

Was evidence of the telephone call inadmissible hearsay?

■ **DECISION AND RATIONALE**

(Bryant, J.) No. A voice over the telephone may be identified as being that of a particular person if there is evidence that shows the person identified is the only one who could have uttered the speech under the circumstances. To make the statements admissible, the state (P) was required to authenticate that the person to whom Ellos spoke was Small (D). A call can be authenticated by several methods, including that a call was made to a particular person's number, or that the voice was recognized. Neither method is available here. A telephone call may be authenticated by the distinctive characteristics of the caller, and a caller may be identified by direct and circumstantial evidence that reasonably identifies the person as a party to the conversation. It is not sufficient that a caller identify himself as a particular person, but the contents of the conversation, the characteristics of the speech, or the circumstances of the call must make it improbable that the caller was anyone else.

The conversation between Ellos and Dominique contains sufficient evidence to identify Small (D) as Dominique. "Dominique" had a Jamaican accent, and claimed Medhin owed him money. Small's (D) wife testified that Small (D) was known as Dominique, had a Jamaican accent, and was owed money by Medhin. It was highly improbable that the person answering the phone was anyone other than Small (D). In addition, the call was made by Ellos, who testified that he did not know Small (D) or Small's (D) wife. The chance that an imposter would have a Jamaican accent and respond to an unexpected telephone call in a way that would incriminate Small (D) is very slim. The evidence was properly authenticated. Affirmed.

Analysis:

In discussing the general rule for authentication, the court states that the Rules of Evidence contemplate identification of a caller "because only he could utter the speech under the circumstances." When applying the rule to Small's (D) case, however, the court mentions only the improbability that someone other than Small (D) was a party to the call, not the impossibility that it was anyone other than Small (D). It may have been highly improbable that Medhin owed money to another person with a Jamaican accent who called himself Dominique, but that is not the same as saying it was impossible that anyone other than Small (D) could have had that particular conversation.

Simms v. Dixon

(Accident Victim) v. *(Driver)*

291 A.2d 184 (D.C. Ct. App. 1972)

PHOTOGRAPHS WIL BE ADMITTED IF THE PICTURE IS ACCURATE

■ **INSTANT FACTS** Simms (P) was not allowed to introduce photographs of her car taken after a collision with Dixon (D).

■ **BLACK LETTER RULE** A photograph is authenticated for evidentiary purposes if a witness with knowledge of the facts is able to testify that the photograph is a correct portrayal of those facts.

■ **PROCEDURAL BASIS**

Appeal from a verdict for Dixon (D).

■ **FACTS**

Simms (P) and Dixon (D) were involved in an automobile collision. Simms (P) claimed that Dixon (D) collided with the rear of her car when she was making a right turn. Dixon (D), however, claimed that he hit Simms (P) in the center of her car when she turned suddenly in front of him. At trial, Simms (P) attempted to introduce into evidence six photographs of her car taken after the collision. Simms (P) stated that she was introducing the photos in order to show where the impact occurred. Simms (P) stated that she would lay the proper foundation through her testimony. The trial court refused to admit the photos without the testimony of the photographer who took them. The photographer could not be located, and the trial court refused to allow the admission of the photos.

■ **ISSUE**

Were the photographs of the accident admissible without the testimony of the photographer, if a witness could corroborate their accuracy?

■ **DECISION AND RATIONALE**

(Fickling, J.) Yes. A photograph is authenticated for evidentiary purposes if a witness with knowledge of the facts is able to testify that the photograph is a correct portrayal of those facts. It is not necessary to have the photographer lay the foundation for the photographs. It is enough that photographs accurately represent the facts allegedly portrayed in them.

In this case, dimensions and perspective were not critical to the admissibility of the photos. In the absence of a finding that Simms's (P) testimony was insufficient to show that the photographs were an accurate representation of her car immediately after the accident, the photographs should have been admitted. Reversed.

Analysis:

The former requirement that photographs be authenticated by the person who took them grew out of a suspicion that photos could easily be doctored to represent anything the proponent of the evidence wanted. The photographer could testify about how the film was handled and processed, and so could banish any thought that the photo had been doctored. Of course, the photographer couldn't testify that the objects being photographed had not been altered before the pictures were taken. If the concern is for the accuracy of the representation of the relevant facts, the photographer would ordinarily not be the only one suited to testify on that issue.

■ CASE VOCABULARY

FOUNDATION: The basis on which something is supported; especially, evidence or testimony that establishes the admissibility of other evidence.

Wagner v. State

(Accused Drug Seller) v. *(Prosecuting Authority)*

707 So.2d 827 (Fla. Dist. Ct. App. 1998)

___

PICTURES ARE ADMISSIBLE IF THE PROCESS IS ACCURATE

___

■ **INSTANT FACTS** A videotape of Wagner (D) selling drugs to an informant was introduced at Wagner's (D) trial.

■ **BLACK LETTER RULE** Pictorial evidence is admissible if there is an adequate foundation attesting to the accuracy of the process that produced the image.

___

■ **PROCEDURAL BASIS**

Appeal from a conviction for selling cocaine within 1,000 feet of a school.

■ **FACTS**

A police investigator enlisted the help of an informant to make drug purchases. The informant made the purchases from a car that was equipped with a video camera. The officer gave the informant twenty dollars, turned on the recorder, and recorded the date and time. He sent the informant to make a purchase. The officer followed the informant for a time in his own vehicle, but drove away form her when she approached the purchase area. The officer did not watch the informant make a purchase, for fear of being observed. The videotape showed Wagner (D) handing something to the informant in exchange for money. The informant returned to the officer and handed him a rock of cocaine. The officer then turned off the video camera. He took the tape from the recording device and kept it in his control until it was viewed at trial. The officer explained how the recording system was operated and testified that the apparatus was in good working order during the investigation. There was no evidence that the tape had been altered or tampered with. The informant was unavailable to testify at trial. Wagner (D) claimed that the videotape was inadmissible because there was no witness who testified that the tape fairly and accurately portrayed the events depicted.

■ **ISSUE**

Was the videotape of the drug deal admissible?

■ **DECISION AND RATIONALE**

(Lawrence, J.) Yes. Pictorial evidence is admissible if there is an adequate foundation attesting to the accuracy of the process that produced the image. An adequate foundation will allow the admission of the pictorial evidence on the theory that the camera was a "silent witness" to the occurrences. The evidence may be admitted when the trial judge determines it to be reliable, after consideration of the following:

1. Evidence establishing the date and time of the recorded occurrence;
2. Any evidence of editing or tampering;
3. The operating condition and capability of the equipment as it relates to the accuracy and reliability of the image;

4. The procedure employed in preparing, testing, operating, and ensuring the security of the equipment; and

5. Testimony identifying the participants in the pictorial evidence.

In this case, convincing evidence was presented to the judge on all of the enumerated factors. Affirmed.

Analysis:

The "silent-witness" theory is used to admit several different types of evidence in addition to pictorial or film representations. The theory has been invoked to admit X-rays, DNA testing, and photo-radar devices used to catch speeding motorists, among other things. Although it is possible to alter any of the evidence produced by such a "witness," experts point out that alterations and tampering are readily detectable by those with training in the field.

■ CASE VOCABULARY

SILENT–WITNESS THEORY: A method of authenticating and admitting evidence (such as a photograph), without the need for a witness to verify its authenticity, upon a sufficient showing of the reliability of the process of producing the evidence, including proof that the evidence has not been altered.

Seiler v. Lucasfilm

(Artist) v. *(Filmmaker)*

808 F.2d 1316 (9th Cir. 1986), *cert. denied*, 484 U.S. 826, 108 S.Ct. 92 (1987)

CONTENTS OF WRITINGS MUST BE PROVED BY THE ORIGINALS

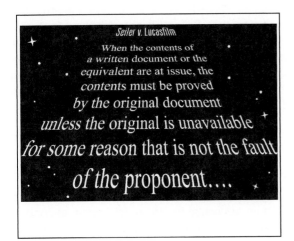

Seiler v. Lucasfilm

When the contents of a written document or the equivalent are at issue, the contents must be proved by the original document unless the original is unavailable for some reason that is not the fault of the proponent....

■ **INSTANT FACTS** Seiler (P) claimed that Lucasfilm (D) infringed his copyright in characters he created, but he was unable to produce originals of the characters that were allegedly the subject of the infringement.

■ **BLACK LETTER RULE** When the contents of a written document or the equivalent are at issue, the contents must be proved by the original document unless the original is unavailable for some reason that is not the fault of the proponent.

■ **PROCEDURAL BASIS**

Appeal from an order granting summary judgment for Lucasfilm (D).

■ **FACTS**

Seiler (P) claimed that Lucasfilm (D) used some of his concepts and illustrations in the film *The Empire Strikes Back.* Seiler (P) claimed that he created and published work in 1976 and 1977 that contained giant walking machines that were similar to those that appeared in the production by Lucasfilm (D). Seiler (P) registered his copyright in 1981, depositing with the Copyright Office "reconstructions" of his original drawings. Lucasfilm (D) claimed that Seiler (P) did not obtain his copyright in the creatures until after the release of the film, and that Seiler (P) could produce no documentation of his creatures that came before the film. Lucasfilm (D) objected to the introduction of the reconstructions of the creatures. The court found that Seiler (P) lost or destroyed the originals in bad faith and fabricated or misrepresented the nature of the reconstructions. The court held that the reconstructions were therefore inadmissible. The court granted summary judgment for Lucasfilm (D).

■ **ISSUE**

Were the reconstructions of the original drawings admissible?

■ **DECISION AND RATIONALE**

(Farris, J.) No. When the contents of a written document or the equivalent are at issue, the contents must be proved by the original document unless the original is unavailable for some reason that is not the fault of the proponent. Oral testimony about the contents of writings is subject to a great risk of error. Memory does not often allow a person to recite the precise terms of a writing, and only the writing itself, or a true copy, can provide reliable evidence. In this case, there can be no proof of "substantial similarity" unless Seiler's (P) work is compared with the work published by Lucasfilm (D). Seiler (P) claims that Lucasfilm (D) copied his originals, but has no proof of what those originals were.

The dangers of fraud in this situation are clear. Proof of the infringement claim should consist of the works that were allegedly infringed. Reconstructions that may have no resemblance to the original do not suffice as proof of infringement. Rule 1002 of the Federal Rules of Evidence states that originals

---

must be produced of a "writing, recording, or photograph." The term "writing" is defined by Fed. R. Evid. 1001 as "letters, words, numbers, or their equivalent." It would be inconsistent to apply Fed. R. Evid. 1002 to photographs or other literary works but not to artwork in other forms. The definition of writing cannot be restricted only to words and numbers, without considering "the equivalent." Affirmed.

Analysis:

The trial court made detailed findings to support its conclusion that Seiler (P) acted in bad faith. The court found that his claim that the originals had been destroyed in a flood was not credible, in large part because Seiler (P) could not prove that there ever was a flood. Seiler (P) also could not offer any other proof that the drawings he claimed were copied by Lucasfilm (D) ever existed, or were offered for sale as he claimed. In addition, Seiler (P) was found to have fabricated evidence that he did present to the court. *See Seiler v. Lucasfilm, Ltd.*, 613 F. Supp. 1253 (N.D. Cal. 1984).

■ CASE VOCABULARY

BEST–EVIDENCE RULE: The evidentiary rule providing that, to prove the contents of a writing (or a recording or a photograph), a party must produce the original writing (or a mechanical, electronic, or other familiar duplicate, such as a photocopy) unless it is unavailable, in which case secondary evidence—the testimony of the drafter or a person who read the document—may be admitted. Fed. R. Evid. 1001–1004. Also termed *documentary-originals rule; original-writing rule; original-document rule.*

INFRINGEMENT: An act that interferes with one of the exclusive rights of a patent, copyright, or trademark owner.

United States v. Jackson

(*Prosecuting Authority*) v. (*Accused Predator*)

488 F. Supp 2d 866 (D. Neb. 2007)

CHAT LOGS, TO BE ADMISSIBLE, MUST BE ACCURATELY RECORDED

■ **INSTANT FACTS** Jackson (D) moved to bar introduction of copy-and-paste notes that allegedly recorded parts of online chats he participated in.

■ **BLACK LETTER RULE** In order to prove the contents of a writing or recording, the best evidence rule requires the introduction of either the original or an accurate duplicate of the original.

■ **PROCEDURAL BASIS**

Decision on a motion in limine.

■ **FACTS**

Jackson (D) was charged with using a computer in an attempt to "persuade, induce, and entice a minor to engage in sexual activity." Magritz, an agent of the Postal Identification Service (P), identified himself as a fourteen-year-old girl in online chats with Jackson (D). Magritz and other officers set up a meeting with Jackson (D) on August 14, 2001. On that day, Jackson (D) drove to a park but did not stop. Officers went to Jackson's home and arrested him, and also seized his computers.

The U.S. (P) assigned an attorney to handle the case on November 3, 2002, but he did nothing with the case. On September 28, 2004, another attorney was assigned to the case. Jackson was indicted on February 24, 2005.

Before trial, Jackson (D) made a motion in limine prohibiting introduction into evidence of a cut-and-paste document of alleged online conversations. Both Jackson (D) and the U.S. (P) agreed that there were no original transcripts of the conversations, either because computers were missing or because instant-message conversations were not archived or maintained on the computers. The parties also agreed that there were no original computer printouts or copies on floppy discs, hard drives, or disc drives that captured the conversations. None of the conversations were saved, and Magritz testified that he wiped his computer clean during a routine upgrade a couple of years after the investigation of Jackson (D). The evidence Jackson (D) moved to bar consisted of notes made by Magritz during the investigation. Magritz testified that, at the end of each conversation, he saved it by clicking and dragging to highlight the complete conversation, and then copying and pasting the selection into a Microsoft Word document. Each conversation was saved chronologically in an ongoing log. Magritz also testified that he made another copy of the conversation for himself and added certain notes and edits to that copy. Magritz testified that it was possible to leave out words that were not properly highlighted and dragged, but he claimed that there was no error in this case because he took "great pains" to make sure everything was copied accurately before he closed the chat window. Magritz also testified that he never modified the document in any way.

A computer forensics expert, Peden, testified on behalf of Jackson (D). Peden testified that, when he conducted investigations, he always produced a bit-stream image of the hard drive, which was the forensic copy of the hard drive and the best way to confirm the chat. He also testified that the bit stream image would be the only way to see the evidence exactly as it appeared during the conversations, and that the copy-and-paste method used by Magritz was the least effective way to capture the chat log. Other more accurate methods were available, according to Peden, but they were not used. Peden also testified regarding multiple errors in the cut-and-paste exhibit that he attributed to operator error. Peden testified that there were several missing offline messages, several instances of selective cutting and pasting, time-sequence errors, missing data, and a four-minute gap in one conversation. Magritz acknowledged that not all of the offline messages appeared in the cut-and-paste document.

Jackson (D) made a motion in limine, arguing that the cut-and-paste document was not the best evidence. He claimed that his intent in agreeing to the meeting was to introduce his grandniece to the fourteen-year-old girl, and that such information was excluded from the cut-and-paste document or from a lost audiotape of a phone conversation between Jackson (D) and Magritz.

■ ISSUE

Was the cut-and-paste document admissible?

■ DECISION AND RATIONALE

(Bataillon, J.) No. In order to prove the contents of a writing or recording, the best evidence rule requires the introduction of either the original or an accurate duplicate of the original. The court finds the testimony of Peder credible, and also finds that the document offered by the U.S. (P) does not accurately represent the entire conversations between Jackson (D) and Magritz. In addition, Magritz changed the document by including his editorial comments. It is clear that the document offered does not accurately reflect the contents of the original.

Jackson (D) contends that the missing evidence contained exculpatory evidence. No hard drive is available, and because of the delay in prosecuting Jackson (D), electronic records have been erased, other evidence is missing, and Jackson cannot verify the accuracy of Magritz's document. The fact that the file sat for two years is significant and "very intentional." There was an intentional decision not to make this a priority case, not to preserve evidence, and not to prosecute the case. If charges against Jackson (D) had been promptly and properly filed, reliable evidence would likely have been available and not destroyed. The conduct by the U.S. (P) that caused the delay was at the very least extremely reckless. Motion in limine granted.

Analysis:

Conceptually, there is no difference between Magritz's copy-and-paste or cut-and-paste document (the court uses the terms interchangeably) and a handwritten copy of a paper document. While it is possible both could be accurate reflections of the contents of the original, the accuracy of either copy depends on the skill and the integrity of the person doing the copying. There is no question that a handwritten copy that contained many errors and omissions, as well as the scrivener's own commentary, would be inadmissible, and a different rule does not apply because the scrivener used a computer mouse instead of a pen.

CHAPTER ELEVEN

Privileges: General Principles

Jaffee v. Redmond

Instant Facts: Redmond (D) sought psychotherapy after being involved in a shooting and claimed that the records of her treatment were privileged.

Black Letter Rule: Evidentiary privileges are justified by an imperative need for confidence and trust in a relationship, if that privilege also will serve public ends.

In Re: Grand Jury Subpoena, Judith Miller

Instant Facts: Miller (D) and Cooper (D), reporters, were held in civil contempt when they refused to respond to a grand jury subpoena that asked for the name of a confidential source.

Black Letter Rule: There is no First Amendment privilege that protects journalists from providing evidence to a grand jury.

Morales v. Portuondo

Instant Facts: Morales (P) was convicted of murder, but the true killer had told a priest and a lawyer that Morales (P) was not involved in the crime.

Black Letter Rule: An assertion of privilege may not bar the admission of evidence if the exclusion of the otherwise privileged evidence would be fundamentally unfair.

Jaffee v. Redmond

(Administrator of Estate) v. *(Police Officer)*

518 U.S. 1, 116 S.Ct. 1923 (1996)

PSYCHOTHERAPIST–PATIENT PRIVILEGE IS RECOGNIZED

■ **INSTANT FACTS** Redmond (D) sought psychotherapy after being involved in a shooting and claimed that the records of her treatment were privileged.

■ **BLACK LETTER RULE** Evidentiary privileges are justified by an imperative need for confidence and trust in a relationship, if that privilege also will serve public ends.

■ **PROCEDURAL BASIS**

Appeal from an order of the Seventh Circuit Court of Appeals reversing and remanding for a new trial.

■ **FACTS**

Redmond (D), a police officer, was involved in an incident in which she shot and killed Allen. After the incident, she received extensive counseling from a licensed clinical social worker. Jaffee (P), the administrator of Allen's estate, filed suit against Redmond (D) in U.S. District Court. The suit alleged that Redmond (D) violated Allen's constitutional rights by using excessive force. During discovery, Jaffee (P) learned of Redmond's (D) sessions with the clinical social worker. Jaffee (P) sought access to the notes of those sessions, for use in cross-examination. Redmond (D) claimed that the notes were protected from disclosure by a psychotherapist-patient privilege. The court denied the claim of privilege, but Redmond (D) did not comply with the order to release the notes. The judge instructed the jury that Redmond (D) had no legal justification for refusing to turn over the notes, and that the jury could presume that the contents of the notes would have been unfavorable to Redmond (D). The jury entered a verdict for Jaffee (P) against Redmond (D).

The court of appeals reversed and remanded for a new trial, holding that "reason and experience" compelled the recognition of a psychotherapist-patient privilege. The court found that the relationship between a psychotherapist and patient is unique and depends upon the ability to communicate freely. The court also noted that all fifty states have adopted some form of privilege for communications to a psychotherapist. The privilege would not apply, however, according to the court of appeals, if in the interests of justice the evidentiary need for disclosure of the communication outweighed the patient's privacy interests.

■ **ISSUE**

Is there an evidentiary privilege protecting communications to a psychotherapist?

■ **DECISION AND RATIONALE**

(Stevens, J.) Yes. Evidentiary privileges are justified by an imperative need for confidence and trust in a relationship, if that privilege also will serve public ends. A psychotherapist-patient privilege meets that requirement. Effective psychotherapy depends upon an atmosphere of trust in which the patient is willing to make a free and frank disclosure of facts, emotions, memories, and fears. Disclosure of matters discussed during psychotherapy could cause embarrassment or disgrace. The mere possibility of disclosure may impede the trust necessary for successful treatment. A privilege for psychotherapist communications also serves the public by facilitating the treatment of those who suffer from a mental or emotional problem. The benefits of the privilege far outweigh the likely evidentiary benefit that would result from denying the privilege. If the privilege were rejected, there would be a chilling effect on the communications between psychotherapists and their patients, particularly when it is obvious that the matter for which treatment is sought will result in litigation. Much of the evidence that litigants seek would not come into being.

All fifty states and the District of Columbia now recognize some form of the psychotherapist-patient privilege. Policy decisions of the states are an important factor in deciding whether federal courts should recognize a new privilege. Denial of the federal privilege would undermine the value of the state privilege. The psychotherapist-patient privilege was one of the nine specific privileges recommended by the Advisory Committee for the Federal Rules of Evidence when it proposed privilege rules. When the Senate rejected the proposed draft that included the enumerated privileges, the Senate Judiciary Committee explicitly stated that its action should not be read as disapproving recognition of a psychotherapist-patient privilege.

The privilege that extends to licensed psychiatrists and psychologists should also extend to communications made to licensed social workers in the course of psychotherapy. Social workers provide a significant amount of mental health treatment, so the reasons for recognizing the privilege apply equally to communications with social workers. The court of appeals was wrong to make the privilege contingent on a balancing of interests. If the privilege is to be effective, the participants in the conversation must be able to predict whether a particular discussion will be privileged. Affirmed.

■ **DISSENT**

(Scalia, J.) A privilege will result in occasional injustice, as reliable and probative evidence will be excluded. It is not clear that psychotherapists play such an essential role in mental health that a privilege is necessary. In addition, it is also not clear that individuals will be deterred from seeking therapy by a lack of privilege. A person who wishes to receive the benefits of psychotherapy should also accept the adverse consequences of telling the truth.

The majority's conclusion that the privilege should extend to social workers is even less persuasive. The training required of social workers is less rigorous than that for the other professionals to whom a privilege has been accorded.

Analysis:

Privileges are not favored, because they act as an absolute bar to evidence that is often highly probative. The scope of a privilege is construed strictly, because of this disfavor. This strict construction, however, often ignores the reality of the way many professions are practiced. For example, it is not unusual for nurses or other medical professionals besides physicians to provide much of the care a patient receives. There would seem to be no logic to deny the scope of the privilege to communications with other professionals, just because they are not, strictly speaking, "physicians."

■ **CASE VOCABULARY**

PSYCHOTHERAPIST–PATIENT PRIVILEGE: A privilege that a person can invoke to prevent the disclosure of a communication made in the course of diagnosis or treatment of a mental or emotional condition by or at the direction of a psychotherapist. The privilege can be overcome under certain conditions, as when the examination is ordered by the court.

In Re: Grand Jury Subpoena, Judith Miller

(Reporter)

397 F.3d 964 (D.C. Cir.), *cert denied* 545 U.S. 1150 (2005)

JOURNALISTS MUST REVEAL THEIR SOURCES TO GRAND JURIES

■ **INSTANT FACTS** Miller (D) and Cooper (D), reporters, were held in civil contempt when they refused to respond to a grand jury subpoena that asked for the name of a confidential source.

■ **BLACK LETTER RULE** There is no First Amendment privilege that protects journalists from providing evidence to a grand jury.

■ **PROCEDURAL BASIS**

Appeal from orders finding Miller (D) and Cooper (D) in civil contempt.

■ **FACTS**

In his 2003 State of the Union address, President Bush stated that the British government had learned that Iraqi President Saddam Hussein had recently tried to buy significant quantities of uranium from Africa. A few months later, the New York Times published a piece by former Ambassador Wilson, in which he stated that he had been sent to Niger in 2002 by the CIA to investigate whether Iraq had attempted to purchase uranium from Niger, and that he found no credible evidence of such an attempt.

Shortly after Ambassador Wilson published his piece, Novak, a columnist, published a column in which he stated that two "senior administration officials" told him that the selection of Wilson for the Niger investigation was made at the suggestion of Wilson's wife, Plame. Novak described Plame as a CIA "operative on weapons of mass destruction." After Novak's column, other media outlets reported that reporters had been told that Wilson's wife worked for the CIA, monitoring weapons of mass destruction, and that she was involved in her husband's selection for the mission to Niger. Cooper (D) wrote one such article, which was published by Time.com (D).

The Department of Justice (P) began an investigation into whether government employees violated federal law by the unauthorized disclosure of the identity of a CIA agent. In cooperation with that investigation, a grand jury issued a subpoena to Cooper (D) and Time.com (D) seeking all documents that related to Cooper's (D) story about Wilson. Another similar subpoena was issued to Miller (D). Cooper (D), Time.com (D), and Miller (D) refused to comply, claiming that the information sought was privileged. The district court found the refusals to comply to be without just cause, and held all three in civil contempt.

■ **ISSUE**

Is there a constitutional or common law privilege that allows reporters to refuse to divulge their sources?

■ **DECISION AND RATIONALE**

(Sentelle, J.) No. There is no First Amendment privilege that protects journalists from providing evidence to a grand jury. It is not certain that there is a common law privilege but, even assuming the existence of such a common law privilege, that privilege may be overcome by an appropriate showing. In the case of *Branzburg v. Hayes,* 408 U.S. 665 (1972), the Supreme Court considered a claim of constitutional

---

privilege and rejected such a claim on facts materially indistinguishable from this case. In *Branzburg,* a reporter was subpoenaed by a grand jury after he wrote an article describing the manufacture of illegal drugs. The reporter refused to identify the persons he saw engaged in the drug manufacture, and he was held in contempt. The Supreme Court recognized that a grand jury's subpoena power is essential to its task. Grand juries and courts operate under the principle that the public has a right to every person's evidence, unless that evidence is protected by a constitutional, common law, or statutory privilege. The Court stated that it could not seriously entertain the notion that the First Amendment protects a journalist's agreement to conceal the criminal conduct of a source on the theory that it is better to write about a crime than to do something about it. The Supreme Court went on to say that there was likewise no privilege in situations in which a source is not engaged in criminal conduct but has information suggesting criminal conduct by others. The public's interest in possible future news about crime does not take precedence over the public's interest in pursuing and prosecuting those crimes reported to the press. The Court recognized that the press is not required to publish information that it has, but the right to withhold news is not equivalent to a First Amendment exemption from the duty of all citizens to furnish information to a grand jury. Cooper (D), Time.com (D), and Miller (D) have been asked for some distinction between their cases and *Branzburg,* but have been unable to supply one. The Supreme Court has spoken on this issue: there is no First Amendment privilege to refuse to provide evidence to a grand jury.

Cooper (D), Time.com (D), and Miller (D) argue that, even if there is no First Amendment privilege protecting their confidential source information, the court should recognize such a privilege under federal common law. They claim that, even though such a privilege did not exist in 1972 when *Branzburg* was decided, "much has changed" in the intervening years. The court is not of one mind on the existence of a common law privilege, but all members of the court agree that, if there is such a privilege, it is not absolute and may be overcome by the proper showing. If the privilege applies here, it has been overcome. Affirmed.

■ CONCURRENCE

(Sentelle, J.) Reporters refusing to testify before a grand jury about confidential sources have no common law privilege beyond the protection against harassing grand juries conducting groundless investigations available to all other citizens. This conclusion is based on precedent, policy, and the separation of powers. *Branzburg* is as dispositive of the question of a common law privilege as it is of the question of a constitutional privilege. The Court discussed the privilege question in common law terms, and noted that courts consistently refused to recognize the existence of a privilege allowing a reporter to refuse to reveal the sources of information. It is indisputable that the Supreme Court rejected a common law privilege, especially since it would have made little sense for the Court to consider the constitutional issue that it would not have needed to consider if there had been a common law privilege.

The argument that the courts have the authority to adopt a common law privilege despite the *Branzburg* precedent is based on Fed. R. Evid. 501. The Rule, which was enacted after *Branzburg,* states that privileges in federal criminal cases "shall be governed by the principles of the common law.... " The language of Rule 501 merely states the law as it existed prior to, and at the time of, *Branzburg.* Thus, the enactment of Rule 501 does not work any change in the law that allows the court to depart from the clear precedent in *Branzburg.*

Cooper (D), Time.com (D), and Miller (D) point out that, at the time of *Branzburg,* only seventeen states had laws to protect journalists from forced disclosure of sources, but now, thirty-one states and the District of Columbia have such laws. The adoption of the privilege by legislatures is instructive as to how the federal government should proceed if it is to adopt the privilege. The statutes differ greatly as to the scope of the privilege, and the identity of the persons entitled to claim the privilege. Defining the persons entitled to the privilege is a vexing issue. As the Court noted in *Branzburg,* freedom of the press is not confined to newspapers or periodicals, but includes every sort of publication. Is a distinction to be drawn between a reporter for a large magazine or newspaper and a person with a desktop printer producing a newsletter, or a blogger? Could such a distinction be drawn that is consistent with a broadly granted personal right? If so, it would be possible for a government official who wishes to leak information unlawfully to have a trusted friend set up a web log and then leak to him under a promise of confidentiality. State laws deal with this question differently. Some states are restrictive, and would seem to apply only to the "established" press, while others are more inclusive and apply to any medium of communication. If the privilege is extended only to a defined group, is there a danger of creating a "licensed" or "established" press? Conversely, if the privilege is extended too broadly, are the legitimate investigative ends of grand juries defeated?

A decision that requires the resolution of so many difficult policy questions smacks of legislation. The creation of a reporter's privilege, if it is to be done at all, looks more like a legislative than an adjudicative function.

■ CONCURRENCE

(Henderson, J.) Any federal common law privilege for reporters that may exist is not absolute. The court should proceed cautiously when creating privileges. The legislature is the more appropriate institution to reconcile the competing interests that inform any reporter's privilege to withhold information from a grand jury.

■ CONCURRENCE

(Tatel, J.) The balance in this case favors compelling the testimony. The consensus of forty-nine states, the District of Columbia, and even the Department of Justice, would require protection of reporters' sources if the leak at issue were either less harmful or more newsworthy. Fed. R. Evid. 501 delegates the congressional authority to create privileges to the courts, even if Congress would be the more appropriate institution.

A common law analysis starts with the interests that call for recognition of a privilege. Reporters depend upon an atmosphere of confidence and trust. If litigants and investigators could easily discover reporters' sources, the press's truth-seeking function would be severely impaired. The likely evidentiary benefit of denying the privilege is modest, but the public harm that would come from undermining source relationships would be immense. Miller (D) testified that her articles on terrorism relied on information from confidential sources at high levels of the government. Cooper (D) testified that his stories on White House policy would have been impossible without confidentiality. Such stories show the role of the press as the constitutionally chosen means for keeping officials responsible to the people, so reason and experience support protecting crucial newsgathering methods.

Turning to the consensus among the states, there is undisputed evidence that forty-nine states and the District of Columbia offer at least qualified protection to reporters' sources. Given these state laws, denial of the federal privilege would frustrate the purpose of state legislation by exposing confidences protected under state law to discovery in federal courts. In addition, federal authorities also favor recognizing a reporters' privilege. Federal courts have limited discovery of reporters' sources in civil and criminal litigation. Justice Department guidelines also establish a federal policy of protecting the news media from compulsory process that might impair news gathering.

The shift in favor of the privilege since *Branzburg* means that the claim of privilege should be assessed in light of "reason and experience" today. Privilege rules may require refashioning as experience may dictate, and Rule 501 shows an affirmative intention not to freeze the law of privilege but to leave the door open to change. It does not matter that unconventional forms of journalism may raise definitional problems later. A rule that authorizes the recognition of new privileges on a case-by-case basis makes it appropriate to define the privilege in a similar manner. While any meaningful privilege must encompass Cooper (D) and Miller (D), future opinions can elaborate more refined contours of the privilege.

The protection for source identities cannot be absolute. Courts should not protect sources whose leaks harm national security while providing minimal benefit to the public debate. Of course, a leak's value may far exceed its harm. The approach should be to strike a balance between the public's interest in the free flow of information and the public's interest in effective law enforcement and the fair administration of justice. Specifically, the court should weigh the public's interest in compelling disclosure, measured by the harm caused by the leak, against he public's interest in newsgathering, measured by the leaked information's value. The authorities may thus obtain evidence when the leaked information does more harm than good.

Cooper (D), Time.com (D), and Miller (D) argue that the qualified privilege does not provide the certainty their work requires because sources are unlikely to disclose information without a prior guarantee of secrecy. Reporters will be unable to provide such advance guarantees, because they cannot balance the harm of a leak against its news value until they know what the leaked information will be. Reporters, however, are not the ones who must do the balancing—sources are. The point of the qualified privilege is to create disincentives for sources. As with other recipients of confidential information, a reporter can do no more than alert sources to the limits of confidentiality. The clash of fundamental interest makes a categorical privilege inappropriate.

Applying these standards to the case at bar, the leak was a serious matter. It may have jeopardized Plame's activities, and also placed those from whom she obtained information in danger. The leak of her employment had marginal news value. While Plame's relationship with the CIA could bear on Wilson's selection for the Niger trip and on his credibility, the news value of that information, when compared to the damage of undermining covert intelligence gathering, does not justify making the identity of the leaker privileged.

Analysis:

Unlike Cooper (D), Miller (D) did not publish a story identifying Plame, but was subpoenaed because she was thought to have evidence relating to the leak. She had access to top government officials, and had done extensive reporting on the decision to go to war in Iraq. In a notebook that contained Miller's (D) notations about Iraq and nuclear weapons, the name "Valerie Flame [sic]" appeared. This case makes clear the complex interplay among privilege, journalism, and First Amendment rights.

Morales v. Portuondo

(Convicted Murderer) v. *(Prison Warden)*
154 F. Supp. 2d 706 (S.D.N.Y. 2001)

DUE PROCESS MAY DEFEAT CLAIMS OF PRIVILEGE

Father, I have a little problem.

Why does "little" never mean "little"?

stus.com

■ **INSTANT FACTS** Morales (P) was convicted of murder, but the true killer had told a priest and a lawyer that Morales (P) was not involved in the crime.

■ **BLACK LETTER RULE** An assertion of privilege may not bar the admission of evidence if the exclusion of the otherwise privileged evidence would be fundamentally unfair.

■ PROCEDURAL BASIS

Decision on a petition for a writ of habeas corpus.

■ FACTS

In 1987, Morales (P) was charged and convicted of murder. A few days after his trial, another man, Fornes, told at least four other people, including a priest, a Legal Aid attorney, the mother of Morales's (P) co-defendant, and Morales's (P) attorney, that he and two others had committed the crime, and that Morales (P) was innocent. Fornes invoked his Fifth Amendment privilege and refused to testify at a post-trial motion to set aside the verdict. The statements he gave to Morales's (P) attorney and the mother of his co-defendant were ruled inadmissible hearsay.

Fornes spoke to the priest informally, not as a part of a formal confession. The priest encouraged Fornes to go before the court and tell what happened. The priest granted Fornes absolution at the end of their conversation. The priest accompanied Fornes to the office of a Legal Aid attorney and told the attorney that Fornes had something he wanted to "get off his chest." Fornes told the attorney that he had committed the crime. The attorney advised him not to confess in court to the crime. The attorney said that his confession would not necessarily exonerate the two defendants, but would only cause problems for Fornes. Fornes followed his attorney's advice and refused to testify.

Fornes was killed in an accident in 1997. In 2000, the priest he spoke with executed an affidavit in which he described the statements made to him by Fornes. The priest stated that he had concluded that his conversation with Fornes was not a formal confession. In the unique circumstances of the case, the priest concluded that he was permitted to disclose the statements. Morales (P) brought a petition for a writ of habeas corpus, claiming that exclusion of the statements of the priest and the lawyer violated his due process rights.

■ ISSUE

Were the statements made by the true killer to the priest and the lawyer barred by privilege?

■ DECISION AND RATIONALE

(Chin, J.) No. Privileged communications may not bar the admission of evidence if the exclusion of the privileged evidence would be fundamentally unfair. The statements must first be evaluated under the normal rules of admissibility. The statements here do not qualify as statements against penal interest, but they are admissible because they are vital to Morales's (P) defense, Fornes is unavailable, and the statements bear sufficient indicia of reliability. The statements were made to four different people in four different circumstances, and the circumstances show that Fornes had no motive to lie. Fornes felt genuine remorse and guilt about what he had done, and there was evidence to corroborate his statements.

Evidentiary privileges may be waived by the person who makes the privileged statements. In this case, Fornes made his statements not only to the priest and to the lawyer, but to others as well. The priest advised Fornes to acknowledge his responsibility for the crime, and Fornes intended to do that. He acted in a manner inconsistent with a desire to maintain the privilege, and he thus effectively waived that privilege. In addition, his conversation with the priest was not a formal confession, but more like a "heart-to-heart" talk. The priest concluded that he was free, after Fornes died, to disclose the conversation. His ecclesiastical superiors also approved his decision to disclose the conversation.

The conversations Fornes had with his attorney are also not privileged. Although privileges generally survive the death of the person making the privileged statement, the privilege may be waived if the client voluntarily discloses the communication to a third party, or if the communication is made in the presence of a third party in whom the client has no reasonable expectation of confidentiality. Although there is nothing to indicate that Fornes acted in a manner that showed that he waived the privilege, fundamental fairness demands that the statements be admitted. When Fornes spoke with his lawyer, he was merely repeating what he had told others. Under these circumstances, the attorney-client privilege should not bar the evidence of Fornes's statements to his lawyer. Petition for habeas corpus relief granted.

Analysis:

The result reached here was no doubt made easier by the fact that Fornes was dead, and there was no one to object to the rejection of the privilege claims. The priest concluded that he was not bound by any promise of confidentiality. The manner in which the court dealt with the statements to the lawyer, however, is a little more troubling. If Fornes were alive, his statements would not only have exonerated Morales, but they would have incriminated Fornes. Query whether Morales's (P) right to present a complete defense should trump Fornes's right to have his conversations with his attorney kept confidential.

■ CASE VOCABULARY

HABEAS CORPUS: [Latin, "that you have the body."] A writ employed to bring a person before a court, most frequently to ensure that the party's imprisonment or detention is not illegal (*habeas corpus ad subjiciendum*). In addition to being used to test the legality of an arrest or commitment, the writ may be used to obtain review of (1) the regularity of the extradition process, (2) the right to or amount of bail, or (3) the jurisdiction of a court that has imposed a criminal sentence.

CHAPTER TWELVE

The Lawyer–Client Privilege and the Privilege Against Self–Incrimination

People v. Gionis

Instant Facts: Gionis (D) made incriminating statements to Lueck, an attorney who did not represent Gionis (D).

Black Letter Rule: The attorney-client privilege applies only to statements made to an attorney in his or her professional capacity, for the purpose of seeking legal advice.

Howell v. Joffe

Instant Facts: Lynch (D) sought a protective order against the introduction of comments she and Kagan (D) left on Howell's (P) voicemail.

Black Letter Rule: A conversation is protected by the attorney-client privilege if the conversation originated in confidence that it would not be disclosed, was made to an attorney in his or her legal capacity to secure legal advice or services, and was kept confidential.

Koch Foods of Alabama, LLC v. General Electric Capital Corp.

Instant Facts: Koch Foods (P) included a privileged e-mail in a response to a discovery request, and GE Capital (D) claimed that Koch (P) inadvertently waived the privilege.

Black Letter Rule: The question of whether the attorney-client privilege has been waived is determined by a balancing test that looks at the reasonableness of the precautions taken to prevent the disclosure, the time taken to correct the error, the scope of the discovery, the extent of the disclosure, and the overriding issue of fairness.

Swidler & Berlin v. United States

Instant Facts: Swidler & Berlin (D) claimed that notes of a meeting with a deceased client were privileged.

Black Letter Rule: The attorney-client privilege survives the death of the client.

United States v. Zolin

Instant Facts: The Government (P) urged the trial court to undertake an *in camera* review of evidence before making a ruling that the evidence was protected by the attorney-client privilege.

Black Letter Rule: The court should undertake an *in camera* review of evidence to determine if the crime-fraud exception will bar a claim of attorney-client privilege only if there is a factual showing adequate to support a good faith belief that a review of the materials may reveal evidence that establishes the claim that the exception applies.

In Re: Grand Jury Investigation [Rowland]

Instant Facts: George (D), former counsel for the Governor (D), claimed attorney-client privilege and refused to testify about the substance of her conversations with the Governor (D).

Black Letter Rule: The attorney-client privilege applies to government attorneys to the same extent that it applies to private attorneys.

United States v. Hubbell

Instant Facts: Hubbell (D) produced documents pursuant to a subpoena and a grant of immunity, and the Independent Counsel (P) used information in those documents to indict Hubbell (D) for other crimes.

Black Letter Rule: The Fifth Amendment privilege against self-incrimination protects a witness both from being compelled to answer questions about the existence of sources of potentially incriminating evidence and from responding to a subpoena that seeks discovery of those sources.

People v. Gionis

(Prosecuting Authority) v. *(Accused Conspirator)*

9 Cal.4th 1196 (1995)

PRIVILEGED STAEMENTS ARE THOSE MADE TO OBTAIN LEGAL ADVICE

■ **INSTANT FACTS** Gionis (D) made incriminating statements to Lueck, an attorney who did not represent Gionis (D).

■ **BLACK LETTER RULE** The attorney-client privilege applies only to statements made to an attorney in his or her professional capacity, for the purpose of seeking legal advice.

■ **PROCEDURAL BASIS**

Appeal from an order of the court of appeal reversing a conviction.

■ **FACTS**

Lueck was an attorney. In the course of his practice, he referred clients to Gionis (D), a physician, for medical evaluations. One night, Gionis (D) called Lueck and asked him to come over to his house. Gionis (D) had just been served with divorce papers and said that he needed someone to talk to because he was upset. Lueck agreed to meet with Gionis (D) after making it clear that he would not be willing to having any involvement as a lawyer in the dissolution case. When Lueck arrived at Gionis's (D) home, Gionis (D) was very upset. He showed Lueck a declaration in support of an order to show cause and indicated he would like to change the venue of the dissolution case from Orange County to Los Angeles County. Gionis's (D) wife was the daughter of the actor John Wayne, one of Orange County's most famous residents. Lueck said that he thought a change of venue would be a good idea, but did not offer to do it. Lueck also told Gionis (D) to retain a good attorney quickly. Gionis (D) also showed Lueck some holes in a wall and a damaged closet door. Gionis (D) said that the altercation that resulted in the holes was nothing compared to what he was capable of doing. Gionis (D) told Lueck that his wife did not know how easy it would be for Gionis (D) "to pay somebody to really take care of her." Lueck told Gionis (D) that Gionis (D) would be the primary suspect if something were to happen to his wife. Gionis (D) said that he would wait until "an opportune time and circumstances" so that he would not be a suspect.

A few months later, Gionis (D) came to Lueck's office with some papers prepared by his attorney in the marriage dissolution case. Gionis (D) told Lueck that his wife was attempting to keep him from his daughter at her baptism, and Gionis's (D) attorney was unavailable. Lueck went with Gionis (D) to court on an *ex parte* basis, but the judge said that arrangements had already been made. Lueck was paid $750 for his services.

Approximately one year later, Gionis's (D) wife and another man were attacked. Gionis (D) was charged with conspiracy, on the theory that he hired the assailants. Gionis's (D) statements to Lueck were admitted, despite Gionis's (D) claim that the statements were privileged communications. Gionis (D) was convicted, but the court of appeal reversed his conviction, holding that the statements to Lueck were privileged communications.

■ **ISSUE**

Were the statements to Lueck protected by the attorney-client privilege, even though he made it clear he could not represent the defendant?

■ DECISION AND RATIONALE

(Baxter, J.) No. The attorney-client privilege applies only to statements made to an attorney in his or her professional capacity, for the purpose of seeking legal advice. The privilege does not apply to all discussions of a legal matter with an attorney. The conversation must be for the purpose of seeking legal advice from the attorney in his or her professional capacity. It does not matter whether the attorney was ultimately not hired to represent the client. The privilege does not apply to statements made after the attorney declines employment. A client who continues to speak after it is clear that the attorney will not represent him or her, for whatever reason, does not need or deserve the protection of the privilege.

In this case, it is clear that Lueck did not go to Gionis's (D) home as an attorney. Lueck was a friend of Gionis (D), and the two shared a business relationship. Before he went to Gionis's (D) house, Lueck made it clear that he would not represent Gionis (D) in the dissolution action. It does not matter that some legal matters were discussed. Lueck advised Gionis (D) to retain an attorney and made it clear that he would not become involved in the matter. There is no evidence that Gionis (D) did not understand Lueck's position. His insistence on speaking to Lueck after it was made clear to him that Lueck would not be involved in the action gives rise to the reasonable inference that Gionis (D) wanted to speak with him as a friend, not as an attorney. The conclusion is not undermined by Lueck's agreement to represent Gionis (D) on a one-time, emergency basis. Statements made to Lueck in the course of that representation were properly held to be privileged. Reversed.

■ CONCURRENCE IN PART, DISSENT IN PART

(Kennard, J.) The determination of whether an individual is seeking advice from an attorney in the attorney's "professional capacity" depends on the circumstances of the case. In rendering the legal advice to seek a change of venue, Lueck was acting in his professional capacity as an attorney. Those statements were irrelevant to the prosecution, so their admission was harmless error. When Gionis (D) made the inculpatory statements to Lueck, however, the conversation had nothing to do with the change of venue. The statements were not made while Gionis (D) was seeking legal advice on any other matter. Those statements were not privileged.

■ DISSENT

(Mosk, J.) The existence of the privilege does not depend on whether an attorney accepts or refuses employment. It depends on whether the client was consulting the attorney for legal advice. The nature of the relationship between Lueck and Gionis (D) showed that Gionis (D) did not consult him as a friend, but as an attorney. Nothing indicates that Gionis (D) intended his conversations with Lueck to be anything other than confidential. Moreover, Lueck's role as an attorney and his status as a friend cannot neatly be separated once Lueck agreed to represent Gionis (D) at the *ex parte* hearing. Attorneys often hear things from clients that are not strictly law-related. Courts do not distinguish between privileged and non-privileged statements made during the same communication.

Analysis:

Attorneys often have friends who are not lawyers. Legal advice or opinions given to those friends on a casual or informal basis—sometimes called a "curbstone opinion"—can cause serious problems. Some courts have held those informal opinions a sufficient basis for a legal malpractice action. In this case, the question of confidentiality is a complex one. Clearly, some of what Gionis (D) said to Lueck was confidential. The question is, which statements qualify for the privilege and which do not? The *per se* rule urged by Justice Mosk's dissent has the advantage of making a clear delineation for the attorney, the client, and the courts.

■ CASE VOCABULARY

ATTORNEY–CLIENT PRIVILEGE: The client's right to refuse to disclose and to prevent any other person from disclosing confidential communications between the client and the attorney.

SHOW–CAUSE ORDER: An order directing a party to appear in court and explain why the party took (or failed to take) some action or why the court should or should not grant some relief.

Howell v. Joffe

(Abuse Victim) v. *(Priest)*
483 F. Supp 2d 659 (N.D. Ill. 2007)

NOT ALL STATEMENTS MADE TO A LAWYER ARE CONFIDENTIAL

Wanna be my new lawyer? The only job criteria is that you know how to hang up a phone.

stus.com

■ **INSTANT FACTS** Lynch (D) sought a protective order against the introduction of comments she and Kagan (D) left on Howell's (P) voicemail.

■ **BLACK LETTER RULE** A conversation is protected by the attorney-client privilege if the conversation originated in confidence that it would not be disclosed, was made to an attorney in his or her legal capacity to secure legal advice or services, and was kept confidential.

■ **PROCEDURAL BASIS**

Decision on a motion for a protective order.

■ **FACTS**

Howell (P) brought suit against Joffe (D) and St. Mary's School (D), alleging that he had been sexually abused by Joffe (D) while Joffe (D) was associated with St. Mary's (D). Lynch (D), an attorney for the Diocese that operated St. Mary's (D), contacted Howell (P) by telephone. She left a voicemail message saying that she was "getting back" to Howell (P). The voicemail recording then had a clicking sound on it, as if Lynch (D) were attempting to hang up, and then Lynch (D) was recorded conversing with Kagan (D), a representative of the Diocese. Lynch (D) and Kagan (D) commented about Howell's (P) voicemail recording, and Kagan (D) made comments about Howell's (P) voice. Lynch (D) and Kagan (D) discussed how Howell (P) compared to others who had made allegations of sexual abuse, and Kagan (D) expressed an opinion about the sexual abuse victims allegedly targeted by Joffe (D).

Howell (P) alleged that the voicemail recording caused him to suffer severe emotional anguish, and he brought claims against Lynch (D) and Kagan (D) for negligent and intentional infliction of emotional distress. Lynch (D) and Kagan (D) sought a protective order barring introduction of the voicemail recording, on the grounds that the conversation was protected by the attorney-client privilege.

■ **ISSUE**

Was the conversation privileged?

■ **DECISION AND RATIONALE**

(Bucklo, J.) Yes. A conversation is protected by the attorney-client privilege if the conversation originated in confidence that it would not be disclosed, was made to an attorney in his or her legal capacity to secure legal advice or services, and was kept confidential. The beginning part of the message, in which Lynch (D) left a message for Howell (P), is not covered by the privilege. The part of the conversation after the "clicking" noise was for the purpose of securing legal advice. Most of the comments made after that are an analysis of the sexual abuse claimants, and imply an analysis of which claims have merit. While some of the conversation—such as when Howell's (D) vocal characteristics are commented upon—are not obviously related to evaluating claims or seeking legal advice, the primary purpose of the conversation was to share information protected by the privilege. Even though there are some extraneous comments, it cannot be concluded that they are somehow unprotected. The purpose of the privilege is to encourage attorney-client communications, so that parsing out different elements of the conversation might undermine a client's ability to speak with his or her attorney without carefully considering each sentence or word.

Kagan (D) and Lynch (D) both testified that they believed that the telephone call had ended when Lynch (D) left her message and placed the receiver back on the telephone cradle. They both believed that they were speaking in confidence and that Howell (P) could not hear what they were saying. Howell (P) argues that they intended for him to hear the conversation in order to cause him emotional distress. This is only an allegation, and Howell (P) has introduced no evidence to support it. Lynch (D) and Kagan (D) have sustained their burden to show that the conversation was intended to be confidential.

The final question is whether leaving the recording on the voicemail was a waiver of the privilege. Lynch (D) and Kagan (D) have shown that any disclosure was inadvertent and unintentional. Illinois courts are split on the issue of whether an inadvertent disclosure can amount to a waiver of the privilege. While some Illinois courts have adopted a rule that inadvertent disclosure can never be a waiver of privilege, it is most likely that the Illinois courts would adopt a balancing test. The question of an inadvertent waiver of privilege would be answered by looking at the reasonableness of the precautions taken to prevent the disclosure, the time it took to correct the error, the scope of the discovery, the extent of the disclosure, and the overriding issue of fairness. Under this balancing test, Lynch (D) and Kagan (D) have not waived the privilege. They both believed that Lynch (D) replaced the receiver, and although this was an error, there is no reason to believe it was not an innocent (and not uncommon) mistake. In addition, Lynch (D) testified—and Howell (P) does not contradict her—that she asserted privilege the same day she learned that Howell (P) had a copy of the recording. The scope of the discovery, the extent of the disclosure, and the overriding issue of fairness also support a finding of privilege. Lynch (D) and Kagan (D) did not waive their right to assert privilege over the privileged portion of the recording. Because the conversation was privileged, it follows that Lynch (D) and Kagan (D) did not intend for Howell (P) to hear it. The finding of privilege therefore bars Howell's (P) intentional infliction of emotional distress claim. Motion for a protective order granted.

Analysis:

Courts are not going to allow every communication between an attorney and a client to be privileged. Apart from the basic requirement that the communication be made to secure legal advice or services, the parties to the conversation must make some efforts on their own to guard the confidentiality of what they say. A lawyer may give legal advice in many situations in which confidentiality is not expected (such as the legal advice often solicited in social situations), even though the same conversation in a different context—an office consultation, for example—would be intended to be confidential.

Koch Foods of Alabama, LLC v. General Electric Capital Corp.

(Privilege Claimant) v. (Waiver Proponent)

531 F. Supp. 2d 1318 (M.D. Ala. 2008)

INADVERTENT WAIVER OF THE ATTORNEY–CLIENT PRIVILEGE DEPENDS ON THE TOTALITY OF THE CIRCUMSTANCES

I'm going to apply a balancing test-- On the one hand, I want to punish you for carelessness. On the other hand, I feel sorry for your client that he has you for his lawyer.

stus.com

■ **INSTANT FACTS** Koch Foods (P) included a privileged e-mail in a response to a discovery request, and GE Capital (D) claimed that Koch (P) inadvertently waived the privilege.

■ **BLACK LETTER RULE** The question of whether the attorney-client privilege has been waived is determined by a balancing test that looks at the reasonableness of the precautions taken to prevent the disclosure, the time taken to correct the error, the scope of the discovery, the extent of the disclosure, and the overriding issue of fairness.

■ PROCEDURAL BASIS

Decision on a motion for a protective order.

■ FACTS

Koch Foods (P) produced 3,758 pages of documents in response to a discovery request by GE Capital (D). In the middle of one of the documents produced was the second page of a three-page e-mail exchange between the Chief Financial Officer of Koch (P) and counsel for Koch (P). Koch (P) learned that the e-mail had been produced when GE Capital (D) produced it at a deposition of Koch's (P) Chief Financial Officer. Koch (P) immediately objected that the document was privileged and should be returned. The e-mail had been identified in the privilege log of documents Koch (P) identified as withheld on grounds of privilege. Koch's (P) counsel stated that he did not intend to produce the e-mail, did not see it despite several reviews of the documents produced, and would have removed it if he had seen it. GE Capital (D) agreed that the e-mail was privileged, but claimed that Koch (P) had inadvertently waived the privilege. Koch (P) moved for a protective order.

■ ISSUE

Did Koch (P) inadvertently waive the privilege?

■ DECISION AND RATIONALE

(Thompson, J.) No. The question of whether the attorney-client privilege has been waived is determined by a balancing test that looks at the reasonableness of the precautions taken to prevent the disclosure, the time taken to correct the error, the scope of the discovery, the extent of the disclosure, and the overriding issue of fairness. Courts have taken three general approaches to the issue of inadvertent waiver. The traditional approach is one of strict liability: a party is responsible for maintaining the confidentiality of its information, and must pay the price of waiver if it accidentally discloses a privileged document. Other courts look at the intent of the party and treat the waiver of attorney-client privilege like the relinquishment of other known rights. Under this approach, a waiver could not be "inadvertent." The balancing-test approach lies between these two extremes and considers the totality of the circumstances instead of applying a per se rule. This analysis serves the purpose of protecting communications that the client fully intended would remain confidential, but at the same time does not relieve those claiming the privilege of the consequences of their carelessness if the circumstances do not clearly demonstrate that continued protection is warranted. In some cases, the intent-based approach may appear to merge with the totality-of-the-circumstances approach, because precautions taken to avoid disclosure help to decide whether the waiver was intentional.

Alabama law does not set out clear standards for deciding whether privilege has been waived. The Rules of Evidence say that the waiver must be "voluntary," but "voluntary" could mean either "intentional" or "uncoerced." Case law also provides no guidance. Ethics opinions from the Alabama State Bar and the American Bar Association also do not point to a standard for inadvertent waiver of privilege. Two Alabama opinions concern themselves with the duty of the attorney who receives the inadvertently disclosed materials, and recommends that the attorney refrain from examining them and return them to opposing counsel. One of the Alabama opinions relies, however, on an ABA opinion that was later withdrawn, and the other opinion states that waiver of a privileged status is a matter of law beyond the scope of the ethical rules. The ABA opinion on the matter endorses a totality-of-the-circumstances approach to waiver, and states that case law shows that mere inadvertence will not constitute a waiver. Something more, such as a failure of counsel to review the documents to be produced, is required before waiver will be found.

The totality-of-the-circumstances approach appears to be the modern trend. More importantly, it allows for a more comprehensive and sensitive assessment of the concerns presented by inadvertent waivers. The protective order is granted.

Analysis:

The idea of the inadvertent waiver of privilege presents a paradox. An inadvertent waiver typically will result from an error or omission of counsel. The privilege, however, belongs to the client, and in most other circumstances cannot be intentionally waived without the client's consent. It is not the carelessness of the party claiming the privilege that determines the waiver, it is the carelessness of counsel—a factor most clients cannot control—that could give rise to an inadvertent waiver.

Swidler & Berlin v. United States

(Law Firm) v. *(Prosecuting Government)*
524 U.S. 399, 118 S.Ct. 2081 (1998)

THERE IS NO GENERAL POSTHUMOUS EXCEPTION TO THE ATTORNEY–CLIENT PRIVILEGE

Foster is survived by his wife, his children, and the attorney-client privilege.

stus.com

■ **INSTANT FACTS** Swidler & Berlin (D) claimed that notes of a meeting with a deceased client were privileged.

■ **BLACK LETTER RULE** The attorney-client privilege survives the death of the client.

■ **PROCEDURAL BASIS**

Appeal from an order of the court of appeals reversing an order quashing a subpoena.

■ **FACTS**

Foster consulted with Hamilton (D), an attorney with Swidler & Berlin (D), regarding representation in congressional or other investigations of the firings of certain White House personnel. Foster and Hamilton (D) met for two hours, and Hamilton (D) took three pages of handwritten notes during their meeting. One of the first entries in Hamilton's (D) notes was the word "Privileged." Foster committed suicide nine days after his meeting with Hamilton (D).

At the request of the Independent Counsel, a grand jury issued subpoenas for Hamilton's (D) notes of his meeting with Foster. Hamilton (D) and Swidler & Berlin (D) filed motions to quash the subpoenas, arguing that the notes were protected by the attorney-client privilege. The district court agreed and quashed the subpoena. The court of appeals reversed, holding that the risk of posthumous revelation of confidential communications would have little to no chilling effect on client communications, but that the cost of protecting those communications was high.

■ **ISSUE**

Does the attorney-client privilege survive the client's death?

■ **DECISION AND RATIONALE**

(Rehnquist, C.J.) Yes. The attorney-client privilege survives the death of the client. Courts that have addressed the question, with only two exceptions, have either held that the privilege survives or presumed that it does. In *Cohen v. Jenkintown Cab Co.*, 238 Pa.Super. 456 (1976), a civil case, the court held that the privilege generally survives death, but that the court could make an exception when the interest of justice was compelling and the interest of the client in preserving the confidence was insignificant.

Case law and statutes in some states also allow for a waiver of the privilege in testamentary disputes. In those cases, the waiver is allowed to fulfill the client's testamentary intent. The Independent Counsel (P) argues that this exception supports the termination of the privilege at death because, in practice, most courts have declined to apply the privilege. The Independent Counsel (P) also argues that the existence of the exception reflects a policy judgment that the interest in settling estates outweighs any posthumous interest in confidentiality. By analogy, the argument goes, the interest in determining whether a crime has been committed should trump client confidentiality. The Counsel's (P) argument

---

does not square with the implicit acceptance of the survival of the privilege and with the treatment of testamentary disclosure as an exception. The rationale behind the exception is to further the client's intent, and there is no reason to assume that grand jury testimony about confidential communications furthers that intent.

The Independent Counsel (P) notes that many commentators have urged that the privilege should be abrogated after the client's death. Those commentators, however, all recognize that established law supports the continuation of the privilege, and that a contrary rule would be a modification of the common law. In addition, despite the criticism, there are good reasons for the posthumous application of the privilege. The knowledge that the privilege will continue even after death encourages free and frank communication with counsel. Some clients may fear posthumous disclosure as much as disclosure during their lifetime. In this case, in which the client may have been contemplating suicide, a client may not have sought legal advice if he had not known that the conversation would be privileged.

The Independent Counsel (P) suggests that the proposed exception might have minimal impact if confined to criminal cases. There is no authority for the proposition that the privilege applies differently in civil and criminal cases. A client may not know, at the time of the communication, whether it will be relevant to a civil or criminal case, let alone whether it will be of substantial importance. Balancing the importance of the information against client interests introduces substantial uncertainty into the application of the privilege. The Independent Counsel (P) suggests that the impact of one more exception to the attorney-client privilege will be minimal. Existing exceptions do not demonstrate that the impact of a posthumous exception would be insignificant, and there is little empirical evidence on that point. The existing exceptions are consistent with the purpose of the privilege, while a posthumous exception in criminal cases appears to be at odds with the goals of encouraging communications and protecting the interests of the client.

Cases cited by the Independent Counsel (P) for the proposition that privileges are to be strictly construed are not on point. *United States v. Nixon,* 418 U.S. 683 (1974), and *Branzburg v. Hayes,* 408 U.S. 665 (1972), dealt with the creation of new privileges not recognized by the common law. In this case, the Court is asked to narrow one of the oldest privileges recognized by the law. Reversed.

■ DISSENT

(O'Connor, J.) Evidentiary privileges are not favored and must give way in some circumstances. The potential that disclosure of confidences after a client's death will harm the client's interests has been greatly diminished, and there is no danger of criminal liability. The encouragement of free disclosure will not be diminished if the privilege terminates on death. The posthumous continuation of the privilege means that important evidence often will be lost forever. The costs of recognizing the privilege could be inordinately high, such as in a case in which a criminal defendant seeks a deceased client's confession. When the privilege is asserted in the criminal context and a showing is made that the communications contain necessary factual information not otherwise available, courts should be permitted to assess whether interests in fairness and accuracy outweigh the justifications for the privilege. There already exist a number of exceptions to the privilege that are not consistent with the goal of full and frank communication. Those exceptions reflect an understanding that there are circumstances in which the privilege ceases to operate as a safeguard on the adversary system.

Analysis:

The situation in which Foster was involved was an investigation of the firing of the staff of the White House Travel Office. Shortly after President Clinton took office, several employees of the Travel Office—which had long been the subject of allegations of corruption and mismanagement—were dismissed. The firings became the subject of an intense investigation and scandal. In a note written by Foster, found a few days after his death, he said that "ruining people is considered sport" in Washington, D.C.

■ CASE VOCABULARY

INDEPENDENT COUNSEL: An attorney hired to provide an unbiased opinion about a case or to conduct an impartial investigation; especially, an attorney appointed by a governmental branch or agency to investigate alleged misconduct within that branch or agency.

United States v. Zolin

(*Prosecuting Authority*) v. (*Clerk of Superior Court*)

491 U.S. 554, 109 S.Ct. 2619 (1989)

IN CAMERA REVIEWS OF EVIDENCE MAY DETERMINE IF IT IS PRIVILEGED

■ **INSTANT FACTS** The Government (P) urged the trial court to undertake an *in camera* review of evidence before making a ruling that the evidence was protected by the attorney-client privilege.

■ **BLACK LETTER RULE** The court should undertake an *in camera* review of evidence to determine if the crime-fraud exception will bar a claim of attorney-client privilege only if there is a factual showing adequate to support a good faith belief that a review of the materials may reveal evidence that establishes the claim that the exception applies.

■ **PROCEDURAL BASIS**

Appeal from an order of the court of appeals affirming a finding of privilege.

■ **FACTS**

The IRS (P) conducted an investigation of the tax returns of Hubbard (D), founder of the Church of Scientology (D). As a part of that investigation, the IRS (P) sought access to documents that had been filed in state court in connection with litigation against a former member of the Church (D). The documents included two tapes that had been filed under seal. The Church (D) claimed that the tapes were privileged. The IRS (P) claimed that the tapes fell within the crime-fraud exception to the attorney-client privilege, and requested that the court listen to the tapes when considering its privilege ruling. The IRS (P) submitted declarations from an agent, setting out his reasons for believing that the tapes were relevant and describing the contents of the tapes. The IRS (P) also submitted partial transcripts of the tapes, which it had obtained lawfully from a confidential source. The court did not review the tapes, but held that they were protected by the attorney-client privilege. The court held that the partial transcripts did not show a clear indication that future fraud or crime was being planned. The court denied a renewed request by the IRS (P) that it listen to the tapes in their entirety. The IRS (P) appealed, arguing that it was error for the court to refuse to listen to the tapes *in camera*. The Church (D) argued that the court should not have relied on the partial transcripts, claiming that evidence independent of the communications themselves must be used to determine if the crime-fraud exception applies.

■ **ISSUE**

Did the district court, in refusing to review the proffered evidence in its entirety, apply the proper standard in reviewing the privilege claim?

■ **DECISION AND RATIONALE**

(Blackmun, J.) No. The court should undertake an *in camera* review of evidence to determine if the crime-fraud exception will bar a claim of attorney-client privilege if there is a factual showing adequate to support a good faith belief that a review of the materials may reveal evidence that establishes the claim that the exception applies. The lower courts erred by applying a strict "independent evidence" requirement for the claim that the privilege does not apply.

Two provisions of the Federal Rules of Evidence could be read as barring any consideration of the communications claimed to be privileged. Rule 104 (a) states that the law with respect to privileges shall apply in determining preliminary questions of the existence of a privilege. Rule 1101 (c) states that the rules regarding privileges apply at all stages of a case. Taken together, these rules could be read as requiring that attorney-client communications not be considered in making a crime-fraud exception ruling. This interpretation would make it virtually impossible to prove that the crime-fraud exception applies. Such an interpretation goes against the plain language of Rule 104 (a), which does not require that all materials as to which a claim of privilege is made be excluded from consideration. It also does not make sense to assume that attorney-client communications must be treated as presumptively privileged until the privilege is defeated by proof that the communications took place in the course of planning future crime or fraud.

The disclosure of allegedly privileged materials to the court for the purposes of determining a claim of privilege does not terminate the privilege. The question is whether the policies underlying the privilege and its exceptions are best served by permitting *in camera* review of the materials, or by prohibiting it. The costs of imposing an absolute bar for the purposes of establishing the crime-fraud exception are intolerably high. There are many blatant abuses of the privilege that cannot be established by extrinsic evidence. On the other hand, a rule that such review is always permissible would place the policy of encouraging open and legitimate disclosure between attorneys and clients at risk. There also is reason to be concerned about the due process implications of the routine use of *in camera* proceedings, as well as the burden *in camera* review places on the courts. There is no reason to permit a party who opposes a claim of privilege to engage in groundless fishing expeditions. The IRS (P) acknowledged that a district court would be mistaken if it reviewed documents *in camera* solely because it was requested to do so with no reason to suspect crime or fraud.

An *in camera* inspection is a lesser intrusion upon the confidentiality of a communication than a full public disclosure. A lesser evidentiary showing is needed to trigger *in camera* review than is required to overcome the privilege. A factual showing adequate to support a good faith belief that the privilege will be overcome is required. Once that showing is made, the decision to conduct a review is within the discretion of the trial court. Factors to be considered include the amount of the material to be reviewed, the relative importance to the case of the allegedly privileged information, and the likelihood that the evidence produced through the review, along with other evidence before the court, will establish that the crime-fraud exception applies. The court may also defer its ruling if it concludes that additional evidence in support of the exception that is not allegedly privileged may be available, and that production of the additional evidence will not unduly disrupt or delay the proceedings. Reversed and remanded.

Analysis:

The crime-fraud exception does not apply to communications that involve past fraud or crimes. Discussions about what happened in the past are the types of free discourse promoted by the attorney-client privilege. On the other hand, the privilege is not meant to act as a shield for the client who plans a fraud or a crime with the help of his or her attorney. An attorney who conspires with a client will not be immunized from prosecution by the attorney-client privilege.

■ CASE VOCABULARY

CRIME–FRAUD EXCEPTION: The doctrine that neither the attorney-client privilege nor the attorney-work-product privilege protects attorney-client communications that are in furtherance of a current or a planned crime or fraud. *Clark v. United States*, 289 U.S. 1, 53 S.Ct. 465 (1933); *In re Grand Jury Subpoena Duces Tecum*, 731 F.2d 1032 (2d Cir. 1984).

IN CAMERA: [Latin, "in a chamber."] In the judge's private chambers, or in the courtroom with all spectators excluded; (of a judicial action) taken when court is not in session.

In Re: Grand Jury Investigation [Rowland]

(Governor)

399 F.3d 527 (2d Cir. 2005)

COMMUNICATIONS WITH GOVERNMENT ATTORNEYS ARE PROTECTED BY THE ATTORNEY–CLIENT PRIVILEGE

Everything I tell you is totally confidential, no matter how heinous, right?

stus.com

Desk of the Governor

■ **INSTANT FACTS** George (D), former counsel for the Governor (D), claimed attorney-client privilege and refused to testify about the substance of her conversations with the Governor (D).

■ **BLACK LETTER RULE** The attorney-client privilege applies to government attorneys to the same extent that it applies to private attorneys.

■ **PROCEDURAL BASIS**

Appeal from an order compelling testimony before a grand jury.

■ **FACTS**

A grand jury investigating possible criminal violations by Connecticut public officials and employees subpoenaed George (D), the former legal counsel to Rowland (D), the Governor of Connecticut. The U.S. Attorney (P) sought information regarding communications between Rowland (D), his staff, and counsel, but was unsuccessful. The U.S. Attorney (P) also asked George (D) for a private interview, but she declined after the Office of the Governor notified her that it believed the information sought was protected by the attorney-client privilege. Before George (D) appeared before the grand jury, the U.S. Attorney (P) moved to compel George (D) to testify about the contents of confidential communications between Rowland (D) and his staff and George (D). The court withheld decision pending George's (D) grand jury testimony.

George (D) appeared before the grand jury and testified that she had conversations with Rowland (D) and his staff about the receipt of gifts, state ethics laws, and the practice of sending state contracts to the Governor (D) for approval. She testified that the conversations were in confidence and for the purpose of providing legal advice, so the Governor's (D) office considered the conversations protected by the attorney-client privilege, which it declined to waive. George (D) asserted the privilege on behalf of her client and refused to answer questions regarding the content of the conversations.

The district court entered an order compelling George (D) to testify. The court concluded that "reason and experience" dictated that, in the context of a grand jury investigation, the privilege must yield because the interests served by the grand jury's fact-finding process clearly outweigh the interest served by the privilege. The court held that a government lawyer's duty does not lie solely with his or her "client agency," but also with the public.

The day before oral argument on the instant appeal, Rowland (D) resigned as Governor. The privilege claimed was held by the Office of the Governor, and Rowland's (D) successor in office declined to waive the privilege.

■ **ISSUE**

Were George's (D) conversations protected by the attorney-client privilege?

■ DECISION AND RATIONALE

(Walker, C.J.) Yes. The attorney-client privilege applies to government attorneys to the same extent that it applies to private attorneys. Courts have concluded that a consistent application of the privilege over time is necessary to promote the rule of law by encouraging consultation with lawyers, and in light of the principle that safeguarding client confidences promotes, rather than undermines, compliance with the law, it is best to proceed cautiously when asked to narrow the privilege's protections in a particular category of cases.

There is no dispute that a governmental attorney-client privilege exists, and the U.S. Attorney (P) concedes that the privilege may be invoked in a civil action. Although the governmental attorney-client privilege is not expressly set out in the Federal Rules of Evidence, its existence has been assumed by many commentators and by case law. In many of these cases, the privilege question has arisen in the context of an exemption in the Freedom of Information Act for documents that would not be available by law to a party other than an agency. Courts have construed this exemption as covering materials protected by the attorney-client privilege and have thus assumed that the privilege attaches when the attorney is a government lawyer and the client is a governmental agency. The U.S. Attorney (P) argues that, while there is some privilege, the privilege for governmental attorney-client relationships is weaker than the privilege afforded to private attorneys. The U.S. Attorney also claims that the reasons for the traditional attorney-client privilege do not apply with the same force in the context of a federal grand jury investigation into potentially criminal government conduct. The U.S. Attorney (P) bases its argument on the theory that George (D), as a government attorney, has a fundamentally different relationship with her client, the Office of the Governor, than a private attorney representing a private individual has with his or her client. George's (D) client is a public entity, accountable to the general citizenry. The Office of the Governor serves the public, and therefore George (D), as counsel to that office, serves the public as well. According to the U.S. Attorney (P), George's (D) loyalty to the Governor (D) must yield to her loyalty to the public, to whom she owes ultimate allegiance, when there are alleged violations of the criminal law.

Although the public has an interest in allowing a grand jury to collect all the relevant evidence it can, the public also has an interest in allowing high state officials to receive and act upon the best legal advice possible. The people of Connecticut have decided that the public interest in allowing officials to receive legal advice outweighs the interest in allowing grand juries to collect all possible evidence. Connecticut statutory law provides explicitly for a governmental attorney-client privilege in all civil or criminal proceedings. Although the Connecticut statute is not conclusive, it does show that the public interest in this matter is not as clear-cut as alleged by the U.S. Attorney (P).

The traditional rationale for the privilege applies with special force in the government context. Government officials are charged with upholding and executing the laws. They could face criminal prosecution for failing to do so. It is crucial that these officials are encouraged to seek and receive fully informed legal advice. Upholding the government attorney-client privilege furthers a culture in which consultation with government lawyers is a normal, desirable, and even indispensable part of conducting public business. Limiting the privilege undermines that culture and thus impairs the public interest.

It is true that the relationship between a government attorney and a government official is not the same as the relationship between a private attorney and his or her client. In the government context, the individual consulting with an official attorney may not control waiver of the privilege. Even if he or she does control waiver, the possibility remains that his or her successor might waive the privilege exercised by a predecessor. Thus, some commentators doubt that a government attorney-client privilege will in fact encourage public officials to confide in counsel. Whatever merit there is to this reasoning, it is not sufficient to jettison the attorney-client privilege. There is also no merit to the argument that the privilege is less important when applied to government counsel because government employees may have private counsel represent their individual interests. The privilege serves to promote the free flow of information to the attorney as well as to the individual with whom he communicates. The government attorney requires candid information from those employed by the office served so that he or she may better discharge the duty owed to that office.

Having determined that the attorney-client privilege applies to the communications at issue in this case, the court will not fashion a balancing test or establish a rule that an assertion of privilege must yield to a demonstrated need for evidence. The Supreme Court has instructed that, when the attorney-client privilege applies, its protections must be reliably enforced in order to effectuate the goal of promoting compliance with the law. There is no persuasive reason to abandon that logic. Nothing in this holding derogates from traditional doctrines, such as the crime-fraud exception, that apply to the private attorney-client relationship and that have been developed to limit egregious abuses of the protections of the privilege.

In essence, the U.S. Attorney (P) is asking the court to assign a precise functional value to the protections of the privilege and then decide whether, and under what circumstances, the cost of these protections is too great to justify. The assumptions underlying this approach are illusory, and the approach itself potentially dangerous. The public interest in disclosure is not always readily apparent, and it cannot be assumed that a public official's willingness to consult with counsel will not be affected by the abrogation of the privilege in the face of a grand jury subpoena. In the end, the question before us is not whether to "extend" the privilege to the government, but whether to abrogate the privilege in circumstances to which its purposes fully pertain. Reversed

---

Analysis:

The U.S. Attorney (P) is, in essence, looking at the public interest solely from the viewpoint of law enforcement and criminal prosecution. The court's view is arguably broader, and looks at the public's interest in the functioning of government. While recognizing a government attorney-client privilege in this case may make a criminal prosecution more difficult or even impossible, in many other cases allowing a government official to obtain legal advice freely and routinely may make prosecutions unnecessary, by ensuring (or at least providing a basis for) compliance with the law. The possibility of prevention thus overrides the ease of prosecution.

United States v. Hubbell

(Prosecuting Authority) v. *(Accused Defrauder)*

530 U.S. 27, 120 S.Ct. 2037 (2000)

DECIDING WHAT DOCUMENTS TO PRODUCE MAY ITSELF BE A TESTIMONY

The good news is that Hubbell just disclosed 13,120 pages. The bad news is you can't go home until you find some juicy new charges.

stus.com

■ **INSTANT FACTS** Hubbell (D) produced documents pursuant to a subpoena and a grant of immunity, and the Independent Counsel (P) used information in those documents to indict Hubbell (D) for other crimes.

■ **BLACK LETTER RULE** The Fifth Amendment privilege against self-incrimination protects a witness both from being compelled to answer questions about the existence of sources of potentially incriminating evidence and from responding to a subpoena that seeks discovery of those sources.

■ **PROCEDURAL BASIS**

Appeal from a decision of the court of appeals affirming a dismissal of an indictment.

■ **FACTS**

Hubbell (D) was served with a grand jury subpoena that asked for the production of eleven categories of documents. He appeared before the grand jury and invoked his privilege against self-incrimination. In response to questions from the prosecutor, Hubbell (D) refused to answer questions regarding the existence of documents in his control that were responsive to the subpoena. The prosecutor produced a grant of immunity that directed Hubbell (D) to respond, but provided him with immunity "to the extent allowed by law." Hubbell (D) then produced 13,120 pages of documents and records. He also testified that those were all of the documents in his custody or control that were responsive to the subpoena, with a few exceptions. The contents of the documents provided the Independent Counsel (P) with the information necessary to indict Hubbell (D) for various tax-related crimes and wire fraud.

The district court dismissed the indictment against Hubbell (D). The trial court held that the evidence that would be introduced against Hubbell (D) at trial derived directly or indirectly from Hubbell's (D) immunized act of producing the documents. The district court characterized the subpoena as "the quintessential fishing expedition," because the Independent Counsel (P) was not investigating tax issues when the subpoena was issued, and the crimes were uncovered only after studying the contents of the records. The court of appeals vacated and remanded, holding that the district court should not have relied on the fact that the Independent Counsel did not have prior knowledge of the contents of the subpoenaed documents. The district court should have addressed the extent of the Government's (P) independent knowledge of the existence and authenticity of the documents and Hubbell's (D) possession or control of them. The court stated that the indictment would have a proper basis if the Independent Counsel (P) could demonstrate with reasonable particularity a prior awareness that the documents sought in the subpoena existed and were in Hubbell's (D) possession. The Independent Counsel (P) acknowledged that he could not meet such a standard and entered into a conditional plea agreement with Hubbell (D). The agreement provided that the charges against Hubbell (D) would be dismissed unless the Supreme Court's decision made it reasonably likely that Hubbell's (D) "act of production immunity" would not pose a significant bar to his prosecution.

■ ISSUE

Did the grant of immunity for the production of documents bar the prosecution of Hubbell (D) based on information found in the documents?

■ DECISION AND RATIONALE

(Stevens, J.) Yes. The Fifth Amendment privilege against self-incrimination protects a witness both from being compelled to answer questions about the existence of sources of potentially incriminating evidence and from responding to a subpoena that seeks discovery of those sources. It is clear that Hubbell (D) could not avoid compliance with the subpoena merely because some of the requested documents contained incriminating evidence. On the other hand, the act of producing documents may have a compelled-testimonial aspect. The Fifth Amendment protection extends to compelled statements that lead to the discovery of incriminating evidence, even if those statements are not themselves incriminating.

The compelled testimony in this case is not found in the documents produced in response to the subpoena. The testimonial aspect of a subpoena *duces tecum* ordinarily does nothing more than establish the existence, authenticity, and custody of the items to be produced. The Independent Counsel (P) has stated that he has no intention of introducing any of the documents produced in response to the subpoena at trial. The Government (P) has, however, made "derivative use" of the testimonial aspect of the production by seeking the indictment against Hubbell (D). The subpoena served on Hubbell (D) requested a broad category of documents. Producing those documents required Hubbell (D), in effect, to testify that these were the documents that were responsive to the subpoena. Providing a catalog of existing documents fitting within the eleven broad categories of documents requested in the subpoena could provide the prosecutor with a lead to incriminating evidence or a link in the chain needed to prosecute. The record shows that is what happened.

The Government's (P) possession of the documents was not the fruit only of the physical act of turning the documents over. It was necessary for Hubbell (D) to make use of the contents of his own mind in identifying the many documents responsive to the requests in the subpoena. Possession of the records was not a foregone conclusion. The Government (P) has not shown that it knew of either the existence or the whereabouts of the documents. This deficiency cannot be cured by the overbroad argument that a businessman like Hubbell (D) will always possess business and tax records that fall within the broad categories described in the subpoena. The Government (P) must show that the evidence it used in obtaining the indictment and proposed to use at trial was derived from legitimate sources wholly independent of the testimonial aspect of Hubbell's (D) response to the subpoena. The Government (P) cannot make such a showing. Affirmed.

■ CONCURRENCE

(Thomas, J.) The majority's opinion correctly applies the act-of-production doctrine, which provides that a person may invoke the Fifth Amendment in response to a subpoena *duces tecum* only if the act of producing the evidence would contain "testimonial" features. This doctrine may be inconsistent with the original meaning of the Fifth Amendment's Self–Incrimination Clause. A substantial body of evidence suggests that the Fifth Amendment privilege protects against the compelled production not just of incriminating testimony, but of any incriminating evidence.

■ DISSENT

(Rehnquist, C.J.) The judgment of the court of appeals should be reversed in part, for the reasons set out in Judge Williams's dissent in that opinion. That dissent held that the Fifth Amendment privilege and the statute conferring use immunity would only protect the witness from the use of any information resulting from the subpoena response beyond what the Independent Counsel (P) would have received if the documents appeared in the grand jury room or in his office unsolicited.

Analysis:

The Court does not retreat from earlier holdings that the Fifth Amendment does not protect the contents of business documents. In this case, the contents of the documents are derivative of Hubbell's (D) testimonial act of deciding which documents met the demand in the subpoena. The result in this case may have been different if the Government (P) had not made such a broad demand for disclosure. The subpoena requested, among other things, all documents relating to the source of any money or thing of value provided to Hubbell (D), his wife, or his children over a three-year period.

■ CASE VOCABULARY

GENERAL WARRANT: A warrant that gives a law-enforcement officer broad authority to search and seize unspecified places or persons; a search or arrest warrant that lacks a sufficiently particularized description of the person or thing to be seized or the place to be searched. General warrants are unconstitutional because they fail to meet the Fourth Amendment's specificity requirements.

TRANSACTIONAL IMMUNITY: Immunity from prosecution for any event or transaction described in the compelled testimony. This is the broadest form of immunity.

CHAPTER THIRTEEN

Familial Privileges

Tilton v. Beecher

Instant Facts: Tilton (P) brought an action for criminal conversation against Beecher (D), alleging that Beecher (D) had committed adultery with Tilton's (P) wife on several occasions.

Black Letter Rule: None provided.

Trammel v. United States

Instant Facts: Trammel's (D) wife voluntarily chose to testify against him at his trial for drug smuggling and conspiracy.

Black Letter Rule: A witness may be neither compelled to testify nor barred from testifying against his or her spouse.

United States v. Rakes

Instant Facts: Rakes (D) was prosecuted for perjury for testimony he gave about extortion attempts, and he claimed that the marital privilege barred his wife from testifying about their conversations.

Black Letter Rule: The privilege for marital communications permits an individual to refuse to testify, and to prevent a spouse or former spouse from testifying, regarding any confidential communication made by the individual to the spouse during the course of the marriage.

In Re Grand Jury Proceedings

Instant Facts: A father (D) was called to testify against his son, and a daughter (D) was held in contempt for refusing to testify against her father.

Black Letter Rule: There is no testimonial privilege for parent-child communications.

Tilton v. Beecher

(Journalist) v. *(Clergyman)*
2 Abbott's Repts. at 49, 87 (N.Y. 1875)

THE MARITAL PRIVILEGE PROTECTS THE MARRIAGE REALTIONSHIP

■ **INSTANT FACTS** Tilton (P) brought an action for criminal conversation against Beecher (D), alleging that Beecher (D) had committed adultery with Tilton's (P) wife on several occasions.

■ **BLACK LETTER RULE** None provided.

■ **PROCEDURAL BASIS**

Arguments of counsel regarding the marital privilege.

■ **FACTS**

Tilton (P) brought an action against Beecher (D) for criminal conversation. Tilton (P) alleged that Beecher (D) committed adultery with Tilton's wife several times over the course of several years. Tilton's (P) counsel argued that the rule that prevents one spouse from testifying against another is necessary to preserve the purity, the dignity, and the strength of the marital relationship. The common law says that a man and his wife are one, and it is said that no man shall put asunder those who are thus joined together. The administration of justice shall not pull and tear asunder this conjugal relationship.

Beecher's (D) counsel argued that the traditional marriage relationship has been much changed. Women are no longer confined to the home but are active and independent in modern life. The identity of husband and wife has already been torn asunder, not only by legal theory, but by the practical applications of it to the ordinary concerns of life.

■ **DECISION AND RATIONALE**

Only the arguments of counsel were provided in the casebook. No decision was set out.

Analysis:

The diction of counsel hints at the high-Victorian melodrama of this case. Beecher (D), the brother of novelist Harriet Beecher Stowe, was the most famous clergyman in the United States at the time of the trial. Tilton (P) was a newspaper publisher and former disciple of Beecher (D). Tilton's (P) alleged marital troubles began when his opinions on a variety of religious and political issues grew more radical than those of his former mentor and he began spending more time away from home on lecture tours. The trial consumed six months, ending with a jury deadlocked in favor of Beecher (D). Historians generally agree that the truth of the allegations may never be known. Mrs. Tilton confessed to the adultery on several occasions, but recanted all but one of her confessions.

■ **CASE VOCABULARY**

CRIMINAL CONVERSATION: *Archaic.* A tort action for adultery, brought by a husband against a third party who engaged in sexual intercourse with his wife. Criminal conversation has been abolished in most jurisdictions.

MARITAL PRIVILEGE: The privilege allowing a defendant's spouse not to testify, and preventing another person from testifying, about confidential communications between spouses during the marriage; the privilege allowing a spouse not to testify in a criminal case as an adverse witness against the other spouse, regardless of the subject matter of the testimony; the privilege immunizing from a defamation lawsuit any statement made between husband and wife.

Trammel v. United States

(Accused Drug Smuggler) v. *(Prosecuting Authority)*

445 U.S. 40, 100 S.Ct. 906 (1980)

SPOUSES MAY TESTIFY AGAINST EACH OTHER

■ **INSTANT FACTS** Trammel's (D) wife voluntarily chose to testify against him at his trial for drug smuggling and conspiracy.

■ **BLACK LETTER RULE** A witness may be neither compelled to testify nor barred from testifying against his or her spouse.

■ **PROCEDURAL BASIS**

Appeal from an order of the court of appeals affirming convictions for importing heroin and conspiracy to import heroin.

■ **FACTS**

Elizabeth Trammel was arrested bringing heroin into the United States. After discussions with law enforcement officers, she agreed to cooperate with the Government (P). The Government (P) obtained an indictment against Otis Trammel (D). Trammel (D) moved to exclude Elizabeth's testimony against him, claiming that he held a privilege to bar her adverse testimony against him. At the hearing on Trammel's (D) motion, Elizabeth testified that she and Trammel (D) married a few months before her arrest. When she was asked if she and her husband contemplated divorce, Elizabeth testified that Trammel (D) had said that he would go his way and she would go hers. Elizabeth explained that her cooperation with the Government (P) was based on assurances of lenient treatment, and she went on to describe in detail her role and the role of her husband in the heroin distribution conspiracy. After hearing her testimony at the motion hearing, the court ruled that Elizabeth could testify as to any acts she observed during the marriage and to any communication made in the presence of a third person. Confidential communications between Elizabeth and Trammel (D) were held to be privileged and inadmissible. Elizabeth testified at trial within the limits of the court's ruling, and Trammel (D) was convicted. Trammel (D) claimed it was error to allow Elizabeth's testimony over his objection. He based his argument on the case of *Hawkins v. United States,* 358 U.S. 74 (1958).

■ **ISSUE**

May a criminal defendant bar the voluntary adverse testimony of his or her spouse?

■ **DECISION AND RATIONALE**

(Burger, C.J.) No. A witness may be neither compelled to testify nor barred from testifying against his or her spouse. The privilege, and the decision of whether to testify, is vested solely in the witness-spouse.

The rule that prohibits one spouse from testifying against the other has its origin in two rules of medieval law: the prohibition against an accused testifying in his own behalf; and the unity of husband and wife, with the wife having no separate legal existence. The rule has survived into the twentieth century, with the modern justification being the perceived role of the privilege in fostering the harmony and sanctity of the marital relationship. The rule has been sharply criticized, with many commentators

---

and drafters of evidentiary rules calling for its abolition. Several state legislatures have abolished the privilege, retaining a privilege for confidential communications between spouses.

In *Hawkins v. United States,* the Court declined to abandon the privilege. The Court left open the possibility that the rule might change in the future, as dictated by "reason and experience." Since *Hawkins* was decided, support for the existence privilege has continued to erode. At present, most states permit one spouse to testify against the other. Drafters of revisions to the Uniform Rules of Evidence have rejected the privilege. The trend in state law toward abolition of the privilege is especially relevant, because marriage and domestic relations traditionally have been questions of state law.

The question now is whether the privilege against adverse spousal testimony promotes important interests that outweigh the need for probative evidence in a criminal case. The privilege against adverse spousal testimony is broader than other privileges. Most privileges protect only confidential communications and are rooted in the need for trust and confidence in a particular relationship. The spousal testimony privilege, however, is not limited to confidential communications. The ancient foundations for the privilege have disappeared. Women are not regarded as chattel and are no longer denied a separate legal existence. The contemporary justification for the privilege also is unpersuasive. When one spouse is willing to testify against the other, for whatever reason, there is probably little marital harmony left to preserve. The rule is more likely to frustrate justice than to promote family peace. In cases such as this one, the rule may actually harm the marital relationship, as the Government (P) is unlikely to offer lenient treatment if it knows that the other spouse could bar the testimony. "Reason and experience" no longer justify such a sweeping rule. The rule therefore is modified so that the witness-spouse alone has a privilege to refuse to give adverse testimony against the spouse. The witness-spouse may be neither compelled to testify, nor foreclosed from testifying. Affirmed.

Analysis:

Barring testimony by a witness is more akin to a disqualification than a privilege. Most disqualifications of witnesses are based on matters outside the control of the witness—age, mental incompetence, etc. The marital disqualification is based on a voluntary relationship, which provides an opportunity for fraud. Note that in this case, Trammel (D) and Elizabeth were married only a few months before her arrest, and her testimony casts doubt on the intended permanence of the relationship. Marrying a co-conspirator would provide a convenient way to guarantee silence.

■ **CASE VOCABULARY**

CHATTEL: Movable or transferable property; personal property; especially, a physical object capable of manual delivery and not the subject matter of real property.

CONSPIRACY: An agreement by two or more persons to commit an unlawful act, coupled with an intent to achieve the agreement's objective, and (in most states) action or conduct that furthers the agreement; a combination for an unlawful purpose.

United States v. Rakes

(Prosecuting Authority) v. *(Store Owner)*

136 F.3d 1 (1st Cir.1998)

SPOUSAL PRIVILEGE PROTECTS STATEMENTS MADE DURING THE COURSE OF THE MARRIAGE

Great news! I sold our liquor store to the mob so they won't kill us.

stus.com

■ **INSTANT FACTS** Rakes (D) was prosecuted for perjury for testimony he gave about extortion attempts, and he claimed that the marital privilege barred his wife from testifying about their conversations.

■ **BLACK LETTER RULE** The privilege for marital communications permits an individual to refuse to testify, and to prevent a spouse or former spouse from testifying, regarding any confidential communication made by the individual to the spouse during the course of the marriage.

■ **PROCEDURAL BASIS**

Interlocutory appeal from an order granting a motion to suppress evidence.

■ **FACTS**

Rakes (D) and his wife, Julie, operated a liquor store in Boston. The Government (P) alleged that Rakes (D) and his wife were threatened by unnamed people who were angry that Rakes (D) and his wife were underpricing their competitors. A man named Bulger allegedly visited the liquor store and threatened to kill Rakes (D) unless Bulger or his associates were made partners in the store. A few months later, Rakes (D) and his wife transferred the store to an alleged associate of Bulger. The Government (P) alleged that the transfer was for a fraction of the actual value of the store.

Rakes (D) was twice called before the grand jury to testify about the sale of the liquor store. Both times, Rakes (D) testified that he sold the store to make a profit, and because it was too much work for him to run. Rakes (D) also testified that no one threatened him to make him sell the store. Rakes (D) was charged with perjury based on his grand jury testimony. Rakes (D) moved to suppress evidence of conversations he had with his wife concerning alleged threats and the sale of the liquor store. Rakes (D) based his motion on the marital communications privilege. The district court granted the motion, with the exception of one statement made in the presence of a third party. The Government (P) appealed, claiming that the privilege did not apply.

■ **ISSUE**

Did the marital privilege bar the evidence of the conversations between Rakes (D) and his wife?

■ **DECISION AND RATIONALE**

(Boudin, J.) Yes. The privilege for marital communications permits an individual to refuse to testify, and to prevent a spouse or former spouse from testifying, regarding any confidential communication made by the individual to the spouse during the course of the marriage. The context and the content of the communications here support the implicit finding by the trial court that Rakes (D) intended the communications to be private.

The Government (P) argued that the suppressed conversations are not privileged because they occurred during an ongoing extortion scheme. According to the Government (P), the crime of extortion extended from the time the first threat was made through the transfer of the liquor store, and Rakes (D) participated in the crime by covering it up and transferring the liquor store. There is no general rule that withdraws the privilege from communications that occur during the same time frame as an ongoing crime, although there is a crime-fraud exception to the marital privilege. In this case, however, Rakes (D) and his wife were not participants in the extortion scheme, they were the victims. The privilege is not lost for communications that play a functional role in the crime unless the holder of the privilege was a willing participant in the crime. Rakes's (D) conduct does not approach misprision or accessory after the fact.

The Government (P) also argues that Rakes (D) disclosed the communications to a third party. Rakes (D) allegedly owed one Burke a substantial sum for construction work on the liquor store. When Burke called Rakes (D), the Government (P) alleged, Rakes (D) told Burke, in a dramatic fashion, that he had been forced out of business. This disclosure is weak and unpersuasive evidence that Rakes (D) did not intend his communications with Julie to be confidential. There was likewise no waiver of the privilege. Rakes (D) did not tell Burke about his conversations with Julie, only about the events discussed.

The district court's suppression order was directed towards the communications, not the facts in those communications. The fact that the communications concerned events that took place prior to the communications does not take away their privilege. Contrary to the Government's (P) argument, the privilege is not lost for communications about financial matters. And it is irrelevant that Rakes (D) and Julie were divorced after the conversations. It is likewise irrelevant that some of the conversations may have occurred in the presence of their infant children. Affirmed.

Analysis:

The marital privilege survives the end of the marriage. Once the marriage has ended, the policy reasons for the privilege arguably also disappear—the need for confidence and trust no longer exists. The focus, however, is on the relationship of the parties at the time the communication was made. A person who has a confidential conversation with his or her spouse should not have to worry that future marital difficulties will erase the privilege for communications made well before the end of the marriage.

■ **CASE VOCABULARY**

EXORTION: The offense committed by a public official who illegally obtains property under the color of office, especially an official's collection of an unlawful fee; the act or practice of obtaining something or compelling some action by illegal means, as by fraud or coercion.

MISPRISION: Concealment or nondisclosure of a serious crime by one who did not participate in the crime.

In re Grand Jury Proceedings

(Father Called to Testify Against Son; Daughter Called to Testify Against Her Father)

103 F.3d 1140 (3d Cir. 1997), *cert. denied sub nom. Roe v. United States,* 520 U.S. 1253, 117 S.Ct. 2412 (1997)

PARENT–CHILD COMMUNICATIONS ARE NOT PRIVILEGED

■ **INSTANT FACTS** A father (D) was called to testify against his son, and a daughter (D) was held in contempt for refusing to testify against her father.

■ **BLACK LETTER RULE** There is no testimonial privilege for parent-child communications.

■ **PROCEDURAL BASIS**

Appeal from orders denying motions to quash subpoenas in two separate cases.

■ **FACTS**

In a case that originated in the Virgin Islands, the father (D) of the target of a grand jury investigation was called to testify. The grand jury was investigating transactions that took place when the son was eighteen years old. The father (D) believed that the grand jury would ask him about conversations with his son and moved to quash the subpoena. The father (D) testified that he had a very close relationship with his son, and that that relationship would be damaged if he were forced to testify. The district court denied the motion to quash.

In a case that originated in Delaware, a sixteen year-old daughter (D) was subpoenaed to testify before a grand jury. The grand jury was investigating her father's role in an alleged interstate kidnapping. The daughter (D) and her mother moved to quash the subpoena, and her father also made a motion to quash, on the basis of a claimed privilege for parent-child communications. The district court denied the motions and ordered the daughter (D) to testify. She appeared as ordered, but refused to testify and was held in contempt.

■ **ISSUE**

Is there a privilege for parent-child communications?

■ **DECISION AND RATIONALE**

(Garth, J.) No. There is no testimonial privilege for parent-child communications. The federal appellate courts and state supreme courts that have considered the issue all have declined to recognize such a privilege. No reasoned analysis of Fed. R. Evid. 501 or of the standards created by the Supreme Court or this court supports the creation of such a privilege. Although Congress enacted that rule of evidence so that the law of privilege would not be frozen, privileges generally are disfavored. The Supreme Court has rarely expanded common-law testimonial privileges. Other federal courts, including this court, have likewise declined to exercise the power granted by Rule 501 expansively. Only four states have recognized some variation of the parent-child privilege. The parent-child privilege also was not one of the enumerated privileges submitted by the Advisory Committee on the Federal Rules of Evidence. This omission strongly suggests that the Advisory Committee, along with the majority of state legislatures, did not regard confidential parent-child communications sufficiently important to warrant the protection of a privilege.

When the court adopted a clergy-communicant privilege, the court examined state and federal precedents and concluded that these precedents weighed in favor of recognizing such a privilege. Virtually every state had recognized some form of the privilege. In addition, the privilege had a long-standing tradition in American law. By contrast, the parent-child privilege is of relatively recent vintage and is little more than the product of academic theorizing. An analysis of the four factors suggested by Dean Wigmore for the adoption of a privilege, as was undertaken when considering the clergy-communicant privilege, does not support the privilege. The four factors are:

1. The communications must originate in a confidence they will not be disclosed;

2. The element of confidentiality must be essential to the maintenance of the relationship;

3. The community must be of the opinion that the relationship ought to be fostered; and

4. The injury to the relationship caused by the disclosure would be greater than the benefit gained for the correct adjudication of the litigation.

The second and fourth elements of the test are not met here. Confidentiality is not essential to a successful parent-child relationship, and it is unlikely that the existence or non-existence of a privilege would have any impact on a child's decision to confide in his or her parent. Any injury to the parent-child relationship resulting from the non-recognition of the privilege is likely to be insignificant. The cost of recognizing such a privilege would, however, be substantial. The truth-seeking function of the judicial system would be impaired, and there would be an increased likelihood of injustice resulting from the concealment of relevant information. The parent-child relationship differs dramatically from other relationships, because of the unique duty parents owe their children. A parent owes the child the duty of nurturing and guidance. Creation of a parent-child privilege would have no impact on the parental relationship, and so would neither benefit that relationship nor serve any social policy.

The court has the authority to recognize such a privilege, but if it is to be recognized, that is a matter best left to Congress. The legislature is best equipped to perform the balancing of competing policy interests required to decide whether the parent-child privilege is in the best interests of society. Congress may consider moral, social, economic, religious, and other values, and it may use those considerations to determine the parameters of the privilege. Congress could consider whether it might apply to adult children, to step-parents or grand-parents, or to siblings. Congress could also consider whether the presence of another family member destroys the privilege. Affirmed.

■ CONCURRENCE IN PART, DISSENT IN PART

(Mansmann, J.) The majority's holding with respect to the Delaware case was correct. A different issue is presented by the Virgin Islands case. That case is an appropriate one to recognize a limited form of privilege for communications to a parent for the purposes of seeking parental advice and guidance. The goal in recognizing the limited privilege would not be to guarantee confidentiality, but to shield parent-child relationships from the devastating effects of compelled testimony. Privileges are primarily about the right to be let alone. The exclusion of testimony is secondary. Although a parent-child privilege may sometimes complicate the criminal fact-finding process, the risk is one that is worth bearing.

The only family-based privilege presently recognized by the federal courts is the marital privilege. Many of the same concerns that motivate the spousal privilege support a parent-child privilege. As with a marriage, the optimal parent-child relationship cannot exist without a great deal of communication. The idea of a parent-child privilege is not a novel one. Ancient Hebrew and Roman law barred family members from testifying against one another, as did the Napoleonic Code. Many civil law countries in Europe recognize the privilege. Three states have enacted statutes that recognize some variant of the privilege, and one state, New York, recognizes the privilege by judicial decision.

Cases that have declined to recognize the privilege are all distinguishable. Most of them arose in the context of a child testifying against a parent. Communications from a parent to a child are not as compelling as communications from a child to a parent. Other cases involve children who were significantly older and did not implicate communications seeking parental advice and guidance. These cases do not present the threat to the family relationship posed by the compelled testimony in this case.

Analysis:

The argument for a parent-child privilege gained momentum shortly after this case was decided during the Independent Counsel's investigation of President Clinton's relationship with Monica Lewinsky. Lewinsky had confided in her mother about the President, and her mother was subpoenaed to testify before the grand jury about her daughter's confidences. Many members of the public believed that the Independent Counsel overstepped an ethical or social boundary. That disapproval, however, has yet to manifest itself as a change in the rules of evidence.

■ CASE VOCABULARY

MOTION TO QUASH: A party's request that the court nullify process or an act instituted by the other party, as in seeking to nullify a subpoena.